* THEY ALL WANT TO WRITE *

HOLT, RINEHART AND WINSTON

NEW YORK   *   CHICAGO   *   SAN FRANCISCO

THEY ALL

ALVINA TREUT BURROWS

DORIS C. JACKSON

DOROTHY O. SAUNDERS

* TORONTO * LONDON

WANT TO WRITE

*Written English
in the
Elementary
School*

THIRD EDITION

FOREWORD

The current emphasis on creative writing is a result of a number of related developments in modern education. One of these grows out of the widespread conviction that the primary aim of education is to assist in the development of well-oriented and reasonably well-adjusted young people. Some educational leaders believe that this goal can be attained only by incorporating creative activities in a broad educational program that seeks to offset some of the influences of a technological world. This point of view is endorsed by psychiatrists and psychologists. Both groups direct attention to the basic needs of the child and assert that the curriculum should be built with a primary concern for their fulfillment. One need that is generally mentioned relates to wholesome physical and mental development. Psychologists point out that the normal healthy child is one who is active and spontaneously alive; as he grows older, the persistence of spontaneity and creativity will reflect continuous, wholesome growth.

Was there ever a time when it seemed so imperative that our schools assume a special responsibility for safeguarding the mental health of boys and girls? To do so it is essential to provide and maintain atmospheres for learning that foster spontaneity and creativity, and to offer children recognition, security, and happiness. Release, expression, and continuous growth will surely follow.

To provide escape and self-expression is one important function of creative writing, but there are others that, from the standpoint of mental health, are similarly significant. Creative writing may be so conceived and developed that it will serve a three-fold function, enabling each child to record his significant experiences and to share his activities and interests as well as to express himself freely, spontaneously, and joyously. To serve these ends creative writing must be thought of as composition in which the child is free to select his subject matter and to determine the length and form in which his writing will appear. Conceived in this way, creative writing will not be confined to poetry or any other form of expression; nor will it be considered the prerogative of gifted children.

During the past decade, many teachers have sought to foster creative writing in the classroom. And a number of professional books that emphasize the significance of creative writing have appeared during this period. The writers of some of these books stressed the importance of individual expression; yet they appeared to be interested primarily in the form, rather than in the content, of children's writing.

Another group of writers also emphasized the importance of personal reaction and individual expression; but they considered creative expression as a *means,* rather than an *end,* of instruction. They recommended that creative products be appraised by considering the extent to which they mirror the genuine reaction and expression of the pupil. This point of view was strongly endorsed by progressively minded teachers everywhere. In fact, just prior to World War II, several books appeared in which teachers themselves presented creative writing as a living, vital form of communication. One of the most significant of these volumes was *They All Want to Write,* in which four teachers described work in one school. They discussed two types of writing, the personal and the practical. In personal writing, all factors that hinder free expression were discouraged. . . . "It is getting down in one's own language what one thinks or feels that is important." The second type of writing, to be read by another, "should be as clear as it can be made. The notice, the business letter, the report to be given to the teacher or to be filed as reference material must, therefore, meet high standards of clarity, correctness, and arrangement." In this type of writing, errors were sought and corrected; then the final product was carefully copied.

The revision, like the earlier book, will prove genuinely helpful to many classroom teachers, since it records the steps teachers have actually followed in fostering creative writing. And it sets forth the results in the form of children's own compositions. Moreover, this volume brings out more clearly than any other the fact that creative writing offers an excellent vehicle for recognizing, respecting, and cultivating individuality. Chapter 6, "Individual Differences in Writing," presents ten case studies and gives a clear picture of the varied development of each child through samples of his personal and practical writing. Herein we find the developmental concept of education in operation. Education is viewed as a process that aims to bring about the maximum development of each child in terms of his unique nature and needs. As each picture unfolds, we also perceive the role of the teacher. We note the recognition of, and concern for, each child's many-sided nature, and for his attitudes and values. We observe also the contributions that different teachers make by working cooperatively to promote the continuous growth of each child.

It is the hope of the writer that the revised edition of a remarkable volume will be read by a new generation of teachers whose understanding and appreciation of the art of teaching will be equaled only by their enhanced regard for children and their responsibility for fostering growth through creative expression.

PAUL WITTY

PREFACE

This book is addressed to the many persons concerned with teaching English composition in the elementary school who, like us, are eager to preserve children's normal creativity while assuring correct form in their written work. Teachers know how difficult this task is, and prospective teachers will soon find out. Leaders with many years of experience in creative education and in the teaching of English can attest to the problems of enhancing creativity and maintaining long-term growth in the mastery of language essentials. We present effective solutions to these problems and we describe techniques illustrated by many examples of children's writing. Teachers and students in college courses, curriculum workers, supervisors, and administrators will find this text practical as a guide for day-to-day teaching, as well as a springboard for further experimentation.

The need for excellence in teaching English is greater than ever before. If we are to preserve the individuality dear to the American ideal and at the same time teach reasonable control of mechanics, the procedures that accomplish these goals are paramount necessities. To answer these vital needs, we present this third edition of *They All Want To Write: Written English in the Elementary School.*

Our aims are to teach children to write well and to enjoy writing. In our search for guidance we could find no explicit directions that achieved both excellence in composition and joy in self-expression. Hence we determined to test many methods in our classrooms, to discard those that proved ineffective or served only to make children dislike writing. We knew that we must also merge the apparently opposing goals of nurturing the urge to write and of teaching standard English mechanics and structure. We are proud that we have found ways to do this.

In *They All Want To Write* we offer a detailed, step-by-step description of a *balanced writing program*, which shows how to bring forth superior results in informational, objective composition (termed "practical writing"); in imaginative, subjective composition (termed "personal writing"); and how to attain these goals so that children find joy and pride in both types of communication. Because this book is written by teachers for teachers, we place major emphasis upon the concrete, and we reserve theoretical discussion for the concluding chapter.

The first edition of this book was published in 1939. About one hundred children formed the core of our first study, some sixty of whom we taught over a period of four years. The classes were organized as follows:

GROUP I	GROUP II
31 children	30 children
Grades 3 and 4—Saunders	Grades 3 and 4—Jackson
Grades 5 and 6—Burrows (Treut)	Grades 5 and 6—Ferebee

GROUP III	GROUP IV
31 children	20 children
Grades 3 and 4—Saunders	Grades 1 and 3—Jackson

Since the first four-year experiment, we have taught many children in different schools for either one- or two-year periods. The teaching of writing was but one aspect of our work, for as grade teachers we were responsible for the social adjustment of our groups and for their achievement in all areas of subject matter.

This third edition of *They All Want To Write* reports the growth in understanding and the development of methods that have come about in our twenty-five years of experience since the first publication. To the case studies showing individual growth over four years, we have added three showing development in a one-year period. In response to requests for more stories, we have enlarged the Story Supplement. In the chapter on children's verse, we have reported teaching procedures not discussed before, and we have provided copious illustration of both individual and group composition of poetry. In addition, we now include a Verse Supplement.

We have added new examples but have kept in this volume much of the original material. Although some of it pictures activities that occurred many years ago, we believe that these experiences are as representative now as when butter was 31 cents a pound.

As we have continued to study and to experiment, we have grown increasingly aware of our debt to Hughes Mearns. He stood with us at the fork of the road, and he turned our steps into a new way marked by a signpost that read: "This path leads to a heightened respect for each individual and an abiding faith in his innate power." It is because we followed where Hughes Mearns led that the substance of this book came to be.

Our gratitude goes also to J. Ralph McGaughy, who was our guide and stay in bringing the first edition through to publication.

To the many children, teachers, principals, supervisors, graduate and undergraduate students who have spurred us on to greater effort and to new insights, we express our continuing indebtedness.

June D. Ferebee, who worked with us throughout the experiment underlying the first edition of this book, and who shared in the labor of writing both the first and second editions, died in December 1959. Because of her contribution to these earlier publications and because of her eternal commitment to beauty, we treasure the association of her name and her spirit with this, the third, edition of *They All Want To Write*.

February 1964   A.T.B.
                                                       D.C.J.
                                                       D.O.S.

ACKNOWLEDGMENTS

We gratefully acknowledge our appreciation to

The Bronxville Schools, Bronxville, N.Y., Dr. Louis H. Braun, Superintendent; Ursula Henley, Principal, Bronxville Elementary School

The Montgomery County, Maryland, Schools, Dr. C. Taylor Whittier, Superintendent; Edward Haggerty, Principal, Brookmont School, Bethesda, Maryland

We are grateful to the following for permission to use quotations from their publications:

William Morrow & Company, Inc. (Margaret Mead, *The South Seas*)

Alfred A. Knopf, Inc. (Kahlil Gibran, *The Prophet*. Copyright 1923 by Kahlil Gibran; renewal copyright 1951 by Administrators C.T.A. of Kahlil Gibran Estate, and Mary G. Gibran)

The Literary Trustees of Walter de la Mare and The Society of Authors (Walter de la Mare, *Come Hither*)

D. C. Heath and Company (John Dewey, *How We Think*)

Simon and Schuster, Inc. (E. Dimnet, *Art of Thinking;* John Cowper Powys, *A Philosophy of Solitude*)

The Macmillan Company (*Letters of John Keats to His Family and Friends*, ed. Sidney Colvin)

Doubleday & Company, Inc. (Hughes Mearns, *Creative Youth*)

The *Washington Post* (quotation by Robert Frost, May 10, 1963)

CONTENTS

chapter three

PRACTICAL WRITING 45

chapter four

PERSONAL WRITING 79

chapter five

CHILDREN'S VERSE 117

chapter six

INDIVIDUAL DIFFERENCES
IN WRITING: CASE STUDIES 141

chapter seven

WRITING AND GROWTH   217

❋ THEY ALL WANT TO WRITE ❋

chapter one

❀ ❀ ❀ ❀ ❀ ❀ ❀ ❀

Cʜɪʟᴅʀᴇɴ

AND WRITING

The teacher who walks in the shadow of the temple, among his followers, gives not of his wisdom but rather of his faith and his lovingness.
If he is indeed wise he does not bid you enter the house of his wisdom, but rather leads you to the threshhold of your own mind.—ᴋᴀʜʟɪʟ ɢɪʙʀᴀɴ, *The Prophet*

We believe that writing can play a significant part in a child's development. For that reason we have sought ways that would cultivate the skill of writing with correctness and ease and would release free, genuine self-expression. Our early attempts to accomplish both were so discouraging it seemed questionable that a child could be made the minstrel of his own free spirit and a careful scribe as well. But in time ways were found to foster both kinds of composition—ways that during each succeeding year have yielded a better and more abundant return than before. We are now certain that children can experience deep personal satisfaction in writing as well as develop control of its essential mechanics.

If a child is to be an effective, poised individual, he must have an awareness and appreciation of his own power. Such self-knowledge comes only from his frequent opportunities to experiment and to fumble until out of his effort he fashions something that in his eyes is good. This growth pattern is especially evident when a child is learning to put his thoughts on paper. That his product is often crude and clumsy does not matter. It is important that the child, out of himself and working in his own way, produces something of which

1

he can approve. His inner satisfaction—that momentary kinship with creative power—makes him seem worthy to himself and stimulates him to further affort.

The Distinction between Practical and Personal Writing

Many kinds of experience offer opportunity for such self-expression, and writing is one of those most commonly available. There are two fundamental kinds of writing—one practical, the other personal. A gratifying sense of power comes to any individual when he can fulfill the practical writing demands of his own life, whether it is the first brief direction that goes home from school or a lengthy treatise that terminates an individual study. Even more telling in its expansive effect is the personal writing through which a child expresses his thoughts and feelings spontaneously in stories and verse.

It became evident that these two kinds of writing must be handled differently. We encouraged personal writing for the sheer fun of doing it, and we gave ample training in practical and utilitarian writing.

Practical Writing

Practical writing serves the same purpose for children and for adults. The letter below is one example of a service performed by writing. There are many others—plans, memos, captions, lists, reports. These answer genuine practical needs, and a child's eagerness to meet these needs makes him receptive to a teacher's guidance and suggestion. Because the written product communicates with a real audience, the author knows he must be clear and honest, that he must express himself in accurate form. In this way writing standards take on meaning and children are willing to strive to attain them.

The practical need to write a thank-you note to Mr. Porter was the occasion for the letter that follows. The first draft was edited with the teacher, and Doug made a copy he was proud to send.

Dear Mr. Porter,

I want to express my appreciation to you. We are so glad that you could take your time to go to the museum with us. Your children made wonderful speeches before the trip. I would like very much to be in your class when I am the right age. I would not be surprised if you became famous.

I learned a lot out of that trip, especially from the room with the fire engines. I never knew there was an engine called the Goose Neck. The only ones I ever saw were the ones in use now. I would like to know how much your class enjoyed the trip.

Yours truly,

Doug Williams

In the early grades before children achieve some control over handwriting and spelling, they see their ideas and words take visible form by dictating to the teacher. The brief clear note that tells parents, perhaps, about a needed pair of sneakers or the date of an approaching program comes out of the childen's thought, discussion, and planning. The act of composition is theirs. Once written for them on chart or chalkboard its reading is shared by pupils and teacher. At the very beginning of learning to write, pupils may copy only a fraction of the letter or other missive; part may be duplicated, part may be finished by the teacher for the weary writer. As skill is gained, less writing is done for the child, and he takes on more of the labor of completing a good copy.

In later grades, practical writing reaches correct form by more involved processes. The situation that demands writing is made clear. Perhaps an explanation of a new playground division is needed for the school bulletin board or a newsletter; perhaps each pupil's report on one of the many birds wintering near school is an important part of a class study; perhaps programs must be prepared for parents coming to view a class play. In any case, the need is kept vividly before pupils as they prepare to do clear expository writing. Information is gathered, mulled over, extended, clarified, organized. Children read, discuss, sketch, plan, write. Rough drafts are corrected with the teacher in a conference that is the very essence of teaching. Reading the rough draft aloud and correcting it is only one part of this important meeting of minds. Encouraging the struggling author; affirming what is clear; seeing value in the honest but crude expression that, of necessity, had been hastily written—these are also essentials of the conference.

Making a fine copy of the first draft of a report or letter is another part of the cycle that brings a good piece of practical writing into being. Children, like adults, need time to do this well. Copying correctly is not easy and, once done, merits reward so that pride in good writing will become part of the children's attitude towards language. Each child needs some special bit of approval—perhaps admiration for an appropriate illustration, comment on neat arrangement and accurate spelling, appreciation of correct paragraph indents and punctuation. Deserving the most praise is the accomplishment of clear statement of idea, honesty of information, and vividness of expression. Thus in practical writing, children derive satisfaction from knowing that a job is well done and will affect the audience as intended.

Personal Writing

Personal writing should be a happy spontaneous experience in which children are free to express their ideas through ways uniquely their own. In our early teaching, this was anything but true. The meager and stilted products labeled "creative expression" certainly were not worthy of the name, and children wrote only because they had to. But with the understanding that personal writing needed a different approach from that used in practical writing came the gracious acceptance with sincere appreciation of whatever was offered, no matter how poor. This was not always easy, for sometimes the offering was very bad, and the urge and impatience for improvement were strong. However, tongues were held by the thought that first of all, children must write freely and without anxiety.

As the children came to know that their personal expression was acceptable in the form in which it was presented, that it would not be tampered with, nor would they be asked to do it over to suit our standards, writing periods were transformed. Impulse to write grew stronger and volume increased. The children, unconfused by coercion or arbitrary direction, wrote or dictated their ideas for what primarily should be the normal and honest purpose of all creative effort: each strove to please himself or to entertain others. In his dictation of poetry ideas he used words to paint pictures or to catch a special thought or mood. He wanted his stories to delight the crowd, to trap their interest with the first phrase, to make them laugh or hold their breath. Two examples of many successful ventures were these:

❋ ❋ ❋

Star, what makes you shine
So bright upon the water
Making a path for me,
No one but me?
A little path
Just for me!
I feel like a queen.

(*Dictated by Mary Ellen in the third grade.*)

❋ SOMEBODY CHANGED HIS MIND

It was test time in school. Mo and Eenie didn't think it was so awful because they knew their arithmetic and spelling, but Meenie, Meinie and Tig didn't like it because they had played hooky all the time when the teacher was showing them how to do arithmetic. So they thought maybe they could play hooky again and get out of going to school. But Mother Bear had suspected that maybe they would, so she took them to school in the morning and afternoon every day. It took up some of Mother Bear's time, so the Five Bears didn't get very good meals.

Tig and Father Bear wouldn't stand for that, so Father told Mother Bear that he and Tig wouldn't stand for it.

So Mother Bear said, "Sit down, then." She was in a good mood.

"That's the last straw! Tig and I will split our money in half and eat out!"

A little while later, Father and Tig came downstairs and went into the kitchen where Mother Bear was cooking some scallops. Father Bear said that he and Tig had decided that they liked Mother's cooking and they would settle for scallops and tartar sauce.

So Tig, Meenie, and Meinie went to school and liked it. And Father Bear ate what Mother Bear cooked and liked it. The reason why Father Bear changed his mind was because he and Tig had only twenty-five cents together.

*(Written by Tom in fourth grade,
edited by his teacher to facilitate reading.)*

After much trial and error it became obvious that subjective expression must not be shaped to fit external standards. Now our effort is directed toward building into the child's consciousness a realization of what makes writing good, and the method continues to be that of appreciating the good thing when it appears. The original idea, the fresh invention, or the vivid, individual way of saying a thing is singled out for comment because what is approved determines the direction of growth. This is ordinarily done when the children are sharing their work with one another. As they grow increasingly aware of the elements of good writing, their spontaneous appreciation becomes more discriminating and concrete. Although the teacher seems to be in the background, just listening quietly, in reality she is still directing with utmost care. She injects her guidance so unobtrusively that it does not arouse resistance nor disrupt the wholesome spirit of rapport. Even when an epidemic of crudely violent stories or stereotyped plots breaks out, she does not show dismay nor waste her energy berating them. Instead, she watches closely for those flashes of good writing that always appear, knowing well that offensive things, when ignored, gradually drop away if there are better things to take their place. She takes occasion, also, to read from her collection of children's stories—tall tales, animal episodes, humorous everyday adventures—until she diverts their attention and sometimes starts a counterepidemic.

This way of working achieves the aim of making personal writing a happy spontaneous experience for children. Much of what they write is trivial, but at times they reveal a startling power. Disarmed by the disguise of fictitious characters and incident, they divulge secret yearnings and resentments that they would never consciously betray. Childhood appears to be an alien land in which grown-up behavior is frankly appraised according to its immediate effect upon the children themselves. This is a point of view that adults rarely encounter, because boys and girls, for their own protection, have learned to conceal it. When they are writing freely out of their inmost selves, however, it is bound to be exposed, and the teacher has to be ready to hear the truth as they see it. Only by accepting their real feelings can we get the sincerity and vigor we want to nurture.

Principles

We have tried to preserve for each child the privilege of writing out of the depths of his own nature and in the rhythmic pattern peculiar to himself. The teacher has to take responsibility for creating a schoolroom atmosphere in which the child can express himself happily and abundantly without fear or strain. Appreciative comment on attributes of good writing is used to encourage observation, invention, clear vivid expression, and honest individual flavor. And finally, at times quite apart from the writing periods, we have presented good literature that has been enjoyed in a friendly, unhurried fashion with time enough to see in our minds the pictures, and to chuckle or to "shiver in our boots" together.

Because it is difficult at best to catch on paper one's very own ideas, in personal writing the disregard of all factors that hinder is frankly allowed. Spelling, penmanship, appearance are not considered, although the child is encouraged to keep his copy clear enough to read smoothly. It is the getting down in one's own language what one thinks or feels that is important. The child does not write a paper to be inspected; he makes a purely personal recording to be shared or privately enjoyed as he may choose.

On the other hand, writing that is to be shared by another, both because of courtesy and practicability, should be as clear as it can be made. Therefore, the notice, the business letter, the report must meet high standards of clarity, correctness, and arrangement. Different ways of expressing an idea and different forms of organization are experimented with until the most satisfactory one is chosen. Mechanical errors are searched out and corrected, and, finally, a careful copy is made, for the child knows that a draft to be used by others merits his best craftsmanship.

Items of mechanics and sentence form learned in practical writing eventually become matters of common use in what a child writes for his own satisfaction. The absolute fearless honesty of expression exercised in all personal writing gives color and conviction to his practical writing. Furthermore, all these elements of good writing gradually fuse into an enlarged and strengthened writing power.

Through the elementary years, children continue to write with eagerness and with increasing maturity. They find it fun to fix an evanescent, beautiful thought in words, or to make up a good story for their crowd; and they get no less pleasure from their ability to report factual material with aliveness and clarity. To have writing a joy instead of a drudgery is an experience still so unique that we think our discoveries are worthy of more detailed explanation.

chapter two

❀　❀　❀　❀　❀　❀　❀　❀

CHILDREN
BEGIN TO WRITE

The desire for writing grows with writing.
—ERASMUS, *Adagio*

For weeks the first-grade group had been looking forward to their own picnic. Throughout the winter there had been parties, of course, but every single one of them had been planned for others. Now, at the end of the year, the long-promised time had come, and the thought of doing something "just for us" was highly exciting. Naturally, the most important part of a picnic is what there is to eat. Interest in that discussion needed no boost. When the kinds of sandwiches and fruit were agreed upon, the menu was translated into a store order, which was written on the chalkboard for all to see. Three children were chosen to go to the local grocery and find prices that very day. Since first-grade children could not cross the streets alone when the traffic officer was absent, several sixth-grade boys were asked to go along. It would be difficult to say who were the more proud, the elder guides or the three young messengers. Each took his list, which he had copied from the board, and each recorded the prices given by the grocery man. One of the lists is reproduced here.

When the shoppers returned to school, the prices they brought were added to the order that was still on the board. The teacher found the total and did the necessary division. Every youngster watched closely to see how much money he would need to bring,

Harry

Price of 5 lb, 2 bananas @ 7¢ .35

3 lbs. butter @ 31¢ .93

6 sliced bread @ 10¢ .60

4 tomatoes @ 15¢ . 6 0

4 Carrots @ 7¢ .28

3 oranges .07

i pt. mayonaise .33

wax paper 15

This grocery list was planned by the children, recorded by the teacher, and copied by the shoppers. Though this episode occurred in the 1930s, as indicated by the prices, the situation is a timeless one.

and when the result was found, wrote on a slip of paper, "I need 14 cents for the picnic."

This, of course, made it official. Mother could see that a bona fide request was being made. The slips were taken home at lunch time and by the next day every single child brought his 14 cents. Important matters are not likely to be forgotten even by six-year-olds.

Then the same three children who had gone on the morning errand went back to the store and bought the food. They took the same lists again and *used* them, this time as shopping memoranda. A few others went along to help carry packages. When they re-

turned, everything was ready to begin the actual preparation of the picnic lunch.

During the process of washing carrots and making sandwiches, a child remarked: "You know, we ought to thank Miss Wetzel's children for taking us to the store."

"A fine idea," we agreed. "They did something very nice for us and we should thank them. Who wants to do it?"

A few volunteered. The letters were written almost immediately and sent to the older children who had been their guides during the morning.

Dear Miss Wetzel's Class,

Thank you for taking our children across the street. If three of our children went alone they would get run over by a car.

Love from

Sam

A facsimile of another letter follows:

A first-grade letter of appreciation.

We doubt that the drawing up of a business contract is more important to an adult than the writing of the grocery order was to these first-graders. The copying had to be exactly right; the success of the picnic depended on it. Through many concrete experiences children come to know the practical value that writing can have in their own lives and to appreciate why it must be carefully done. Its results are often visible, tangible, or even edible.

In October, a first-grade class dictated and Carolyn copied this brief note.

Beginnings of Composition

In other ways, too, the child discovers that writing is useful in his daily living. He learns to write his name so that he can identify his own materials. He copies a word or phrase from the chalkboard so that he will remember to bring his lunch money or his sneakers. Here are further suggestions for writing allied to a genuine need:

Signs on collections
Lists of children's names and telephone numbers
Lists of birds seen on bird walks
Daily temperature records

Memoranda concerning material to be brought from home
    for cooking
Captions for pictures or movies
Lists of supplies needed for making a terrarium
Calendars
Greeting cards for special holidays and birthdays
Signs to advertise a cooky sale
Invitations or ads for Book Week

As soon as the composition of ideas, no matter how simple, enters into a writing experience, we talk about the ideas first. At this time the children decide what they want to say and we write it on the blackboard so that they may copy it. For example, it may be necessary to tell the parents the exact hours of the new afternoon session. One class formulated and many children copied the following message:

> We come at 1:00.
> We go at 2:30.

Each child carried his note home proudly because he was telling his mother something she needed to know.

Copying from the chalkboard is hard work at first. There are always some whose concentration and muscular skill are not sufficiently developed for them to do as much as the others. Encouragement needs to be given to these children so that their first faltering steps in writing will bring them satisfaction. Always we stand ready to give approval to those who are making a sincere effort, no matter how meager their accomplishments. Occasionally we do part of the writing as illustrated, or we excuse certain individuals from the task.

As time goes on, however, we make sure that even the slowest children write enough to grow in independence. Situations frequently arise when only a single copy of a letter is necessary. Here is an example:

To the School Store:
    Please bring a large roll of brown paper to our room. We want to make a big picture. We are in Room 136.

Mrs. Jackson's Class

After the class has composed the message, a child is selected who needs either the additional practice or the stimulus to do the copying. Donald was chosen to prepare the order. Having such a responsibility touched his pride, and he set to work to do the best he could. He could write at his own slow tempo without the discouragement of being outstripped by more capable neighbors working at the same task. Finally, after considerable labor, he finished the order and delivered it to the school store. When the paper arrived, Donald obviously felt that he had done a good job. Satisfactions like this compensate for struggling effort and spur a child on toward mastery.

Often when writing is finished, the children display their products so that everyone has a chance to view them. Because children thoroughly enjoy looking at one another's work, the bulletin board receives careful inspection. Frequently, we talk with them about the good points in each paper, commenting upon neat arrangement, careful formation of letters, and appropriate illustrations. Taking time to enjoy what they have done offers immediate dividends for their investment of effort.

After many experiences in which the group makes up the message and the class copies it from the board, the children are ready to compose individually. There is the usual class discussion, when they talk over the main points to be included in their letters. Following this, each dictates his own message and the teacher writes it. Then the child puts in the date, the greeting, and the close. To make it more his own, he invariably adds some sort of decoration.

In the thank-you note shown, Pat, of course, decided what he wanted to say; his teacher typed it for him; and then he finished the job. Naturally the illustration was to him an important part of the message. The "Dear Children" were an older group in the school who had taken the first graders on a sleighing party. Before many weeks Pat had sufficient muscular control to enable him to copy a whole letter including the dictated message.

In the daily life at school there are many opportunities for children to write messages that are important to them. A child may dictate a note to his mother asking for a smock or one to the science teacher inquiring how to set up an aquarium. Perhaps he helps others phrase a short letter to a neighboring group inviting

Jan. 18, 1950

Dear children,

It was very nice of you to give the class a ride.
I liked the ride very much and so did the other children.
Thank you for giving Mrs. Jackson a ride.

Pat

One of the first individually composed letters, dictated to the teacher and completed by the child.

them to inspect the new lighthouse just built in the classroom; or he helps to plan a class note requesting permission to go on a trip, and he makes a copy for Mother to sign. Sometimes he dictates a letter to Father "just for fun"—one that is brief enough for him to copy by himself and illustrate eloquently.

All possible variations of the telling-dictating-helping-copying procedure occur at this early age. At the same time the children continue to write the lists, labels, and memoranda that are needed to make their daily living go more smoothly. However, the amount of writing that can be expected in the first school year depends, of course, upon the children's emotional stability and their mental and physical maturity. We have found it wiser to expect too little rather than too much. Young children should not write so frequently or at such length that writing becomes a task they dread.

Milk   Bill   March
                              4

          through   May
                              3

T   weeks   at   22¢ - 1.54

Good   Friday   .09
One   day   we   forgot } - $ 1.45
                                      paid

A child in charge of milk delivery submitted this bill. The experience was sufficiently meaningful to sustain his effort.

Building Standards

In the notes and letters our children write we take pains to stress the value of the individual touch, calling it "something in your letter that is just like you." We begin with the first copied notes by commenting on anything in the decoration that is unique or distinctive, and when letters are independently composed we transfer our attention to the ideas they express. As a child holds up his finished work so that the class can see, we read it aloud, and someone—child or teacher—points out any parts that show the writer has done some personal thinking and feeling about what he has said. Thus in referring to Vicki's thank-you note we commented on the way she described the butter churn, and we called attention to Ruth's quite different reaction. Hearing and seeing one another's work stimulate writing interest and growth.

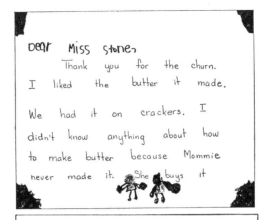

Dear Miss Stones
      Thank you for the churn.
I liked the butter it made.

We had it on crackers. I
didn't know anything about how
to make butter because Mommie
never made it. She buys it

from the A+P

from Ruth

Pupil dictation preserves originality of composition.

Very gradually children acquire writing skills, which sooner or later enable them to dispense with the teacher-stenographer. Although they cannot spell all the words they want to use, they ask for the ones they need, and they have the ability to hold a thought while putting it on paper. This transition from dictating and copying to the independent writing of each sentence as it is composed is a big step. Often, in order to preserve the all-important idea of "making it sound like you," we come to a child's aid by writing the final portion from dictation. Countless letters have been saved from commonplace endings by this device.

Dear   Miss   Greve,
                    Thank   you
for   taking   the   chickens
home.   Did they   get   out

of   the   bath   tub?
               There   is   one
black   one   that   looks   like

he   has   a   flag   on

his   wing.
        How   can   they   sleep
standing   up ?   I   should   think
they   would   fall   down.   I   get
so   tired   on   my   feet   that
I   do.   love   from   Danny.

The personal flavor of this letter was sustained because the child
was given the opportunity to dictate the final portion.

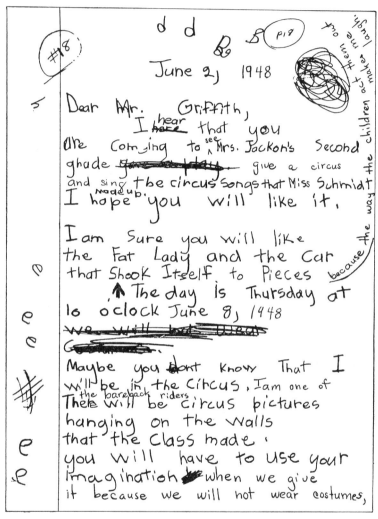

First draft was written by the child and edited with his teacher.

A letter is corrected by the child and teacher together. It may be copied if necessary. Not all writing requires more than one draft, but by the time a child arrives at the middle of the third grade he has had a number of experiences in which copying has been es-

The cut

Fat Lady

June 5, 1948

Dear Mr Griffith,
I hear that you are coming to see Mrs. Jackson's second grade give a circus and sing the circus songs that Miss Schmidt made up. I hope you will like it. I am sure you will like the Fat Lady and the cat that shook itself to pieces because the way the children act them out makes me laugh. The day is Thursday at 10 o'clock June 8, 1948. Maybe you didn't know that I will be in the circus. I am one of the bareback riders. There will be circus pictures hanging on the walls that the class made. You will have to use your imagination when we

The second draft shows how the writer made necessary corrections and decorated his copy.

sential. This is usually due to the rapid and oftentimes untidy writing that results from trying to get ideas down before they are forgotten. Since children recognize the importance of having in "good shape" anything that is to be read by someone else, they accept the job of making a fresh copy.

The checking of first drafts affords opportunity to teach punctuation, such as commas after the salutation of a letter and between the numbers in the date, periods after the abbreviation of the name of a month and at the ends of sentences, and capitals for proper names and the beginnings of sentences. This is by no means the first exposure to these items of mechanics. Over and over again, as the teacher has been writing on the chalkboard, she has indicated the need for such marks of punctuation.

In correcting first drafts the teacher works with each child individually. As they read the letter aloud together, she might pause to ask: "What goes here?"; "Why do we need a period after Feb.?"; or, "Where does the sentence stop?" The time devoted to this is governed by individual needs and abilities. With the child who has had to struggle to express his ideas clearly or for whom writing has been a laborious process the checking is finished quickly; but with one who is more mature and who writes with relative ease, the editing is done more slowly, so that he can take the initiative. The spirit of joint endeavor enhances the experience for both teacher and child.

Varied Opportunities for Writing

Of high value are the situations that lead children to care enough about what they are composing to give it a personal flavor. We believe a child will grow in power in written language if he learns early to respect his individual way of saying things.

Because one third grade found their lockers so small that precious papers were getting crumpled and torn, they welcomed the suggestion of making storage folders for their unfinished work. Since the folders would be kept on a shelf where visitors could easily spot them, it was necessary to indicate that they held material being worked on. Certainly the class did not want "company" to examine them with the notion that their contents were finished samples of writing. Here was a chance to dramatize the fun of "thinking up a title that fits and that belongs only to you." "Of course," it was suggested half-heartedly, "you could call it, 'My Folder of Unfinished Papers.' How do you like that?" By giving a title so obviously dull that everyone could disapprove, hopefully any child would be forestalled from taking the easy, unimaginative way out. The next question, "Has anyone a better idea?" brought no response, and was followed by the suggestion, "Here's one— 'Work under Way'; but," it was added quickly, "that's mine. No one else may use it."

Suggestions came slowly at first, but no effort was made to hurry the children. Instead fresh and fitting ideas were commended in titles such as "I'm Loaded with Unfinished Work"; "Girl at Work— Do Not Disturb"; "Approaching the Finish Line." When invention seemed at a standstill, the class moved to a chalkboard demonstration on how to arrange titles for good placement. As each one was written, its capitalization was discussed. The reasons for lingering over these details were not only to produce attractive covers, but also to permit the children to know the excitement and challenge of achieving individuality even in performing a uniform class assignment.

During this teaching period most of the children had thought of titles; so all were given cheap newsprint on which to try out spacing, penmanship, and decoration. The teacher went about the room, giving help or encouragement where it was needed. Sometimes the class was interrupted to share a pleasing arrangement or a design that carried out the idea conveyed by the title. This often led other children to think of different names or plans for their papers. Since the amount of writing involved was small, anyone could, if he wished, make several trial pages without growing fatigued. Such opportunities for experimentation are of great value because they strengthen a child's feeling of personal responsibility for the quality and the individual character of his output. He tastes the vitalizing pleasure of working, not for the teacher's approval, but for his own.

The making of the real folder came at a later period. Each child was given a large piece of colored paper, which brought forth pleased comments as it was placed on the desks. The use of this paper was deliberate; it was something to live up to.

With their samples to help them, they tackled this final step soberly. Some used folded paper as a guide to keep their writing straight. In a few instances children asked permission to change the

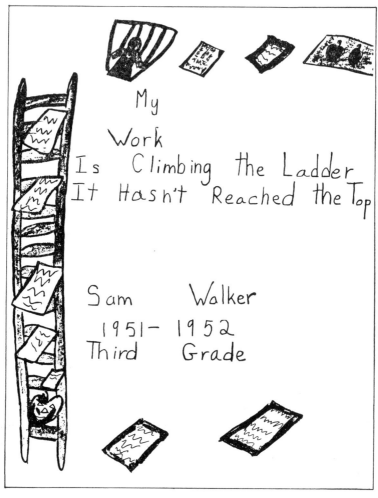

My
Work
Is Climbing the Ladder
It Hasn't Reached the Top

Sam Walker
1951— 1952
Third Grade

First draft of cover design for a folder to hold unfinished work.

names of their folders. Many decided to use designs that were different from their samples. All these changes were approved after quick experiments had been made on scrap paper to make sure that the new ideas were satisfactory.

As soon as the covers were completed, they were placed on the

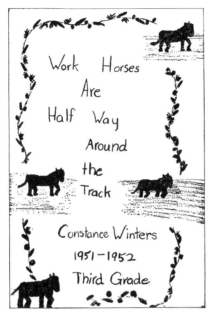

Originality shows in both the title and
illustration for a folder in which to keep
unfinished work.

bulletin board where they remained for a day before they were put
into actual use. No discussion was given to their appraisal, but the
appreciative scrutiny that they received from their makers revealed
how much the youngsters cared about what they had done.

Children thoroughly enjoy writing all kinds of advertisements
and posters to publicize coming events. It is fun to invent slogans
and write copy that will bring buyers to a cooky sale or mothers to
a book talk. Here, as in the making of titles for work folders, the
emphasis is on thinking, and there is a generous amount of oral
exchange. Selecting a few essentials to present dramatically makes
for stronger writing than including many trivial items. The writing,
when it is finally done, is so limited in quantity that it is possible
to exact a high standard of appearance and correctness. Illustration,
especially if it reinforces the idea of the poster or the ad, is always
encouraged, for it is one more way in which a child may put his

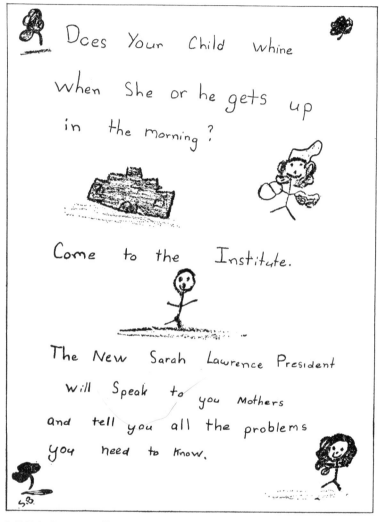

Does Your Child whine when She or he gets up in the morning?

Come to the Institute.

The New Sarah Lawrence President will Speak to you Mothers and tell you all the problems you need to Know.

A P.T.A. Institute offered opportunity for writing an advertisement instead of a letter.

individual stamp upon his product. We have found that when children care about what they are doing, they work far harder than any teacher would have the heart to expect.

Even though the sending of letters and notes provides an opportunity to give meaning and purpose to practical writing experiences, it is unwise to use this type of communication too often. Through having to write too many letters, children frequently acquire more distaste for the activity than skill in doing it. So on occasion we have used posters, slogans, and advertisements as invitations and announcements, and have reserved letter writing for the special occasions when the warmth of their feeling helps to carry children through the sustained and usually arduous task of composing a good letter.

Oral Language Is Basic to Writing

Although the foregoing experiences play an important part in the initiation of written expression, they constitute but one phase of the approach to writing. From the first day in school the program provides children with the opportunity and time for them to express their ideas orally. It is through the patient handling of this form of self-expression that we help them grow in the power to state their thoughts with honesty and clarity. *In the primary grades abundant experience in oral expression is more important in the development of ability to write than the actual writing itself.* Through discussing plans, telling stories and experiences, and simply chatting with each other, children exchange ideas freely and develop the ease and power necessary to fluent writing.

Always, of course, the important element in this sharing of ideas is the classroom atmosphere in which each individual knows his thoughts and feelings will be welcomed. At first some participate very little, but they enjoy listening to others and eventually make contributions of their own.

Some subjects entice all children to take part in group discussions. Experiences during thunderstorms or being in parades, stories about pets, accounts of "the time I had the measles," or "when I went to the circus," reports of dreams—these and many more may start the ball rolling. Topics of this kind are popular when small groups are working and talking together informally. Often we join them and take part in the casual visiting. Such conversations inevitably draw other children to the scene, and in this atmosphere many an inhibited child talks for the first time in an audience situation.

First Reports

Besides encouraging the offhand exchange of ideas, we occasionally inaugurate a class study that is purposefully designed to stimulate inquiry and discussion. This enterprise is of necessity an oral one, fitted to the capacities of young children, but it follows the pattern used to guide the preparation for written reporting in later years. First graders, too, explore a subject in great detail, using such source material as fits their abilities; they work with it long enough to accumulate a supply of facts and to clarify their understandings about them; and they prepare an end product that calls for expression in their own language. Although this book concerns itself primarily with written English, we know that oral reporting in the early grades is a necessary prelude to written reporting in the later ones.

It is essential to start with a congenial subject—some project that will kindle interest quickly and hold it for a considerable length of time. Live things always have an immediate appeal. Through the care and observation of some kind of animal—rabbits, polliwogs, a baby hamster—children learn exciting new facts and taste the satisfaction that comes from realizing that some living thing is dependent upon them. Having something alive in a classroom is not without its problems for the teacher, but it can yield dividends of far-reaching value.

One of our most rewarding ventures was the raising of some baby chickens. The children were so eager for this opportunity that they sat through several sessions of earnest consultation with the science teacher while they planned the right home and food for their guests-to-be. The talk was animated and full of curiosity. These children knew nothing about little chickens except that they were "cute and cuddly," and they had much to learn before they could take over the responsibility for their care. Questions spilled out al-

Please   get   US
25 lbs.   of a baby chick mash.

Mrs.   Jackson's   room
210

A genuine need for writing is illustrated by
this order written in first grade.

most faster than they could be listed on the chalkboard, and many
meetings with enthusiastic discussion were required to answer them
all.

At last the day came when a roomy cage was set up at just the
right height for viewing and handling; and with much ceremony
the children added clean newspaper and food and water and gravel
to make it a comfortable and healthful place for chickens to live.
The next few minutes were tense with expectancy. Then the door
opened and a lusty peeping announced that the chickens had
arrived.

Each child served many turns as caretaker, and the responsibility
was always carried out with dependability and pride. Every morning the appointed children were on hand early, often before the
teacher had arrived, and they set to work at once to clean the cage,
remove the babies from the warm box where they had spent the
cool spring night, and watch with beaming faces while their little
black and yellow charges chirped and ate busily. Always in the
before-school time there was a gallery of fascinated observers. Older
brothers and sisters, even teachers and mothers, stopped by for a
look at the chickens, and on those occasions the first graders were
the experts who answered their questions with surprising accuracy
and with the confident air of authority.

During class time there was abundant opportunity to talk, to

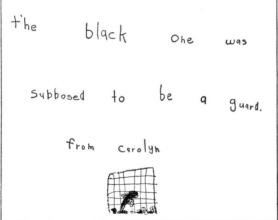

A letter written in connection with the chicken study.

watch, to question, and—most important of all—to enjoy. This was such an absorbing interest that there was no need to hunt up things to talk about. It was a stirring and releasing experience that lasted long enough and was sufficiently dramatic to strike below the surface and affect each child so that he cared mightily about what he was learning.

Eventually the chickens became too big for the cage, and our custodian offered to add them to his flock. Parting with their pets was not easy for the young guardians. To help them over this emotional hurdle we proposed giving a chicken program for the mothers. Again the room was full of bustling excitement. There was much work to be done: decorating the room, making a frieze, drawing large pictures to illustrate facts, writing invitations to mothers, and finally planning a program in which each child would play a significant role.

On the day of the program the room was lined with pictures and by 10 o'clock most of the mothers were sitting in a large semicircle on the small first-grade chairs. The children sat on the floor in front so that they could stand easily and face the audience when their turns came. Anne made the speech of welcome and introduced the guests of honor—the chickens, of course. Shy little Ruthie was the announcer. She sat at one side holding big cards on which were written the questions previously dictated by the class.

Her voice trembled as she read the first one: "Billy, how do baby chicks get born?" But by the time Billy had explained the hatching process she had gained enough composure to go on. "Penny, why are they so fluffy when they are little?" "Jonathan, when they get a drink why do they stretch their necks when they swallow it?" "Jerry, how do we take care of chickens at night?" "Lloyd, how do chickens chew their food?" "David, why do they have little bumps on the sides of their heads?" And so it went until every child had spoken. The mothers listened intently, as one by one, each child stood up and gave an accurate answer to his question, usually in words quite different from the ones he had used when we had practiced.

Such unmemorized answers are factual reports at the first-grade level. They are the culmination of an undertaking that involved the whole child, both his mind and heart; that added to his growing store of knowledge; and that extended his language power.

Oral and Dictated Stories

Just as experiences in oral reporting provide the necessary background for report writing, so do the telling and dictating of original stories furnish the preliminary steps that eventually lead into the more mature technique of story writing. Fortunately most little children are interested in this form of self-expression, and with very little encouragement from us—by merely allowing them time enough for storytelling before an appreciative audience—their stories show gradual but very definite improvement in invention, form, clarification of ideas, content, and individual flavor.

In one second grade almost every day children signed their names on the chalkboard under the caption: "Who Has a Make-up Story?" At the beginning of the year, day after day, the same five children were the ones who wanted to tell stories, although with no exception the whole class enjoyed listening to them. As the weeks went by, new children volunteered and their stories were received with enthusiasm. The approving remarks made by the class had a definite effect on the stories that followed, although individual gains were often almost imperceptible at the outset. The changes in Kathie's stories illustrate this very gradual growth, as well as the amount of mediocre material that must be accepted.

Early in the fall, when in the second grade, she dictated "The Family of Frogs," to her teacher. In this Kathie portrayed conflict with adults—an idea that runs through all of her stories and that was true in her own daily living. Although there is no evident story pattern, it was probably somewhat connected in her thinking, but it moved so rapidly through her mind that she told only the high spots. The story reveals her vivid imagination and a suggestion of the moving picture she visualized as she told it. The sentences she used are the immature run-on type.

* THE FAMILY OF FROGS

Once there was a father frog and he was a big father frog and he had a great big family and he went for a swim. Mother went downtown to buy some groceries and the children were out playing and the baby was inside his cradle. There was an alligator under the cradle and he jumped out. Baby started to cry. The mother came home and she came in and slid down on the floor. There was this pipe that led right out to the water and she slid right down it. But the baby didn't stop crying and one of the children came in. He was too fat and he decided that he needed a glass of milk. So he gave the alligator some milk and then he tried to push him out, but he got much fatter. The alligator's head was just peeping out of the hole. The mother came in through the hole and the alligator's mouth was open and she slid right down his throat. Down in his stomach there was this little house. She opened the door and she looked in. And she saw three ghosts, but the ghosts were friendly and they would not hurt her for the world of alligator's stomach. So they lived happily ever after.

In "The Naughty Little Duck," told less than two weeks later, Kathie had limited her idea and developed it more logically. This time she was able to catch in words more of what was going on in her mind. The invention all centers about the duck who did not want his face washed, and she piled up incidents to effect this end.

* THE NAUGHTY LITTLE DUCK

Once there was a little duck. The little duck was an awful funny little duck. One day the little duck went out to visit his grandma. His grandmother asked him if he wanted some ice cream. The little duck said, "Yes." And he went down to the ice-cream store and bought some ice cream. He smeared it all over his face and didn't like to have his face washed so when he got home the grandmother wanted to wash his face. He started to run all through the house and he slid on a rug. It happened to be that they had a vase that stood on the floor, and he slid right on top of the vase and it had some lovely roses in it. He landed on top of it and the water spilled all over the nice rug and the grandmother gave him a shellacking for being such a naughty boy. Then she took him up to the bathroom and she tried to wash his face, but every time she tried to get the wash cloth on he put his head down. He slipped and saw stars so he couldn't feel it and the grandmother put him in the bathtub and she washed his face. When he came out of being knocked out, he ran downstairs and he grabbed his scooter and he scooted home and I think that ever since then he never would buy an ice-cream cone. And he lived happily ever after.

A month later she related "The Family of Pumpkins," which shows remarkable growth in Kathie's ability to construct a well-knit story that works to a most interesting and personal conclusion.

* THE FAMILY OF PUMPKINS

Once there lived a very old pumpkin. She had quite a lot of babies. They were very nice. They weren't naughty. One of her pumpkins was pretty. She was the nicest and kindest of all, but the others were jealous, and so she was treated very poor. None of her friends were jealous so she had quite a lot of friends. But her mother didn't think that she should do all the hard work, especially cleaning up the house. So she had the best fun.

"Of all the dirty tricks," said one of her sisters. "We have to do all the hard work while she goes out and plays with all her friends. She has too many friends."

The mother pumpkin said, "She has more manners than you. Until you learn how to behave you'll have to help me."

And so all the children tried to do good work. And pretty soon they had all the best of friends, too. And so they had to leave the mother pumpkin home to do all the hard work.

The last story, "The Fat Old Woman," was given just two months after the first one. Whereas the pattern is not so clear in her mind as the one before, Kathie's power to picture things vividly makes it more alive. The run-on sentence has almost disappeared, and has been replaced by more mature types, showing inversion, introductory clauses, and the use of verbals. There is also a pleasing rhythm effected by the balance of long and short sentences.

* THE FAT OLD WOMAN

Once there lived an old woman. She was very fat, because she ate too much. Whenever anyone would invite her to their house she would say, "Have you got any turkey?" They would say, "No." She would go home. But before she went home she would buy a turkey. When she got home she would eat it. One day when she had come back from her shopping she found her dog gone. He was usually at home. She quickly dropped her turkey on the floor and opened the door and ran down the street. She saw her dog at the corner. Very quickly she went one way while the dog went the other way and they met. The fat old woman thought that she would take him home and she would eat all the turkey herself. She looked on the ground and she saw a run in her stocking. She thought she would go home and sew them, but when she went to get her dog, instead of her getting the dog, the dog got her and ate her up, but it took him a year to eat such a fat lady.

The Contribution of Dramatics

The interaction between story invention and group dramatics merits a thorough analysis that can only be touched upon here. We have found that stories and plays contribute immeasurably to each other. Both stir the imagination of children and help them to grow in confidence and power as they lose themselves in the excitement of living play characters. Our experience has shown, however, that each of these activities flourishes best when it is carried on without competition from the other.

By dramatics we do not mean the memorized-line type of play, for it rarely affords any opportunity for the individual to express his creative self. The plays that we do find invaluable are those created by the children themselves through the dramatization of book stories or tales of their own making. The dialogue for these impromptu plays follows a plot line, but the speeches are never written or "learned by heart" and usually vary considerably with each performance, just as the cast of characters may be adjusted, even at the last minute, to provide enough parts for all. Because there is no set script to be learned, the children are free to invent and to inject color without the awkwardness and the inhibitions that accompany the reciting of memorized speeches and with no congealing fear of forgetting lines. Moreover, these dramatic experiences are an outlet for many youngsters who through the disguise of play characters unconsciously reveal hidden facets of their personalities.

The Good Witch and the Bad
                    Witch

Scene 1
    The good witch is trying to
make some magic.
Scene 2
    The prince came in and
showed her some good magic.
Scene 3
        The prince brings his father
the king to the good witch's
house.
    Scene 4
        The prince gets all excited
about the bad witch.
    Scene 5
        The prince and his father
and the good witch and her
daughter capture the bad
witch.
        Scene 6
        They shake hands and
go home.

This copy was used by the announcer of a small group
play. The description of the scenes served to make the
plot clear to the audience and to remind the players of
the forthcoming action.

Growth in Dictated Stories

Along with the many opportunities for oral expression the teacher
should let the children dictate stories and poetry. One way to
initiate dictation is to offer to write down a made-up story that has
been of particular interest to the group. This invariably leads to a
siege of dictating, with the children continuing their enthusiasm
long after the teacher has been forced to call "time out" to rest
her weary fingers. For a teacher who can type, these dictating

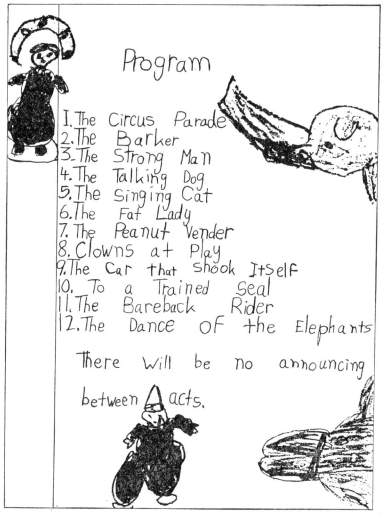

Program

I. The Circus Parade
2. The Barker
3. The Strong Man
4. The Talking Dog
5. The Singing Cat
6. The Fat Lady
7. The Peanut Vender
8. Clowns at Play
9. The Car that Shook Itself
10. To a Trained Seal
11. The Bareback Rider
12. The Dance of the Elephants

There will be no announcing

between acts.

Preparing a program for his mother's use during a second-grade performance gives a child a reason to write in good form.

experiences are not so fatiguing, and they enable a greater number of children to participate.

Little children enjoy dictating stories about pictures they have made. Sometimes a few pieces of Manila paper are folded into a booklet that is then filled with pictures, with care taken to leave sufficient space for the teacher to write down the story that the pictures illustrate. We have found that in many instances children make the transition from this to another stage wherein they themselves write captions under the illustration in these booklets, asking the teacher to spell needed words or phrases.

One of the essential accompaniments of the child's dictating experience is the reading aloud of his product. Often very little has any outstanding quality. The teacher should take this for granted, realizing that out of great quantities of mediocre output only a little of artistic merit will emerge. Insofar as she can, the teacher reads aloud everything that is dictated, but she takes pains to emphasize those bits of writing that, because of their originality and freshness of approach, will raise standards and prove inspirational to the others.

This reading should be planned carefully in order to contribute to the child's recognition and appreciation of the creative expression of thought as well as to his growth in the ability to do it himself. Very few stories should be read at one time, and they should be read well. It is important to choose periods when the children are relaxed, and in a receptive mood. When they are too tired to sit quietly, they can get nothing from the reading. In such a negative atmosphere much that the teacher has been trying to build may be destroyed.

Three illustrations follow with the comments the class made after each had been read. These are stories told by beginning second-grade children.

* THE LITTLE PIECE OF CHALK

Once there was a little piece of chalk. He thought he was walking on the sidewalk, but he was walking on the blackboard. One day he was wandering around the board and he came to a big, big house. It was a doll house. Something was hanging down from one window. It was a big piece of rope. He climbed on the big piece of rope and he ran up into the window. Then he saw the blackboard again. And he went on the blackboard and he drew a little girl holding a basket. The little girl walked in the bedroom with her mother. The mother couldn't see the piece of chalk and she wondered how that was drawn.

The mother said, "Well, I can't do anything about it."

So she went out in the kitchen and cooked the dinner. And the little girl went out to play with her friends. When dinner was ready the little girl came in and ate her dinner. After she ate her dinner she went to bed. The next morning she got up and went to school. And they lived happily ever after.

Tommy said, "I like the idea of making a story about a piece of chalk."

Peggy's comment was, "I think it was nice where the chalk thought he was walking on a sidewalk, but it was really the bottom of the blackboard."

Kathie said, "I liked it where the mother and girl were fooled because they didn't know who had been there."

* TOMMY WITH HIS NEW TEDDY BEAR

Once upon a time there was a little boy named Tommy. Tommy wanted a teddy bear. One day he went out to play. He looked in all the garbage cans. He didn't find any teddy bear. He came home and he asked his mother if they could go to New York. The mother said, "I'll think about it."

So they went to New York. They looked in every store. The mother said she was tired. Tommy said, "Come on, Mother, I want to find a brown teddy bear instead of black ones and white ones." So the mother said, "O.K., we'll walk to the next store."

There was the little brown teddy bear sitting in the window scratching his head. They went in the store. They came out again. Tommy ran all over the town, bumping into everyone with the teddy bear because he was so happy.

Harry thought, "It sounded just cute where Tommy saw 'the little brown teddy bear sitting in the window scratching his head.'"

Ruth liked the ending. She said, "Tommy sounded so happy, and it didn't say 'they lived happily ever after.'"

Frank said, "Grace made me see a picture of Tommy when he ran all over town bumping into everyone."

* THE LITTLE NEW POCKET

Once there was a little pocket. This little pocket was sewed on a dress and he didn't like it. So this little pocket didn't know who wore this dress. So he planned to go away. And the little girl never went out of the house. All she did was look out the window at the big gray buildings. So all he saw was green and gray, because the dress was green and all he looked at was himself. Of course he had two eyes, a nose and a mouth and two legs and two arms, but he didn't have any teeth because he was a new pocket and the dress was new, too.

He planned to get away so he got off his hook that he was hanging on and tried to get out of the closet, but he couldn't get out of the closet. Finally he tried so much that he got out and looked for the scissor box, but he could not find it because it was moved to another place. He dragged the dress all around. Finally he came to the scissor box and just as he was reaching his hands out of the scissor box with the scissors the little girl came in. He lied down and tried to go to sleep, but he couldn't because he wanted to get away. He went snip, snip, snip, and finally he was loose and he wabbled around the room because he was a little pocket and he couldn't walk very straight. But finally he walked out of the door and he saw this man walking along the hall to this middle-sized box and it was very tall. He wondered what it was because he couldn't think very straight, but finally he knew. "It is an elevator," he said. And he saw a man walking out of another apartment.

The man went into the box and the door shut and it disappeared. So the pocket looked through the cracks and only saw the top and he dropped the handkerchief that the little girl had put in him one day.

He said, "I will be found out. They will see this handkerchief so I must take it."

He took it and he dropped the handkerchief through the bars of the elevator. It stuck in one of the ropes and the elevator got stuck coming up. The pocket squeezed through the bars and sailed down into the ventilator of the elevator. He rolled himself up in a long coil and squeezed through the net. He went sailing right on the man's head and he jumped off and thought he would get the handkerchief. He took the handkerchief out of where it was stuck. The man was in such a hurry to try and fix the elevator that he knocked the lever on. He went sailing up, but the pocket jumped up on the lever and pushed it back and stopped it. Then he pushed it the other way and it went sailing down and he went out of the door and out of another door and was outside.

He felt some drops. He thought it was raining, so he looked up and said, "Is that a cloud? No, it isn't." And there was the little girl crying. "My, my," said he, "I wonder why she is crying. Oh, I know—because I am lost. I must go right back."

So he went back and took a needle and thread and sewed himself onto the new dress, and he never took scissors and tried to cut himself loose again.

The children loved this one and talked about it at length. They thought it was a different idea. The part about the pocket's seeing only green and gray interested them. They laughed when John said, "He didn't have any teeth because he was a new pocket and the dress was new, too." They liked the ending because "it was not 'living happily ever after' and it ended quickly." And they especially enjoyed the conversation when the pocket thought it was raining.

Transition from Story Dictating to Writing

Eventually the time comes when children show the desire to take a more active part in the recording of their stories. Usually, in the beginning stages, they dictate a paragraph at a time, copying each in turn until the story is completed. Sometimes they write down the first part of a story and dictate the end of it to the teacher. Finally, they reach the place where they are able to write a story alone, asking only for spelling help.

The transition from a child's dictating to the actual writing of his own stories is a matter of individual growth. In some instances children take over the writing of utilitarian material before they attempt the independent writing of their story ideas. Probably this is because in utilitarian writing they can go back to sources if an idea is lost, whereas in imaginative writing thoughts follow one another so fast that they escape. There is no age limit when dictating becomes taboo. Teachers of older children who allow some opportunities for dictating are amazed at the impetus given to all kinds of writing.

In contrast to their dictated stories children's first independent efforts are meager and disjointed. Although the story may be rich and complete in the child's imagination, his thoughts fly so fast that he catches only fragments of them in writing. The teacher, in her reading aloud to the group, must be able to "sell" these first independently written stories so that the writer feels satisfaction from having worked so hard. To do this, she studies his telegraphic style, talking it over with him, so that when she reads aloud she can fill in the gaps in order to make his story say what he wanted it to say.

A third-grade teacher used the following technique for beginning the independent writing of stories: She offered to help four who had already shown such an interest. Sitting at a large round table, the teacher wrote needed words on slips of paper just as fast as the children asked for them. This enabled them to turn out a finished piece of work before their energy was exhausted. Reading the stories aloud brought forth several requests by other members of the group for such an opportunity to write. In this way story writing was fostered. Always the teacher made it a point to choose only a few for this writing group so that she might give help immediately. Therefore, the continuity of thinking was maintained, and the children had the satisfaction of getting their stories quickly into a permanent form.

The Teacher's Role

It is the school's responsibility to help children know the release and delight of personal writing and to acquire pride in meeting the necessary standards of practical writing. To create a setting in which this power can develop is a constant challenge to the teacher. She must provide a program that is stimulating and varied, but at the

same time she must protect children from being bombarded by so many interests that they become confused and their energies dissipated. The best results are obtained when there is a nice balance between satisfying experiences and time for their assimilation.

Normal growth in writing as in all areas does not proceed in a straight line—but there must be a sense of moving ahead. This development will best take place in a warm and appreciative atmosphere. The quality and sincerity of child writing dwindles to nothing if fear and self-consciousness set in. When children are fed a nourishing diet of experiences, when their underlying need for growth is being fulfilled, and when they are free to write naturally and joyously, they grow in writing power and they mature mentally and emotionally as well.

chapter three

✿　✿　✿　✿　✿　✿　✿　✿

PRACTICAL WRITING

The bond of society consists of reason and speech.
—CICERO, *De Officiis*

Inviting one's parents to a star party, as did David in the following letter, is a serious responsibility. If adults can be made to see the necessity for an eight-year-old's going to school after dark, the much-wanted permission will be forthcoming. If the message is not clear and convincing in tone, the whole plan will result in failure. The long weeks of study during which the third graders had worked with white hot enthusiasm will have a fitting climax if shared with their parents in plain view of the night sky. Reporting knowledge in such a setting would add prestige to the young workers who so obviously seek grown-up importance. Hence the children worked carefully in writing, correcting, and copying these letters of invitation. Similar in purpose to David's but different in phrasing, each presented information essential to parental understanding of the bona fide nature of the evening session.

Letters were but a fractional part of this long study. For the reports that were to accompany the conducted tour of the constellations came from much seeing, working, talking, drawing, painting, listening, and planning. Reading, too, was a source of information: the teacher's oral reading of books too difficult for the children to read themselves; the reading of star charts and pictures, captions and labels. But firsthand experiences were the bedrock for these learnings. These children looked for planets and constellations in the evening sky; they charted in their notebooks what they had seen.

First draft of David's letter to his parents inviting them to the star party his third grade was having. His carefully copied second draft was proudly taken home.

They went to the planetarium to view moving models of the solar system, and to see a film-made procession of the stars showing a whole night's star cycle in a few minutes. They saw and touched specimens of meteorites; they clarified their detailed, concrete experiences through conversation and through making many illustrative renditions of their learnings. Star charts, clearly organized notebooks, and slides would accompany their talks, which were planned to show their parent audience how much they had learned about Saturn, Venus, Orion, Aldebaran, and other ear-delighting members of the heavenly regions.

Writing and Talking Interact

Because of the sheer labor of handwriting, oral reporting seems more productive for third graders. For these children the sound exposition of ideas needs to be oral. Writing skills, for all their usefulness in plans, letters, captions, and explanations, are not elastic enough for the fluency demanded by this age group's swift flow of thought. But segments of the whole cycle of communication inevitably are written; indeed, it appears in the star study, as in many another, that writing and talking complement each other. Recorded plans, titles, charts, and notebooks give permanence to the ephemeral spoken word. Illustrations are also part of the solid structure of ideas. They clarify understanding and provide a reliable nucleus for the oral reports. Further than this, such visible materials to handle and explain contribute markedly to children's self-confidence by relating language both to the manipulation and to the substance of ideas.

Throughout the star study this relation of talking to writing was reciprocal. Daily "star meetings" were held at which facts discovered and rediscovered were gloated over with the joy usually reserved for personal treasures. These informal chats about what the children were finding revealed a deep absorption in factual knowledge. Talking about the many fragments of information not only broadened the children's awareness of the range of man's astronomical knowledge but also led even these young observers to sense the necessity for grouping their many items of information. Plans for another meeting usually had to be recorded on the chalkboard. Questions postponed for future reference were charted so as not to be forgotten. Books needed for special items were often listed. And as the idea took shape that an evening meeting with parents would be the happiest climax for the long study, many plans had to be jotted down: plans as to who would give which topic, and where each part of the program was to be held, since some of it inescapably had to be out-of-doors.

Writing made possible the more precise arrangements for the

anticipated program. Writing brought about the notebooks that represented a serious organizing effort for these third graders. The well-written table of contents suggests the orderliness that helped to make the copiously illustrated books an effective record. The first draft of David's invitation to the parents, at the beginning of this chapter, shows the careful correction he was willing to work out with the teacher before making a final copy. John's full-page drawing of the planet Mars indicates the combining of pictorial representation with verbal explanation. This twofold clarification of ideas served the young astronomers many times in their dealing with the expansive subject matter of stars, moons, and planets.

Table of Contents

	Page
Sun	1,2
Beginning of the solar system	3
Solar System	4
Our moon	5
Mars	6
Jupiter	7
Saturn	8
Saturn's rings	9
Comets	10
Meteors	11
Meteorite	12
List of important Stars	13
Taurus the bull	14
Orion the hunter	15
Canis Major	16
Lepus the hare	17
Cancer the crab	18
Big and little Dipper	19

A third-grade boy made this table of contents for his star notebook.

the planet
Mars

Halley's comet

moon

moon

/s/u

Mars is a little smaller
than the Earth. Mars has
two moons.

Earth/

A page from a third-grade boy's star notebook.

Oral Reporting Precedes Written Reporting

Learning to make a good oral report must precede the still more difficult task of preparing a written one. Even gathering material for oral reports exposes children to the danger of copying whole sections from reference sources. To avoid this risk of plagiarism we give children many firsthand experiences before they read. Then when they return to books, they already know a great deal about the material they are searching for. This knowledge fosters the assimilation of ideas without the helpless feeling of being overwhelmed by new facts one must somehow gather and control.

Children often report their findings in class sessions. They tell interesting facts and ideas that they have discovered in their reading. The mere telling of information lessens the probability of copying or parroting whole pages from some convenient reference. To achieve this independence children are put in the social situation where talking to their peers demands they make things clear in their own words.

During the first weeks of school in one fourth grade, the real experiences that introduced the oral reporting of children's individual animal studies were prerequisite to the integrity of later individual factual writing. As part of a required study of animal adaptation to various climates, the children's own pets and animals living nearby were discussed with much warmth. Interest in these apparently random fact-finding meetings ran high before a beginning of organization was attempted. "What are all the different things it's important to know about animals?" was asked. With a bit of discussion and some re-ordering of suggestions a chart was made that included:

Appearance
Food
Protection
Enemies
Where they live
Their homes

These topics formed the nucleus of further sharing of findings about animals. More data were found in reading matter, in pictures, and from adults.

Getting facts from people who knew and from a number of excellent animal pictures was climaxed by a trip to the zoo. Here the prime questions were: "How does the animal protect himself?" "What kinds of food do they eat?" "How many babies do they have?" This building of factual background before turning to the printed page equipped the children with many meanings for the words they were to meet.

This acquaintance also provided the fourth-grade zoologists with enough contacts for them to begin to select their individual topics. Obviously each child could not report orally or in writing on all the animals of the study that ranged from the small animals near at hand—squirrels, chipmunks, and woodchucks—to those of the jungle and forest. Narrowing one's topic is as necessary in elementary-school reporting as in the graduate school. "Take your time to choose the one you want to report on. Look at lots of books to be sure you can find good reading material before you decide. It's better to take time to choose than to change in midstream," they were counseled.

Searching for Material

When four or five children had decided upon the animals they wanted to study, they were gathered together for some direct instruction in how to use reference books. Contents, indices, and the arrangements of encyclopedias were pointed out and their use demonstrated. A shelf full of the best books on animals was collected. Everyone was caught up in the excitement of the search. And, as so often happens in the quest for material pertinent to a given topic, individuals found as much for their neighbors as for themselves. "Say, you've got to get this book—you're going to need it when you get going on the elephant" was the kind of advice often overheard.

As the children began to find a number of references bearing on their chosen animal they, of course, wanted to preserve many of the details for their reports. Some started copying word for word what was in print. The time had come to lay a foundation for later note taking. Each child was given a half-dozen cards and was told to put down the name of any book especially good for his animal and the page or pages on which he found the material. "But I'll never remember exactly how many bushels of hay an elephant eats in a day," complained Henry. So facts that had to be precise, like sizes or speeds or weights, were agreed upon as the only kinds of notes to take. To copy the exact figures meant also the obligation of noting the name of the book and the page. This was enough of a writing chore to check the impulse to copy too many things verbatim. Sketches and diagrams were often suggested as better ways to get down an idea. It is unlikely that fourth or fifth graders can do other kinds of note taking without descending to outright plagiarism. Hence we learned to keep note taking very simple if done at all.

How much to find out, how many more books to read were questioned one day when the searching and reading were going at full speed. "Look at the chart of things we thought were important to know about animals and see how much you're sure of," they were advised. (See list of topics p. 50.) I know about the bear's appearance pretty well and about his enemies and how he protects himself," said Jon, in such a stocktaking. "I don't know all the places where bears live—there seem to be so many. I'll have to find more about that."

As the children found more of what they were looking for, their eagerness in the quest became more intense. Knowledge added to curiosity. The enthusiasm that springs from working in a company of eager fellow workers became truly electric. A few still feared that they would forget some choice bit of detail, but were willing to accept the adult promise that such matters could be taken care of later. Knowing that they could find the book and page again from their book card substantiated this assurance.

During this period of intensive reading two problems arose. As in almost any group of fourth graders, some children found reference reading discouragingly difficult. They needed help and they needed short periods for concentrated effort. One relatively simple device used in many study sessions was a notice on the chalkboard "Sign Here for Help" under which the children needing help wrote their names. The teacher was then able to get to these children in the order of their signatures, thus avoiding confusion and waste of time. Her help took many forms. Sometimes it was simply a matter of reaching for the right book and pointing out the appropriate section of its index. Quite often a child needed to clear his thinking, and the teacher said, "Tell me what you know about the chipmunk's home." Answering such questions often showed where the pupil needed more information. Occasionally the teacher read to the child a paragraph from a difficult reference and explained it. And there were many times when she told directly the bit of information that an individual was seeking. The other problem was that of fatigue and what the poor readers (or immature readers) might do while waiting their turn for help. They were urged to make illustrations for their reports—pictures, an introductory announcement, a surprising statement of size or kind of protection, or a diagram showing, perhaps, claws and pads on a tiger's feet. The children kept in folders the pictorial material that they were getting ready for their oral reports.

Note Taking in Upper Grades

The most successful approaches to note taking with upper-grade pupils were found when they became concerned about the chance of forgetting data needed in a report whether oral or written. At such a strategic time the several pupils facing the dilemma were called upon to show the class what they had found and why they wanted to record some of it. Then the situation was broadened to include those who were nearing such a hurdle, and it was announced that some periods for special training in note taking would be set aside.

For a whole class or a sizable group of those ready or nearly ready to begin note taking, available texts in science or social studies were used. In one sixth grade the teacher said, "Let's assume that we are all trying to write reports on fruit growing in New York State. It would be ridiculous, of course, for everyone to report on the same topic, but this is just for practice. After we learn how to do it, each person will take notes for his own individual report."

The first step in selection of material for any note taking is to have a clear purpose toward which one is working. On this occasion the goal was gathering interesting data to report to the class audience. Hence, the pupils were asked to skim the selection used for practice work and then formulate orally the three or four topics in the passage that might be worthwhile to their fellows. These topics were jotted down in scattered places on the chalkboard. Then the children were asked to read the section again and to try to tell something about each of the important topics jotted down.

"Put your pencils away," the pupils were advised during these readings. "You take more notes with your mind than with your pencil."

After a few samples of telling the important ideas aloud, the students read again, this time to dictate a brief reminder for recording on the chalkboard. Such "memory clues" encase a whole set of ideas. Different children suggested different clues for the same facts, and these were recorded to dramatize the diverse ways in which people work on this complex job. The pupils needed to realize that even when formulating notes on a selection that all had read they could express ideas honestly and uniquely. It is in such commonplace learnings, as well as in more colorful ones, that respect for individuality can be enhanced. Independence in expression is the goal rather than a close paraphrasing of what one has read.

Because for children long notes are prone to be imitative as well as time consuming, brief word clues were the focus. Sometimes the children counted the words used by the author. They found, for example, that one pupil's phrase contained only eleven words: "Insects—greatest pest to orchards—destroy more than frost or storms". Both the detailed treatment of the original version and the economy of notes revealed special values, and children could see the roles played by each form of writing.

After several attempts at oral formulation and dictation, the pupils were ready to try a bit of independent note taking. They read another paragraph, selected its essential point, and then tried to devise a brief phrase or two that would recall it. While they did this, the teacher was available to give help to those who still needed the step of "saying it aloud." Many wanted to try out their notes orally with the teacher and needed encouragement to sustain rigorous effort.

After two or three sessions of this kind of teaching, some children were ready to go on to taking notes for their individual reports, the goal from which the whole class had been temporarily diverted. Some children needed another lesson focused upon selecting essentials and phrasing them briefly. All needed help when they went back to read various references for their special reports, but they had acquired the basic procedures of skimming, formulating questions, reading and rereading before trying to reduce a long passage to a few brief but revealing phrases. Many refinements remained for later learnings. However, the necessity of clear-cut aims for searching out information and the children's awareness of their obligation to be honest and independent were gratifyingly obvious as they returned to gathering data for their emerging reports.

Organizing and Presenting Oral Reports

After two or three weeks some of the fastest workers declared that they were ready, that there was simply no more to be found about their particular animals. The whole class was assembled to consider how to make an interesting oral report. The children were told, of course, that they might start with any topic on their list of things to know about animals. "Begin with the topic you are most interested in yourself," they were advised. "For instance, if you are reporting on the porcupine you might want to begin with his unusual way of protecting himself."

Because children learn much from one another and because first examples in such a situation are influential, it was found expedient to give really detailed help to those who were ready to report. These first reporters were asked if they needed help on any special part of their work. Perhaps an item of fact had to be checked or a more accurate reference for some moot point decided upon. But the teacher's main job was that of helping the child to organize his material. "What are you going to tell about first?" was followed by her jotting down on a card the topic to use as a beginning. A sample of the sequence worked out with one fourth-grader follows:

* W A L R U S

1. Loose skin and big teeth but real ivory—*Introduction*
2. Where people hunt them and why
   Map
3. The walrus family
   Picture
4. Protection
   Picture
5. Food
6. Future supply of walruses

With this in hand for a guide and with illustrative material arranged in sequence so it could be easily shown, the reporter was ready and confident of his audience's interest.

This individual planning with the teacher took less and less time. As some reports were given in well-ordered sequence, the children became aware of what made a good report. They came to their planning conferences so well-geared to the job that it took only a brief checking to give that sense of certainty for which most fourth graders still look to adults. The careful preparation of content and sequence that each child had made, the sense of group enterprise that had come from the real experiences and from the avid search for materials and sharing of findings, set the stage for active listening. Preparing the group to hear each report was as carefully attended to as when the first graders shared their information about chickens (Chapter 2). Discussion after each report indicated that genuine concern had developed for the success of each speaker as well as interest in his exciting subject matter.

Starting Written Reports

It is not until the end of the fourth grade that most children show the maturity necessary for writing extensive, well-stocked, well-organized informational reports. Indeed, even fourth graders can write well only as the climax of a long series of activities. They must first amass much concrete information; they must become deeply immersed in the subject matter; and, of course, they must share findings through talking, listening, and illustrating before they can write.

In one class, weeks of study about Vikings had preceded the stage of readiness to write about them. This was the first time that fourth graders had used books as a source of much of their information. Prior to this, real and concrete materials were the main sources of data. In third grade few could read well enough to use the variety of books necessary. Furthermore, the more serious danger of merely acquiring words to put down on paper, which is so often mistaken for true writing, had to be avoided. Always the menace of verbalism had to be forestalled by laying a foundation of detailed, concrete information before reading.

One of the most difficult things about informational writing, even for many grownups, is gettings started. This was especially true of the class preparing to write about explorers.

Although these children had devoted much time to the careful reading of reference books, consulted source material, studied pictures, real objects, and other illustrative material, they needed help in finding an organization that would give shape to the mass of information they had accumulated. This presented an opportunity for the economy of class teaching. We brought the group together and asked such questions as, "What are some of the important points you will need to include in writing about Vikings?" The children responded with the following:

Food
Homes
Places explored
Religion and customs
Famous Vikings
Ships
Sagas

The teacher listed the topics on the chalkboard as the children suggested them.

Getting the first thoughts down on paper presents many hurdles. We have found it helpful to ask: "Which of these topics do you know a good deal about?" When Pat said he knew a lot about Viking ships, he was asked to start talking about that subject to the class. Seizing a pencil and paper the teacher momentarily became his scribe. The others watched while she wrote "Ships" at the top of the page and rapidly jotted down his first few enthusiastic sentences as they tumbled out. After a minute or two he was given the chance to read back to the class what was now on paper. Following this demonstration of how one can "talk his ideas to his paper" the children returned to their places and got set for work. Each was given several pieces of paper. All were elated at having so much paper to start with and they were relieved to learn that this first draft did not have to be in perfect handwriting —just had to be sufficiently "clean" copy to make editing and recopying as easy as possible. These new techniques for putting thoughts on paper seemed to break down the Herculean task into controllable parts.

A child could decide for himself which topic he wished to write about first. The topic was written at the top of the sheet and then it was "full steam ahead"—writing fast enough to catch ideas before they escaped. (The teacher, of course, stood at the chalkboard and wrote words children didn't know how to spell.) When a child became fatigued, he was encouraged to set pencil aside and read over what he had written. Often new thoughts came to be added to a topic. If not, that one was set aside, and he wrote another heading on a clean sheet of paper before beginning the next.

The caution to write nothing else on the paper but what was known about ships and to take a fresh sheet for Viking foods seemed a little startling at first. This sudden bounty in the use of paper had many immediately apparent possibilities. Rough drafts always need space for correcting. Further, the evidence that one is covering many pages adds impetus to the process, for children often feel that lengthy writing is related to grown-up status. But the most important outcome is that of arranging material so that all one's ideas about a heading are grouped together logically. When the child eventually decides upon the sequence, reshuffling topics and pages to fit is relatively easy. For most children the sentences written on each topic form a single paragraph. In later grades more discriminating organization of paragraphs is possible, depending upon the maturity of the child and the nature of the topic.

Maintaining Individuality and Interest

Two factors demand simultaneous concern in the writing of reports: the product must be made factually true, and the writing must be kept as individual in style as its writer. Once the children are off to a good start with their packs of paper, the teacher interrupts occasionally to ask who is writing something that is not only true but would also be fun to hear. Free of the inhibitions of adult writers, children are eager to read what they have written. Kim, for example, was excited about the way he had pictured the Vikings setting off across the ocean:

*   *   *

Eric was such a good advertiser that twenty-four ships set sail with him when he left Iceland for Greenland. Imagine twenty-four ships loaded with people and cattle facing all the danger of the sea. It was rough going, and sad enough, only fourteen ships made it.

John's pride in the skill of the Viking navigators showed in the sentence that he wanted to read aloud:

*   *   *

Around the year 1000, the compass did not exist in the northern world, so the Vikings had only the North Star and the sun to guide them.

Bill savored the vigorous picture made by his words:

*   *   *

Nevertheless, the Vikings gathered twenty-four ships and in a short time they were OFF! Some days later a big gale came upon them. They were thrashed around like feathers.

This spilling over of enthusiasm contributes markedly to the enjoyment of the difficult job. It adds the elusive element of group momentum. And further it demonstrates that one's personal reaction adds flavor and color to a recital of facts. To the degree that the writer puts his own stamp on his report, it becomes a part of him. This kind of individualization compels the assimilation of what otherwise would be raw data soon forgotten. Accuracy and the strength of one's writing are of a piece.

Since in spite of enthusiasm, writing is a fatiguing occupation, it has been found wise to make these periods short. Once children have got the feel of the thing, once they have caught on to the idea that they can begin with the topic that interests them most, the teacher plans immediately to forestall weariness. Because the threshold of fatigue was reasonably high for the fourth-grade group described here, the writing was continued for about fifteen minutes. "Finish the idea you're writing," they were then told, "but don't start any new ones now." "Oh, no!" they objected, almost with one voice. "We can't stop yet!"

To stop when vigor is high is productive. The feeling remains that one must get back to the work tomorrow, that one is full of ideas. The next day, a few minutes of reading aloud what some had written set everyone writing with a fervor equal to that of the day before.

Organizing Written Reports

After three or four periods it became obvious that the children were almost "written out," that most of them were coming to the end of either their knowledge or their energies. At this point the class was again gathered together to consider a further step. Facts had been recorded accurately and in an interesting way. But since these reports were to go home for parents, something else was needed. "What would you have to do to catch the interest of a reader who picks up your report cold?" the children were asked.

It was quickly decided that the statement of facts must be preceded by something to make a reader take notice immediately. Some children thought that their own feelings about the topic would prepare for what was to come. As is often the case in adult writing, the children wrote their beginnings after they had written the body of their reports. Here are some sample introductions:

❈   ❈   ❈

About five hundred years before Columbus, the Vikings were tough and bold. They came from Norway, Sweden, and Denmark. The Vikings were the first men to discover America.

Back in the year 1000, some people were Vikings and some people weren't. The Vikings were a kind of explorer. They were also fishermen and sometimes pirates.

The Vikings sailed from Norway to Iceland to start a new life because Eric the Red started trouble in Norway. Again Eric started fights so he was expelled from Iceland. He and his men sailed off to the West.

The following report by a fourth grader contains a great deal of the writer's personality, and is a good example of the results obtained by the technique described.

* HERE COMES THE WOODCHUCK—
BIG, FAT AND HANDSOME

Out in the open spaces where there are rocks the woodchuck builds his home so that the bears and the dogs can't get him. You could find the look-out tower. It is made from the dirt that he has dug out while he was building his home.

A woodchuck's home is a burrow which he digs under stone walls. He spends most of his time eating vegetables like carrots, corn, lettuce and all young vegetables. Farmers do not like it because woodchucks raid their gardens.

If you go over to the woodchuck's home you'd find four to nine babies so that's why every time the farmers shoot one they can't get rid of them because there are so many more than they can shoot.

Their protection is their home mostly. They use their tower to see if any enemies are coming and when they do come, the woodchuck goes in head first and if the enemy comes while their babies are playing outside the woodchuck whistles for them to come in the hole. When the dogs try to get in the hole, the woodchuck just goes out the back door and watches the dog digging away. When the woodchuck is surrounded he'll snap his teeth and claw like a cat.

Extended Reporting in Later Grades

As experience accumulates, the responsibility for saying clearly what one wishes to report continues to be felt personally. Control of factual data, greater reading power, and longer attention span all contribute to the extension of reporting ability. Other factors also influence this greater strength. Children's intimate and genuine association with a wealth of literature means an inevitable absorption with some of the familiar patterns of folklore and fairy tales, and with some of the form and idiom, rhythm and cadence of our language.

The sheer bulk of prose consumed by the average voracious reader of eight-to-twelve years may partly account for the tendency toward more voluminous expression. It also seems true that the respect for honesty in practical writing and the opportunity for sincerity in personal expression make children much more sensitive to color, ruggedness, fragile delicacy, or exact phrasing in what they hear. One group of sixth-grade children upon hearing *Moti Guj, Mutineer* spontaneously picked out many of the elements that make Kipling's style inimitable.

"Oh, read that again, please—where he called him 'warty toad of a dried mud puddle,' " begged Alice.

"And read all those other things Deesa called him," demanded another. "They're good."

"That part, too," remarked Jerry, "where Moti Guj swung the baby up in the air in his trunk—that was awfully smart. Gosh, he *had* Chihun there."

"There's something alike in all Kipling's stories and yet every animal is different. He uses so many big words! If we try to use big words in a story just to use them—well, it sounds queer, that's all."

And again, one snowy winter day when the same group heard

> A prompt decisive man, no breath
> Our father wasted: "Boys, a path! . . ."

Albert stated, "Oh, boy, I know what kind of man he was! Just two lines to say all that." Whittier's economy of description was not lost upon children who had themselves felt the compulsion to make their characters real. Moreover, this heightened awareness made them infinitely more responsive to the few elements the teacher chose to bring to their attention.

These lines of growth are so interwoven with extended reading, personal and practical writing, and genuine literary appreciation, and so tied to the whole business of growing up that it is truly impossible to separate cause from effect. Reading, hearing, telling, listening, and writing become mutually significant. A many-faceted sensitivity emerges through an alchemy difficult to comprehend. But though we do not understand the process, we do know that two of the indispensable elements of this genuine integration are time to assimilate and opportunity to react honestly.

An example of this more facile and extended expression is to be found in a report written by a child of eleven. Though this is an example of practical writing, of reporting information as part of a larger class venture, there is an individual flavor to "many a river has its beginning," "the salmon also have their beginning," or "something like instinct tells them to go back." Carolyn was a spirited child and her interest in the live creature was reflected in the quality of her writing about the journeys and struggles of the live fish. Her description of the canning process is dull by comparison, though the facts are presented in a fashion not greatly inferior to the average adult-written textbook. Carolyn needed checking only on the spelling of "uncertain" and "appearance."

° SALMON

In Washington and Oregon on the tops of mountains, many a river has its beginning. These little streams rush madly along, fed by the melting snows of the glaciers. The salmon also have their beginning in that freezing cold climate. Their eggs are orange mixed with a little pink. When the baby salmon hatch they eat almost everything smaller than themselves. (By the way they are only about one-half inch long.) When they grow bigger they finally start downstream to seek their fortunes. When they reach the ocean they live there about three or four years. After this time, something like instinct tells them to go back to the streams where they were hatched. Millions of salmon start up the long, hard journey. Many of the salmon are caught or killed. The ones that escape continue their fight upstream, leaping falls, and etc. When they reach their destination, the male scoops out a hollow in the gravel. Then the female lays her eggs and the male buries them. Then the two salmon float tail downstream and die an uncertain death.

The salmon that are caught are loaded into scows and taken to the cannery. Their heads and fins are cut off, and the eggs removed. The body is passed beneath circular knives. They are cut into the sizes of the cans they are to go into. Then a machine fills them in correctly. The cans pass on a belt to a weighing machine. Two girls in white uniforms refill any can underweight. Then the cans are lacquered because it gives the cans a nice appearance and also because when a ship is loaded with cans of salmon and is going south, it prevents condensation.

The people that are usually employed are either Chinese or Indians.

References

Atwood and Thomas, *North America*, pp. 244–245
Allen, *United States*, p. 253
Pamphlet, *The Salmon*

It seems illogical that the cover in which a bit of expository writing appears should be of titanic importance. Yet to a child the delight of making a red back for his elephant book is equal to the material itself. Rightly so. For the youngster the product is a total in which size, color, and illustration are inseparable from content. Indeed, let any adult tell a neighbor he's writing a book and the almost invariable comment is, "Oh, I'd like to *see* it." Moreover, quite a few grown-up authors confess in unguarded moments that they see their future book printed, bound, and standing in majesty upon the library shelf long before the first chapter is completed. As children grow up they take great pride in making by hand more interesting and often more complicated kinds of books. In our experience no other activity gives more zest to the growing ability and interest in utilitarian expression.

Opportunities for Brief Practical Writing

Caution must be exercised against requiring too much writing even at nine or ten. Better a child writes one report containing real substance than several that become mere shadows. Of course, there is in most schools a continual need for work that affords practice in the mechanics of sentence formation, writing, and capitalization, such as:

Labels
Keeping one's own reading list, month by month
Recording weather and temperature data
Recording feeding and growth of pets
Invitations and messages of all sorts, to people hard to
  see in person or too busy to be interrupted

Thank-you notes
Notices about assemblies, journeys, school bulletins,
    playground arrangements
Identification cards for various files
Spelling exercises, both the statistically derived lists and
    "our own" words; also dictation exercises
Recording absence and attendance daily for the principal
    and the nurse
Captions
Rules for games
Explanations
Plans for a party or field trip
Homework assignments

It is highly important that children realize the full significance of practical records. Otherwise, their writing can degenerate into a meaningless chore. Doing useful things well either becomes a burden or further establishes the pride of workmanship that in itself is an energizing influence. Though practice for facility in handling paper and pencils is necessary, its amount is largely determined by the meaning of and attitude toward the writing done. Certainly less practice is called for when situations are real and the reasons for accuracy are keenly felt. Then, too, increased maturity leads naturally to somewhat more lengthy expression in many children.

Writing in response to genuine needs is conducive to ease and high standards of both form and content. The occasional isolated repetition of a few difficult items, plus, in intermediate grades, the use of writing in spelling practice, all contribute to the flow of expression and to improved muscular control. Most assuredly, in addition to this craft writing, many children are artists as well as artisans. At ten many write stories for sheer fun. The production of even very mediocre stories, if written spontaneously and joyfully, makes a valuable contribution to a child's fluency, to his control over the mechanics of putting ideas on paper, and to his further experimentation with thoughtful writing.

Clear Structure To Match Clear Understanding

Though we do not tamper with a child's imaginative or personal creations, certainly direct and thorough teaching is needed in the realm of practical writing. Much of this writing is read to the

Fuses

If you will look closely at a blown
out fuse you will see that a piece
of metal was once attached from
one side of the fuse to the other.
When there is a short circuit in
your house—by that I mean if the
insulation should get worn ~~off~~
off two wires—not all the way
off Just scraped off in two
places—and they touched
together The electricity will
go from one wire to the other
one. Then it will go back to the fuse box
and come to the thin piece of
metal. It will try to go theurgh
the metal but the surge
of the electricity behind will push
until that metal gets hot
and melts. This breaks the
Circuit and saves you from fire.

good fuse This is a bad fuse

First draft of an article prepared for a fourth-grade
class book on electricity. The corrections and additions
were made as the child read the report to his teacher.

class, is put into a book, contributes to a group discussion of some
larger subject, or, at the more mature levels, is done just to find out
how. It is often wise for a child who is weak in this field to read his
material first to his teacher alone. The two may then correct sentence
errors together. Usually reading a passage aloud convinces a child
that "it says too much" or "it doesn't sound finished." If he doesn't
observe the weakness, the teacher points it out, gives him several
examples of ways to repair the bad spot, and *sees that he does it.*

Frequently children come for help faster than a teacher can be of real service. Many children as they write feel a need for clarifying an idea but do not know how. "I want to say that there are three ways of tanning leather," complained Ellen, "but one sounds so much like the other that I can't get them straight. One sounds like it talks about softening the hide and the other two sound like tanning—you know, to make it wear. I can't make it clear."

Ellen was really asking for help to clarify her understanding of a process. Wise child! Indeed, without this clear perception, sentence structure is bound to suffer. After she talked it out and saw the point, writing it was not so mysterious.

But Ellen had already half-analyzed her own problem. Another child may only sense a difficulty and feel inadequate and uncomfortable. Then the youngster needs help to spot his trouble and work out the muddle. This is indeed a slow process, but the teacher cannot hand out a glib prescription to all who need aid. She must consider not only the material the child is writing but also his particular level of maturity. She must talk over the concrete problem with him and guide him in straightening out the tangle. Going back to experiment or to reread sources to verify information and then to talk about the matter may be necessary to heighten the understanding. For understanding is basic to adequate and controlled expression. If through conversation the teacher assists a child in clarifying his own ideas enough to write them, and in making construction fit his thought, then he will be permanently strengthened by the experience. Even though costly in time, in the long run such guidance is economical and effective because it makes for increased independence.

Of course the most effective test of clarity comes from the other members of the class. The success of a report is measured by the degree to which it is clear and understandable, or adds to the larger study under way, or illustrates a general notion with concrete detail. These criteria become the children's.

The teacher watches, naturally, for positive illustrations of clarity, good choice of language, or some accidental use of a superior technique. In class discussions she sees that the atmosphere is kept friendly and free of strain. Emphasis of comments should be upon how clearly the ideas were developed, how one thought naturally led to the next, how interesting a certain picture was made. A sportsmanlike attitude of seeing how suggested improvements would make the thought clearer in practical writing can be acquired by almost every child. If he rests secure in the knowledge that in general he is "coming along in fine shape," he can almost always accept suggestion for a needed change. This is a test of mature rapport, achieved only by many months of living together. Whether or not the rest of the group gets the point the child is trying to make in writing is the important thing—a test almost as tangible as seeing that a handmade boat really sails. This is not a matter of pleasing the teacher. She is usually too ready to interpret inadequate expressions and sometimes has to "temper the wind to the shorn lamb" when the child is personally insufficient. Following the reading and discussion, the writers often see changes they themselves want to make. After all, even in the professional world, a play does not "click" until it is tried out on an audience.

Before children begin to write, a rich store of knowledge is as necessary as air for breathing. Days, even weeks of observing, analyzing, experimenting, talking, and reading may precede a story of an automobile's cooling system. It is necessary to know much to say little, if that little is to carry its point home. Certainly much of children's nonsentence writing, of repeated "ands," and ambiguous construction is caused by their having to write before they have anything to say or by having to write purely fictitious or sterile exercises. If any adult doubts this, let him try offhand to write an animated and lucid exposition of "How To Build a Skyscraper" or "An Interesting Conversation between Two Natives of Tierra del Fuego." No more absurd than dozens we were asked to do in early childhood! Moreover, a child needs time to assimilate an experience—whether it is experiment, trip, reading, or observation—before the ideas gained can become part of his own mechanism. In our experience, writing about yesterday's trip to the museum is sadly unsuccessful. Yesterday's picnic, likewise! Even the most glowing enthusiasm cannot provoke a flow of ideas when the reaction to the experience is too raw to be translated into written form. Again and again this has proved true. Time for experience to ripen is as important a phase of the ideas-into-writing cycle as the actual putting of pen to paper. Reflecting, talking, thinking become necessary precursors to the depth of perception that makes clear writing possible. Indeed, even many able children slip back into nonsentence or otherwise faulty construction when forced to write what has not been digested and absorbed. Furthermore, the apparent correlation between repeated "ands" and immature mentality adds weight to the belief that a genuine control of ideas is the main condition for adequate writing.* Content begets form.

Achieving Effective Organization

Not only is clear construction an outgrowth of thoroughly assimilated ideas, but effectiveness of organization, that much-lauded characteristic of real intellectuality, is also closely related to thorough understanding. Sound organization of material depends, too, upon other vital factors. True, a rich background of ideas is important. So, too, is the degree to which these ideas have matured within the individual, a process that takes time and that, if hurried, can produce only a mushroom growth. To let the ideas one has touched lie fallow, to sort and resort them, to talk over what one has discovered or read or observed or thought are as necessary a prelude to logical arrangement as is the gathering of factual data. This casual talking over of experience, reporting the results of one's exploration, is a vitally important stage in developing disciplined expression. Here half-understood ideas and vague impressions begin to take form through casual and informal talking about "what we found out" or "what we have done." New questions arise. Relative values emerge. Some clarification takes place from this simple verbalization of ideas. And the fact that talking is so much faster and less strenuous than writing makes such conversational stock taking an economical step toward the eventual refinement of expression. Thus do ideas become an integral part of the person.

Another factor in a developing power of organization is the clearness of purpose for which the specific material is being gathered and presented. Even to seven-year-olds, preparing a simple program to show their mothers what they had been studying about Scandi-

* R. Salisbury, "Psychology of Composition," *English Journal* (May 1936).

navia offered a problem in organization and likewise set the general scheme of their presentation. Mothers would see first, upon entering the room, the large fireplace and bed set up in one corner.

"We'll have to explain in the beginning about the big things because that's the first thing they'll see. We can tell about the cupboards, the pewter, and the red panels afterward."

Another group of eight-year-olds, in planning a star party for the seven-year-olds, realized that many things they'd like to tell (often just because they're so proud to know them) would not fit into a party, and certainly not in a party for younger children. Seven-year-olds, from the vantage point of being eight, need things made very easy and very clear. Incidentally, explaining anything to younger children obliges one to be very straightforward and direct, a discipline most valuable to writers of any age. Yes, selection and rejection of data for a specific purpose was beginning to be practiced by these children. Even at the university level, choosing facts relevant to a specific problem continues to be an important type of intellectual exercise.

But of equal importance to a wealth of ideas and to a clearly seen purpose toward which these ideas must be organized is the individual's stage of maturity. To give significant help, awareness of the child's development of orderliness must be in the foreground. This again is a very complex matter, influenced by perhaps more unknowns than we have yet dreamed. Differing with every individual, this mental power is a fascinating and subtle one, growing with the growing individual; further, it never shows the same earmarks even in two persons brought up in the same general environment, with apparently the same immediate purpose, and with the same I.Q. To a degree, fortunately, a feeling for organization is a part of everyone. Moreover, it appears that the privilege of writing purposefully and sincerely makes a marked contribution to its natural development.

It is very interesting to observe some of the manifestations of a dawning sense of order. Even quite immature children often want to divide a report or a story into chapters in an effort to satisfy their need for some sort of dividing line. The word "chapter" may seem a bit humorous to the staid adult, but it is by no means to be laughed at. Let the young writer divide his little offering on, perhaps, the fruit fly into chapters if he wishes. In short order he sees that some of his items really belong in another chapter, maybe a new one that should be written about the damage the fly does the world over. This bundling of material to put like things together is one of the first stages of logical and coherent writing.

As children mature it is easy to point out, usually following their own discovery of the matter, that within a chapter is a sequence of ideas—smaller divisions within the larger one, the basis of paragraphing. That each different idea—each part of the chapter—stands out better if seen in a separate paragraph is about as far as it seems reasonable to go with elementary school children in the debatable matter of paragraph division. Certainly much of the trouble in paragraphing arises from forcing the use of a form before the need for it is understood. The groups under discussion had *experienced* the need for paragraph division for greater clarity. They did not learn it in isolated exercises.

Later on, children become aware of another factor of organization, infinitely more involved than the grouping of like ideas and frequently conspicuous by its absence even in adult writing. This is the active principle in sequential arrangement. The marshaling of functional material toward a real goal implies the beginning of a dynamic organization.

A group of fifth graders, for instance, planned to explain the running of an automobile to another group similarly interested. Cogwheels, diagrams, batteries were at hand. Jack told how gas is exploded in the cylinders. Harry expounded upon the gear shift. Peter told how the battery, coil, and generator did their work. After the event was over, the children were talking about it with their teacher. Jim pointed out, "I wouldn't have understood that. You know, we told how each part of the car works, but nobody ever told how they all went together. "

The teacher's opportunity was at hand to show that it is necessary in many kinds of explanation to "tie it together as you go along." The class worked out, with little help, a plan showing how they could have done this with their automobile explanations, how they could have really traced power from gasoline to turning wheels.

A live organization, propellent and galvanic, is difficult to achieve, even for adults. Still, in reflecting upon the automobile report, the genesis of this mature mental faculty was being used. The children had the experience before they could understand the reason for vitalizing their organization. Having sensed the need they could see what to do about it in a setting that was concrete and genuine in intent. These boys had worked from a wealth of content for a period of weeks, had organized their learning for a purpose real and significant to themselves, had analyzed their talks according

The illustration above and the text opposite are from the book *Automobiles*, made for the school library by a group of sixth-grade boys.

to how clearly they had told the story. With further similar experience they will all be well on the way toward exercising an intellectual function cultivated under artificial circumstances by the highly gifted only.

As we patiently encourage the slowly increasing power of organ-

The Cooling System

The cooling system is used to cool the cylinders.
It is a very necessary device, for if it were missing
the terrific heat would stop the action of the cylinders.
To prevent this, the walls of the cylinders are made up
of hollow passages. These passages extend around the cylinders and form what is called the water jacket. (See
figure 4 C) You have probably seen on the front of a
car a honey comb-like thing which is called the radiator.
(See figure 1 B.) The radiator is made up of small,
hexagon-like cells. The walls of these cells are hollow.
(See figure 2 and figure 3.) When the garage man puts
water in the front of your car, the water enters atank
which is joined with the top of the radiator. After
reaching this tank, the water trickles down through the
radiator, or in other words it trickles through the
hollow walls of the hexagonal cells into another tank.
(See figure 1 C.) In the meantime air has been sucked
through the radiator crosswise; so at this stage the
water is quite cool. From the bottom tank the water is
pumped into the water jacket and cools the cylinders. To
recool the water it is pumped through a pipe into the
first tank, and the process is repeated from the beginning. Thus the water is constantly circulating.

ization, it becomes signally clear that whatever plan a child follows
in a piece of writing must be his own. Help may be received, but
only after its need is felt; otherwise, it is superfluous. Following
someone else's scheme of sequence is a purely external procedure of
no help to the individual and perhaps of genuine damage. The

writer does not then *learn to organize*. What the writer learns, in this case, is to imitate some other person's mental processes, to juggle words, perhaps to be clever. At the impressionable age this may be even worse than imitating another's voice, posture, and gestures. As given in one dictionary, the meaning of the word "organize" is "to give life or being to; . . . to cause to unite or work together in orderly fashion; . . . to endow with life."* Hence, one is not organizing thought when one is fitting data into another person's scheme. Obviously one is filling in a formula, fitting together the parts of a puzzle, giving an orderly appearance to the finished product.

The fostering of an individual's organizing ability takes time, but because the process exercises innate faculties, precludes long sessions spent on made-up exercises.

After extended reading, study, talking over, note taking, and more talking over, Elaine, in sixth grade, made the following plan for her report on wheat:

I.   Planting and growing winter wheat
II. Where it grows best
III. Its value to the country
IV. How it is shipped and stored

The last item, that of storage and shipment, was the teacher's suggestion but easily accepted as part of the job when Elaine saw its significance. After having read her account to the class, and while still satisfied with its acceptance by the group, the writer herself noted that she might have discussed the value of wheat to the country last of all, because shipping really "came right along after growing," but value and costs were something quite different and would be a better ending. Thus do experience and guidance interact.

* WINTER WHEAT

Winter wheat is usually planted in September with a drill. It grows several inches high and then droops. It does not die but simply rests for the winter. It begins to grow again in the spring. Its color changes from green to golden yellow. Fields of wheat look like golden sand with a patch of green grass here and there with the wind gently blowing the wheat back and forth.

* *The Winston Dictionary,* College Edition, 1957, p. 684.

In late June or July the wheat is harvested. The harvesting machines have a thresher machine combined with them. The thresher has a little wagon that is attached at the side to catch the wheat as it comes from the thresher. . . .

Only about one sixth of this report can be reproduced here because of lack of space. Maps and graphs added to Elaine's three type-written pages caused serious bulges in the original folder.

English Essentials

Even under the best known conditions—vitality of purpose, richness of background, confidence in the group and the teacher, much satisfaction in knowing "how much better we can do than a year ago"—a few common danger signals in the mastery of technicalities should be watched for. Clarity of expression seems often to be endangered by "thens," "whens," and "ands" used incorrectly. Susan reread her three sentences, omitting "then" to see if she could feel the "then idea" better without saying it.

* * *

Before:

Then the blossom begins to come out. The plants are then two or three feet high. The blossom is first white, then shell pink, rose-pink, and red. Then the petals fall.

After:

The plants are two or three feet high. The blossom is first white, later shell pink, rose-pink, and last red. Then the petals fall.

Another frequent pitfall is the lengthy but incomplete sentence. When, in the process of growing up, the more able children naturally begin to use complex and compound sentences, such errors occur. "The switch on the line which was usually open where slow freights had to be side-tracked to let express trains pass." Having Ruth reread her lines aloud to see what happened to the switch made her see how "where" caused confusion. "Who," "when," "where," "which," and "then" might come to be viewed with caution by the children themselves.

At times it is economical to isolate special ills of writing, observe them closely in one or several class periods, and work on them directly. The ever-present nuisance of showing possession is sometimes abated by a dictated exercise such as the following:

*   *   *

We played "Snatch-Club" with Mrs. Brown's class at noon today. We had two teams and so did they. Jack's team played first and Mary's second. Our opponents were quick and well-organized. They wasted no time forgetting their numbers. We won one game and so did they.

Jack's books
a girl's coat
their balls
their bats

The difficulty illustrated had shown up in previous work and many were aware of it. The teacher has to underscore the problem, clarify it as concretely as she can, and then provide simple practice exercises to work on. Language texts, of course, furnish some helpful ones. A week or two later the genuine writing needs of a group of ten-year-olds may require the same items. Many will remember, but others will not. (Indeed all through high school and college "others" will not. Even in adult writing mechanics need continued attention.)

The following notice was written for an assembly two weeks after the exercise on possessives. It made use of the forms that had been isolated for practice:

*   ASSEMBLY NOTICE

All children will please take their regular seats for assembly on Wednesday, February 10th. Miss Wright's class will give a play from the story, "Jane's Father."

For these and other more difficult items of English form some specific drill seems necessary for almost all children. Correct use of apostrophes, punctuation of conversation, spelling of "its" and "their," for example, need to be spotlighted even after much use in a child's meaningful writing. Comparatively little of such practice is needed, fortunately, when children from the first grade on have held high standards of practical writing, and items of form have been supplied or checked by the teacher and pupils when needed. Such skills can become more nearly habitual after much correct use in concrete situations. Most important of all, after the habit of writing with fluency and with a sense of security and satisfaction has been established, these technicalities can be assimilated more readily into a growing fabric of purposeful written expression, either personal or utilitarian in nature.

No real barrier exists, of course, between practical writing and personal expressions termed "creative." Indeed *practical* writing can also be *creative*. Rather, these are similar, although different, phases of the same social institution of speech and communication—differing notes in the same scale of verbal artistry. And, in spite of the great specificity of learning, some transfer really occurs from the techniques practiced in utilitarian writing to the joyous artistic outpouring done for its own sake. From the beginning the need for clarity has set standards high but possible of attainment for each child. Continued, this has become a discipline, strengthened often by the approval of fine work, by the encouragement of obvious improvement, and on rare occasions by negation. The reality and often the dramatic quality of this approach is perhaps the strongest factor in the carry-over of standards from the practical to the more subjective and more personal writing of stories and lyrical expressions. When almost all of a large group of sixth-grade boys and girls volunteer to rewrite or retype a story to satisfy their own standards, the identification of the individual and his job has been clearly felt. The children have made a real integration between two distinct but related functions of writing, between themselves and the fruits of their labor.

chapter four

✿ ✿ ✿ ✿ ✿ ✿ ✿ ✿

PERSONAL WRITING

*There is no art to writing but having
something to say.*
—ROBERT FROST, The *Washington Post*

Most of us remember all too vividly the ordeal of "composition time." No matter how zealous we may have been in filling private notebooks, we approached the task at school with distaste, if not with dread; and the prim, anemic accounts produced under assignment were a far cry from the entrancing adventures we made up for ourselves when our imaginations ran free. At school we wrote to please the teacher; at home we labored solely for the joy of using our creative power.

Those secret stories that many children write for their personal pleasure or for the delectation of a few special cronies are usually crude, extravagant, and childish, but invariably they have life. Moreover, because their creation is prompted by an inner urge rather than by an external compulsion, marked changes occur in the thinking and feeling of the young writers. This eagerness to write for one's own satisfaction or for a trusted and appreciative audience does many things for children. It stirs and stretches their imagination, it develops a sense of ease in handling language, and it encourages the desire to make words say what they want them to say. These are significant changes that we wish to foster. So in our classrooms we have tried to approximate the conditions under which children write spontaneously for their own fun and satisfaction. The stories they write are read aloud for mutual entertainment, and no direct attempts are made to correct or improve them. In other phases of written expression efforts to fix necessary English forms and mechanics are redoubled; in story time interest is centered on getting more and more stories for when children write copiously and with interest they make surprising gains in language power.

How Story Writing Is Initiated

The question arises, "How is story writing begun in the first place? When a teacher is faced with a new class, how does she go about stirring this storytelling power into life?" Our way has been simple as well as happy and fruitful. It is based on the fact that making up stories is not only a natural impulse but also a contagious one.

During the early days of a new term we use short periods—"rest periods" they are sometimes called—for gathering the group about us and sharing stories other children have written. Apparently the occasion is one for enjoyment only, but actually the necessary groundwork for future growth is being laid. We are establishing the habit of appreciative listening, and we are implanting in the children the desire to make stories of their own. Ten-year-olds, for example, might be introduced to the Bear family and then hear John's story about bathing the cat.

* * *

It was early afternoon on a winter Saturday and Mo was calling his cat. "Here, kitty, kitty. Come, kitty."

His cat appeared, its black fur stained with mud from the melting snow. Ulp! No cat could be that dirty.

"Oh, Mo," called Mrs. Bear, "you'll have to wash your cat next week," but when Mrs. Bear saw the cat she quickly changed her mind. "Er—well, on second thought, you'd better wash it now."

"Now, Mother?"

"Yes, now."

"Well, all right."

Five minutes later Mo had the tub filled with scalding water. "I guess the cat would rather have it hot than cold," he mumbled. Carefully he picked up the cat by its tail. A howl rent the

air, but Mo still held on. Slowly he dipped the cat in the water
after putting half a box of dishwashing soap in.

Yeo-o-o-ow." The cat wriggled loose and fell struggling into
the water. Covered with suds he jumped out, spilling suds all
over the bathroom.

"Darn you," shouted Mo, throwing a drinking glass at the
fleeing cat. Crash! The glass flew into the next room where unfortunately Mrs. Bear was entertaining the principal of Mo's
school.

"Help!" Then the principal came out very red and with the
glass wedged very firmly on his long nose. "Goodbye, Mrs. Bear,
and I must say that I never saw such a—"

The principal's sentence was cut short by the cat, who was
still trying to escape from Mo. Mo tackled the cat, or he thought
he did, but the cat climbed the principal. Mo missed him and hit
the glass on the principal's nose.

A little while later when they had gotten untangled—wack—
crash—bam! Poor Mo! And all that night Mo had to stand up in
bed.

This episode is so full of action and vividly told details that children can readily picture it in their imaginations. Quite likely they
will make under-their-breath remarks about Mo's stupidity or the
"poor cat"; and some adventurous child is sure to laugh aloud at
the predicament of the principal. We laugh, too, because it *is* a
ridiculous sight. Besides, we always deliberately contrive to read
some stories in which children are aggressively clever, and adults
can be tolerantly laughed at; such stories dissolve the fiber of resistance, and are convincing proof to children that they dare to
write freely without fear of the teacher's displeasure.

The impulsive reactions during the reading will be followed, no
doubt, by more comments at the close of the story. If not, we may
chuckle over how clearly we could see the whole thing happen, and
then, for emphasis, reread the lively action of the bath or the escape, or the picture of the irate principal "with the glass wedged
firmly on his long nose." The mood we are trying to induce is a
relaxed, companionable one with sufficient leisure to visualize the
story and savor it to its full. Positive remarks are encouraged. If

someone ventures a negative one, he is reminded that it is always easy to find mistakes, but it is more fun to watch for the things to enjoy.

Since nothing stifles creative effort so quickly as adverse criticism, whether voiced or merely felt, we allow only appreciative comments in the story-sharing time. The tendency to pick flaws is checked in this beginning period when the children are listening to stories from the teacher's stockpile. To this end a few poor ones are always read. At the first negative remark we stop to discuss why we expect only approving comments or none at all. Our point is that if anyone takes the time and effort to write a story for our pleasure, we cannot be so ungracious as to pick it to pieces; and the children, through airing their own experiences, reveal how faultfinding takes the heart out of any activity. The exclusion of negative criticism is an absolute *must* for any successful program of creative writing.

The short periods of reading stories for enjoyment are continued until two things happen: the children begin to show signs that they are ready to write stories, and the pattern of kindly acceptance is so firmly set that even the most humble effort will escape condemnation.

This whole process of initiation is of great importance. Every fall, whether the group is a new or a familiar one, a third grade or a sixth, we go through these same steps. It is essentially a warming-up process; the group has to be drawn into the rapport necessary to happy, easy writing, and the individual's own love of writing must be tempted to the point of action. With some groups two or three weeks suffice; for others the preparation moves more slowly through a month or more, and there are occasional groups that require a whole semester of innoculation before writing gets under way.

Finally, when the time seems ripe, it is suggested that the children begin writing stories. The invitation is intentionally casual, and the way to respond is made easy. A time is provided for those who wish to write, and the others are allowed to turn to some self-chosen quiet work. The nonwriters may do such things as read or draw pictures of story incidents, drill on arithmetic or spelling, finish up some uncompleted task. No stigma is attached to not writing, but acclaim is given to those who make the venture. With the occasional ones who are eager to try but who lack ideas, we visit a little, hoping to make a suggestion that will set their pencils going. If after a short conference no story plans are forthcoming, we counsel them to wait until another day. If a child has no characters in mind, he is free to use any from stories we have been reading. Whereas we once thought of an incident as the necessary starting point of a story, we now realize that many young writers invent with ease and originality when they begin with characters and let them act out their experiences on paper.

Because many children are blocked by their concern for neatness and correctness we urge them to care about nothing but getting their stories down. Any words they ask for are written on the chalkboard.

Stories do not even have to have titles. Starting with a title is often a limiting or inhibiting experience. Creative writers need the freedom that allows thoughts to wander as they will. To help a child feel more daring we sometimes remark, "You can never be really sure how a story is going to turn out; so it's an adventure for you, too. If you want to name it, that can be the final touch before you share it with the class." Many children forego titles entirely. When they finish one story, they grab more paper and promptly lose themselves in creating another. At the peak of writing excitement, ideas often come with a rush.

This whole procedure may sound careless, but we have found that it bears good results. Since the first concern is to free a child so that he can reveal his thinking and feeling through writing, every possible hindrance must be brushed aside. True personal writing wells up from the subconscious, and unless the items that require conscious efforts are minimized, they can easily bar the way.

Reading the First Stories

It is a red-letter day when the first stories are finished, and a glad sense of achievement pervades the sharing time. As teachers we try to let no shadow darken this joy. For the halting or the fearful we read their efforts, having, of course, gone over them with the authors beforehand to make sure we can present them well. The more able or secure children usually choose to read their own. We put away distractions and sit comfortably in order to listen with ease. At first, we thought it strange that the children somehow moved closer and closer together as we went from one story to another. Later we accepted this urge to be near the story reader as part of the joyous communication of spirit generated by spontaneous story creation.

During the reading period the teacher gives herself wholeheartedly to even the simplest story; listening as naturally and eagerly as she likes the class to listen to her. Her eyes do not slide about to see who is wriggling; her mind does not concern itself with other matters. The story takes over completely, holding her in its spell. By some curious form of osmosis this spirit of attentive listening spreads throughout the group. It is courteous listening, but more than that, it is creative listening, which works magically upon the children to release their native gifts and to build up their confidence. Even sophisticated adults are exhilarated and prodded by the *feel* of a responsive audience, and children, who are extremely sensitive to emotional climates, react more strongly still.

No early story is passed by without some sort of favorable notice. If no child volunteers an appreciative comment, the teacher is sure to. In the most meager effort something can be found to enjoy: a hint of lively action or picture-making detail, a touch of invention, a curious name, or a glimmer of humor. Later in the year comments are often by-passed, but in the beginning they are important because they point up the elements that make all stories entertaining and alive. Moreover, they help to make the first story-writing experiences happy ones so that even a hesitant child will want to try again.

What Children Write About

What do children write about when they write just for fun? Why, about themselves, of course. To be sure, they are not aware that this is what they are doing. They think they are making up adventures of an imaginary hero or a mischievous bear. But in reality, when they become absorbed in telling about Uncle Rufftuff or the Bossy King, it is their own experiences—their own thinking and feeling—that they unconsciously reveal.

Strangely enough, when a child begins to write because it is fun, he does not choose the topics that used to be doled out as the easy ones based on immediate experience: A Summer Adventure, My Dog, My Trip to the Farm. He rarely writes openly about himself or about happenings that are recent and therefore fresh in his mind. The reason is plain. If he writes about himself he cannot write well about anything that has not yet become a part of that self. Only when the experiences have had time to sink into deeper levels of a child's consciousness and there be intermingled with the residue of other experiences and other meanings, do they become the stuff from which his imaginings and interpretations are fashioned.

As he grows in writing experience he draws more and more from this reservoir of emotions and ideas, and through the alchemy of his imagination he transmutes them into stories and poems uniquely his own. The world portrayed in this writing is essentially a child's intuitive creation—a most satisfactory world, indeed, in which the familiar and the wished-for are happily blended. He rarely peoples it with everyday characters, perhaps because he does not choose to be limited to pedestrian reality. So animals or half-fairy-tale beings take on the attributes of humans, while at the same time they accomplish with ease what is ordinarily impossible. It is an upside-down world as well, in which the child, not the adult, is the person of importance. By means of magic, shrewd intelligence, or merely a slingshot, he dominates each situation.

More than this concerning the substance of children's writing we are not ready to say. It is true that when they write without restraint, they write about themselves, but even now, with added confidence stemming from increased knowledge of child development, we are not satisfied with our understanding of what those selves are really like. We do know that they are very different from adults in their desires, sense of values, and points of view; and also that they change markedly in the various stages of their growth. Realizing this we are slow to take exception to ideas that at first glance seem discourteous or crude. They may not appear so to a child, and we would only bewilder him with seeming injustice were we to reprove him. So we try not to curb his fun of writing by quibbling over differences inherent in our points of view.

On the contrary, we seek to open the channels through which

natural child thought and language flow. Contagion is one of the most effective means yet discovered. When a few youngsters have grown excited about a group of lively characters or a new pattern of writing, their enthusiasm spreads throughout the group until most of the class gets caught up in the story-making activity. The fact that a familiar thread runs through their stories seems to add to the children's interest, and to free their creative power. Writing comes more abundantly and is of better-than-usual quality. Under such impetus some children produce the only spontaneous writing they ever do.

One fall a group of nine- and ten-year-olds came upon Sterling North's simple adventures of five little bears. The next day an original five-bear story appeared, and immediately the contagion began to spread. Every child wrote at least two or three stories about the bears and one boy wrote more than twenty-five. Although they used the same characters and frequently the same type of mischievous incident, their tales were remarkably varied, both in content and style. Curiously enough, too, of the large number of stories written that year the bear stories were outstandingly the best. Here is one of them; others appear elsewhere in the book.

* A BEAR STORY

"Children," said Mother, "you are going to take lessons in language."

"How many do we have to take?" asked Nig.

"Four," said Mother, "Greek, Latin, German, French—now that I think of it you should have Spanish and, of course, English."

Mother had studied language and wanted the little bears to, but Father disagreed with her. He had gone away for a year, and Mother jumped at the chance.

"You shouldn't have to take them all at once, but you have a year and I won't make you go to school."

Just then they saw Father coming up the walk. "I am going to tell Father unless you promise that we won't have to take languages and you'll promise to take us to the movies ten times each month and let us go swimming every day this month," said Nig.

"All right. Don't tell him."

Father opened the door. "I forgot my suitcase," he said. "The boat doesn't sail for an hour."

The invention of characters is usually a difficult step for children, and newly created ones often produce in their writing the formality and self-consciousness that one feels with strangers. But if children have characters at hand—old friends with whom they have laughed and teased and adventured—they find it relatively easy to use them as vehicles for their imaginings. When we remember the great story cycles, such as Robin Hood, King Arthur, and even our own Paul Bunyan, we realize that the community use of popular heroes has long been the storyteller's privilege and practice.

Furthermore, if these familiar characters are a compound of realism and fancy they make invention easier still. Although such beings may behave like humans, they are not bound by ordinary limitations and standards. This sets a child's imagination free. In his story, people can wander at will between the real world and the unreal, they can combine the magical and the commonplace, and they can act in arrogant and startling ways that children dream of but dare not emulate.

For our own children the roguish bears—Eenie, Meenie, Meinie, Mo, and Nig—have long given lively impetus to story writing. From time to time we have suggested that someone devise a new set of characters, and an occasional child has done so. Dixie had her Otter Family—Big, Middle-Size and Small. When the baby came she named it Tiny. John invented the Great Chimino, and Donald wrote many stories about Droopy, the Little Aeroplane. But by and large, few newcomers have challenged the popularity of the bears. That does not mean, however, that there has been no invention of character, for in the guise of friends, enemies, and relations there have been many colorful additions to the original five until now the group of Bear characters make up a sizable clan. There have been the baby Daisy May, Uncle Upper Bumper, Eenie's boon companion Roy Bear, Meinie's girl friend, and a host of cousins and playmates. When children have a set of old characters as a nucleus, they seem able to evolve new ones readily enough whenever the need arises. For their wonder-working power we have blessed and cherished the Bears, who have released spontaneous, entertaining stories and an abundance of humor.

The tales about such imaginary, childlike creatures are unusual in their fresh originality. This fact shines out more clearly when they are contrasted with the realistic stories that children sometimes attempt. In concocting a horse or dog story a child commonly apes the situation, the vocabulary, and even the cadences of the animal fiction he reads. Almost never is there anything in his tale that bears the stamp of the author—no childish insight, no natural awkwardness of expression, no humor. A similar lack of inventiveness and personal flavor generally marks stories about everyday people. Ordinary characters rarely touch the wellsprings of imagination, but fall instead into dull, conventional molds. It is the half-fanciful characters that set invention working and the disarming familiar ones that reveal most clearly what a child actually thinks and feels.

Encouraging Originality

It follows that because we permit each child to say what he wants to say in his own way, we, for our part, must accept graciously whatever he writes. Writing is a heart-warming delight when children are sure of an eager acceptance of their stories. Although many children like to write in an almost fierce privacy, they usually look for an audience as soon as they have finished. After all, stories are invented to be told to others. The joy of devising a story is only half realized until the tale is shared, and the delight of creation is reinforced by the pleasure of appreciation.

Younger children know of our interest in stories because of their previous happy experiences with dictating and telling them. It is quite natural, then, that they should bring their first stories to us. The word "bring" is worthy of note. We do not collect stories; we do not demand that they be handed in on a given date or as finished; we do not even *ask* to read them; we wait until the children, quite of their own accord, bring them to us. Then we accept them as we would any other gift—with warm appreciation. Criticism is as inappropriate in this situation as it would be at Christmas time.

The teacher is definitely in the role of recipient. And it is a *story* that is offered, not an exercise in composition or punctuation or spelling. A *story* is offered—it would be absurd to talk of periods or paragraphs, of spelling or neat writing. Those matters are taken care of in practical writing. Here is a tale woven out of this child's unique experience, feeling, and imagination. To him the story is satisfactory and complete. We accept it eagerly, just as it is, without suggestion for change or improvement.

This is not always easy, for the desire to show him how to make his story better is a deep-rooted one. We may feel that it could be improved by developing this idea or cutting out that one, but we also know that if it is to be the *child's*, it must be left in just the form which at the moment seems good to him.

Here is a story written by Peggy when she was barely nine. We are unable to reproduce the smudgy, wrinkled paper, but the story is otherwise exactly as she wrote it.

* GRANDMOTHER'S SKIRT

Once there lives an old laddy with gray hair, dubble toes and a very sweet hart but she allways fell down because her peticoat was allways hanging. She lived all alown way way on the tip top of a great big hill one of her hobies was baking pies blueberry chery and apple were her very best. The only one in all the world that she loved was her own grandbaby who hardly ever came to see her. Today however she was in her living room when a nock came at the door. She jumped and ran to see who was coming, she opund the door and to her serprize no one was there she was all setled down again when another nock came. Again she went to the door and there she saw her grandbaby whose mother had got run over she had taken lots of monny so she could live with her grandmother and they bilt a new house and were very happy. After that the grandbaby allways held up her grandmothers peticoat and she never fell

Now it would be easy to criticize this. "What does baking pies have to do with the story? You haven't explained why there wasn't someone there the first time she heard a knock. Why not leave that part out? Whatever are 'dubble toes'? You need a lot of periods and capitals and your spelling is a disgrace."

Of course from the point of view of a nine-year-old, food is always a spendid thing to have in a story, "serprizes" never fail to interest, "dubble toes" sound fascinating, and periods and spelling do not affect a story anyway! So perhaps the very changes that, from an adult point of view, would strengthen the tale, would really spoil it entirely for a nine-year-old audience and would most surely have spoiled it for Peggy.

We read the story eagerly, ignoring the unconventional spelling and punctuation. We admired the amazing idea of "dubble toes" and pointed out that probably no one ever before had thought of writing a story about a hanging petticoat. We commended the way the story was rounded out, beginning with the petticoat and ending with it. Peggy beamed and volunteered that she had "a lot more ideas for stories even better than this." The story was read to the class, who added their approval.

Perhaps if we had criticized "Grandmother's Skirt" or any of the dozen mediocre tales that followed Peggy might never have written this delightful story. For ease of reading we have corrected spelling and punctuation.

* THE HOUSE THAT ECHOED

Once there was a sweet old lady who lived all alone with her parrot in a huge, big house with 143 rooms. She might have been a happy lady but she wasn't because whenever she said anything she heard an echo. There were echoes in every room. When she said, "Good morning, Polly," she heard high and whispery, "Good Morning, Polly." [*The echo was always written very small.*]

When the parrot said, "Polly wants a cracker," the little old lady would hear, "Cracker, cracker, cracker," echoing all over the house.

She was determined to stop the echoes and to live happily every after. She sent for some men to come out from the city to put hangings on all the walls of the 143 rooms. [*New hangings had just been put in our music room to deaden the reverberations there.*]

But when the men had gone she said, "Well, now *that's* fixed."
And all through the house she heard, "Fixed, fixed, fixed."
"What shall I do?" cried the sweet old lady. "I know. I'll open
the windows and doors and then the echoes will slip outdoors."
So she opened and opened all the windows and all the doors in
the 143 rooms.

"*Now* I won't be bothered any more," she said with a sigh,
settling down.

"Any more, any more, any more," whispered the echoes.

"Oh, oh, oh," cried the little old lady and she ran out of doors
into the woods. She walked and walked trying to think what to do
next about the echoes when suddenly she heard an awful crying.
She ran through the woods and found a whole lot of children, 439
children, all sitting in the woods, crying.

"Goodness gracious," said the little old lady. "What are you
crying about?"

"We used to live in an orphan but it burned down," said a boy.

"Well, blow your noses and come home with me," said the little
old lady.

So they did and all those children filled the house so full of
noise because of pillow fights and not wanting to wash, especially
the boys, and asking where things were, that there wasn't any
room for echoes at all. And the old lady was happy. So were the
children.

The following story is typical of the kind of thing we have
learned to accept as cordially as we did "The House that Echoed,"
overlooking the weak, confused plot, but calling attention to the
spark of real insight—in this case, the quick characterization in the
first four sentences.

❋ ❋ ❋

In a bee castle there lived a cross old queen bee. She kept
every bee over-busy. The king was kindhearted. He couldn't bear
the queen himself. Soon he decided to get the "S" band. This
was a band of stingers, stingers and selfish. The queen had many

more ladies than the king had men. She forced the ladies to fight. In two weeks, in our time, the queen got a rose with an invitation written on it. It said as follows: "You are invited to fight the King's 'S' band. Bee-bee." (The bee-bee meant answer soon.) The queen was expecting this and answered back, "Yes."

When the day came there was a carpet of bees' wings they lost during the fight. There was a bee called Octar. He was a "selfish." He was the king of the "selfish."

When the battle was over he was the only dead. Guess who won.

We read this story to the children with sufficient vigor to support the feeble plot. Nancy was happy that everyone liked her picture of the king and queen—and started another story. By accepting this halting tale without criticism we kept the way open for her further writing.

Inevitably there is an occasional tale so utterly hopeless that one's heart sinks before the eager anticipation of the little writer.

* THE CAT SLEEP

One day the cat said. I am ging to sleep. gone to sleep. She went to sleep. By the time I went to sleep I heard a noise. So I went to the bed and I look there and them. I went to the chair and I look there and them. Boo?

P s ti si a Mouse

the end

Certainly this is a challenge to one's ingenuity. How can one present such a story as this in a way that will give the child his bright moment of delight? The teacher chose to read it at the very beginning of the reading period. With Johnny pressing warmly against her shoulder, she summoned every ounce of dramatic ability she had and by her very voice and manner gave importance to the tale. She turned to beam on the child, saying, "O, Johnny, our very first riddle story. What fun!" And then before the other children could sense the obvious inadequacies, she rushed on to the next story. Johnny went on writing and each succeeding tale required less agility and drama of his teacher.

Sometimes the offerings are actually offensive to the teacher's taste, but these, too, are received without adverse comment. This can take considerable forbearance, for children can be very thorough in establishing the tone of a story. Stories about messes are disgustingly detailed and these, by the way, are always very humorous (to the children); war stories involve endless gruesome killings; and many tales are practically dripping with blood. We have learned to ignore the qualms we may have and to listen to these distressing themes, if not with enthusiasm, then at least with courteous attention. This excerpt from "Red Duke" is a sampling of an epidemic of "tough" stories that swept a fifth grade.

❋ ❋ ❋

"So you three mugs thought you'd squeal on Red Duke, eh? Well, there ain't anyone never squealed on Red Duke that really lived to tell about it," said Red Duke, breathing hard.

"Aw, let's kill the dirty squealers and get it over with," said Jake with his finger on his trigger.

"Shut your mouth, I'm running this gang," said Red Duke. "I'll rub these boys out when I'm ready, see?" He glared at the trembling men. "Now you lily-livered yellow dogs, how much does Black Mike know?"

Even this we took quietly with perhaps no further comment than the truthful one that the rough language and vigorous action are admirably suited to the characters. Older children inevitably recognize their teacher's personal likes and dislikes, but by that time their confidence in her genuine interest in every story is well-established. A sixth grader offered his repulsive war story to us with the easy remark, "This isn't the kind of story you like, but I knew you would read it. I think it's keen."

There are stories, too, that verge on impertinence. These are always about imaginary beings who, of course, are not bound by the usual rules of decorum. Even so it may rankle to hear a teacher labeled Miss Pastypuss and described as "a nice old gal," or to see one of our own foibles humorously portrayed. However, this is never a personal attack; it is a natural and mild outburst against adults for the sense of inferiority they make youngsters feel. All children yearn at times "to put grownups in their place," and if they write freely, their hidden emotions are bound to show through. So we listen undisturbed to these revealing stories because we know that only by accepting ideas as they are offered can we cultivate the sincerity and fearlessness so essential to originality.

* MRS. WIDDLE WADDLE TEACHES SCHOOL

One day when Mrs. Widdle Waddle was making her bed, the telephone rang. Then she stopped making her bed and ran to the phone and answered it.

"Hello," said Mrs. Widdle Waddle.

"Hello," said a voice. "I am Mrs. Pickle Puss and I am a school teacher and I am going to go away and visit another school and I was wondering if you would please take my place this morning and I will be back this afternoon."

"Well, all right," said Mrs. Widdle Waddle because she thought she would like it very much. And then Pickle Puss said goodbye and hung up.

"Well," said Mrs. Widdle Waddle, "I am going to like this. I guess I had better not finish my bed but get on my coat and go."

So she got on her coat and locked the door and walked to school. After a while she got to the school and found the children scribbling all over the blackboard and pounding on the piano and messing up her desk.

Mrs. Widdle Waddle said, "Stop it."

The little boys said, "Mind your own business, Madam, will you please?"

Mrs. Widdle Waddle didn't know what to say but rang the school bell. That meant for the children to call the attendance cards. This time the children obeyed her.

"Sammy, Johnny, Jane, Joan, Mary Lou, and Rose," said Mrs. Widdle Waddle. "Well, I guess those three are late and so is Sammy Jay and Mary. Now for Arithmetic."

"Pooh," said all the children. "Recess is what we want." And before she knew it they were out in the court where they played. "Oh, dear," said Mrs. Widdle Waddle as she walked out into the courtyard. "Children, come here." But instead they threw a football at her and laughed.

"Oh well," said Mrs. Widdle Waddle not knowing very well what to do and it hurt a little where the football hit her.

"Well," she said, "I'll let you stay out a little longer."

She really wanted to be alone while she had stomach ache. But she wasn't alone because when she went into the school there were Sammy Jay and Rose and Mary Lou.

Sammy said, "I thought I would be late."

"So did my mother," added Rose and Mary Lou.

"But you are late," said Mrs. Widdle Waddle.

They all looked up in a startled way. "Oh, boo hoo," they all cried at once. "We are late. Boo hoo."

"Oh, well," said Mrs. Widdle Waddle, "I wish Mrs. Pickle Puss would come back." But finally she did come back.

"Well, hello," said Mrs. Pickle Puss. Mrs. Widdle Waddle was so relieved that she got up and said her goodbye and went home.

"Well," said Mrs. Pickle Puss after Mrs. Widdle Waddle had gone, "did you get your Arithmetic O.K. and your Spelling O.K.?"

"Yes, yes," said all the children at once and Sammy Jay added, "No one was late and the Arithmetic and Spelling papers were thrown away because they were all O.K."

"Well, good," said Mrs. Pickle Puss, "good for you."

And at the same time Mrs. Widdle Waddle was saying at home, "I'll never do that again."

Being sure of the teacher's friendly concern adds immeasurably to the joy of writing a story. Children are often eager to read the first part of a tale to her; indeed we have known many who come with shining eyes to show each new paragraph. Still more often youngsters look up from their writing to say, "Just *wait* 'til you read this one." "You'll be crazy about *this* part." It is easy to tell by the tingle in the voice that every sentence has added zest because of the prospect of sharing it with an appreciative friend—added zest and added power, too, for joy releases power just as surely as uncertainty or fear restricts it.

Presentation to the Class

Delightful as the enthusiastic acceptance by the teacher is, the truly exciting experience is the presentation of one's story to the class. A few children may wish to keep their stories "secret," and we respect their wishes even when it means that over a period of years we see but a small fraction of their personal writing. Occasionally, although a child enjoys sharing his story with his teacher, he may hesitate to present it to the group. Usually the temptation, "I know the class would enjoy your story, especially the part where . . . May I read it to them?" is too strong to resist. However, if he truly does not want his story read, we never insist.

At the eight- and nine-year age, youngsters sometimes seek the assurance of our approval before they offer their stories to the class. In the early stages we read the tales to the group, partly because youngsters of this age rarely have enough skill to read effectively their hastily written and often telegraphic accounts, and partly because we can, through dramatic reading, bring out the good points and cloak the insufficiencies.

Later, toward the end of third or the beginning of fourth grade, children begin to take over the presentation of their own stories. In order to achieve the best possible results, the preparation for this is carefully done. When a story is finished the young writer goes off by himself into a quiet corner or out into the hall to practice reading aloud so that he can successfully "put his story across" to his audience. He may discover where words have been omitted or where the meaning is not clear, but these rough places can be quickly mended by the insertion of a few words or phrases. This is the time, too, when the perfect title may pop into his head, although as we have previously stated, the naming of a story is not a required step.

We do not underestimate the importance of setting the stage for this sharing occasion. Paying attention to such details as a comfortable and cozy seating arrangement so that the reader does not have to strain to make himself heard, and choosing a time when the class is in a relaxed and receptive mood make possible the full depth of satisfaction children can derive from these experiences.

These satisfactions in turn produce the enthusiasm and the impetus that carry story writing on and on.

Value of Oral Presentation

The frequent periods of reading and listening are a vital part of the writing process. There is no greater spur to writing than the keen delight of watching one's story "catch" an audience, unless perhaps it is the heart-warming approval that follows the reading. Again and again a nine-year-old sits rigid with happiness or twisting excitedly while his story is being read; and then in a sudden burst of sheer joy makes the announcement, "I'm going to write more stories. My next one will be even better'n this one. I bet I write a hundred stories." And often an older child, though more self-contained, is no less moved by the pleasure of his accomplishment. Donna, in the absorbing excitement of her reading, used to wriggle herself halfway across the room, and sometimes she grew so pleased she laughed aloud.

Although the children are urged to present their own stories simply because they enjoy doing so, in the wake of reading aloud we have discovered three important values that were not foreseen at first. Oral reading itself has improved. Many children who have spoken in dull, halting tones when using books, have read their own stories in an easy, lively fashion. This gain has remained, in part at least, upon the return to book reading. Improvement in writing style is a second by-product. Because of the abundance of reading and listening, the tongue and ear have learned to work together to seek for more pleasing sounds, so that the reiterated "and" or "then," the clumsy connective, the monotonous sentence pattern gradually disappear. Sentences change in length and tempo to fit the changing pace of a story. And lastly, the children make headway in recognizing where sentences begin and end. The scribbled papers may be guiltless of capitals and periods and some of the constructions may be rather involved, but a child never fails to read his story correctly. His ear seems to know without question where to stop and start again.

But far more significant than the gains in English power is the effect upon the personality of the child himself. There is something deeply rewarding in the feeling that accompanies the reading of one's own story to a group. Because each creation is unique, because there in black and white is the idea that until now has been an intriguing but invisible part of himself, because each story is woven out of his own being, the glow of success is a peculiarly personal and vitalizing one. It is obvious to an adult that the child unconsciously identifies himself with the protagonist of his tale and accepts as his own the praise and approval accorded his hero. In addition, he is the manipulator of all the characters of his story. For a brief time he is not a child subject to the limits set by adults, but a being with omnipotent power who moves characters about as he wills. In this dual role of hero and manipulator he stands among his peers as a clever and capable person. Such an experience cannot but add to a child's stature and security. Furthermore, in a world becoming rapidly more mechanized there is little opportunity for a child to know the satisfying experience of identifying himself with his own product. To stand before a group and hold their interest with *his* story awakens in him a sense of innate power and makes him ready for larger ventures.

Blocks to Writing

Once well initiated, story writing usually continues under its own momentum providing nothing is done to check it. With shy and self-conscious children a very little thing may disturb their confidence and thus shut off the flow of their ideas. Praise or blame can be equally devastating. The former, if excessive, may oppress the sensitive child with the fear that he cannot again equal what he has already done; the latter may but strengthen his conviction that he cannot do anything worthwhile. For this reason evaluation is avoided and interest is kept directed to the way the story affects us the audience. "Wasn't that part funny or exciting? Couldn't you close your eyes and see Mo coming bumpity-bump down the stairs?"

Sometimes our overeagerness to be helpful trips us. We have all caught ourselves saying, "That's a wonderful story. Now why don't you . . ." *It never works.* The child seems to feel that what he is doing is not right, and he promptly puts it aside. It is like the touched egg to which the bird will not return. Such an error makes us realize anew that at this stage our concern lies not so much in the specific product as in the sincerity and on-goingness of the writing process.

In fact we have come more and more to treat each story as an ephemeral thing to be relished and laid aside, and we have turned our eyes expectantly toward new stories. When attention is fixed upon a single narrative a child may come to regard it as a standard or model and try to imitate what he has already done. Others whose writing is not equally lauded may lose faith in their own creations. In a few unfortunate instances certain gifted children have been told their stories were good enough to be published. Immediately self-consciousness set in, and there was a quick falling off in the freshness and vigor of their writing. All of these practices lead to stagnation rather than to growth. It is growth that we want—growth that involves the cultivation of spontaneity, the strengthening of the individual voice, and the habit of writing not for commendation, but for the release, the satisfaction, and the power it affords. Therefore we rarely gather stories into more or less permanent booklets nor select "best" stories for school publications. Such activities tend to halt rather than to stimulate growth in writing power. It seems better for children to find their reward in the joy of fresh creation rather than in the preserving and revering of what they have already done.

Another effective block to creative effort is overconcern with the clerical aspects. Imagination is a demanding master; it refuses to operate freely when attention is shared with anything else. Since an elementary-school child has as yet attained but a small measure of control over the details of English mechanics and form, he must be relieved of responsibility for them if he is to create joyfully and well. Spelling, too, can hamper the flow of ideas, so we promptly give the spelling of any words the children ask for, no matter how simple, because in the excitement of creation many actually forget how to spell even everyday words. No time is used for filing or looking up words in a spelling notebook; good ideas are often lost through such delay. The hardship of writing itself is enough of a deterrent. One has only to watch the tightly held pencil stubbing along to sense the labor involved. As Julie remarked one day, "I just can't keep up with my ideas." And Allen, who is almost a year younger, finds transcription such an ordeal that only every fourth or fifth sentence gets on paper, although he achieves an exciting story even in this fashion.

    ☼   ☼   ☼

Once there was a monkey. He was called Minnie, the Monk. One day he was taking a walk through the woods. Then he saw a fire and then he call the fire department. Then he heard a siren. Then he saw the fire truck.

"I rang the bell."

"Where is the fire?"

"This way." (Of course he forgot.) He led them on a wild goose chase.

One fireman said, "You are going to caught."

"Bang! Bang! Bang!" goes the judge's hammer.

"You are going jail."

"But, but, but, but, but, but, but, but, but, but."

"Shut off your motor boat."

"I saw the fire."

"Well, where is it?"

"I'll find it."

"Come on, boys," says one fireman. "Come on, little monkey."

"Okay, okay, I'm coming." (The fire was right out on the back lawn.)

When Minnie stepped out he saw.

He said, "Fire!"

The firemen ran to the engines.

Indeed, unless we mitigate as much as possible the travail of story writing, the child will not only write fewer stories but shorter, duller ones as well. So it is for this very obvious reason that we have confined our teaching of mechanics to utilitarian writing in which the child is not so emotionally involved. *In personal writing there are never any requirements of form or standards of correctness.*

But the school is not the only influence that can curtail a child's expression. Sometimes the home is unwittingly at fault. Tom, who had been writing freely and happily for some time, came to school one day with the troubled announcement, "My mother doesn't think much of the five bears." Now many children in the group had been writing about the bears who had become real and beloved characters. The disparaging remark of Tom's mother, therefore, discredited for him not only his latest story but also the writing of the other children. Tom wrote no more stories that year.

Another child who had begun to write freely was slowed down to a marked degree when his mother belittled his brief but delightful stories by saying, "You're too big to be writing such simple things. When I was your age I could write compositions several pages long." (It is an amusing fact that grownups, even when acting in good faith, tend to glorify their own childhood accomplishments.) Pressure to meet an imposed but shadowy standard undermines a child's confidence in his own power and so confuses him that writing ceases to be gratifying and becomes instead a labored effort to satisfy a demand he does not comprehend but feels obligated to meet.

Unquestionably, the stories created by a child's own urge to write are more crude and ragged than the tidy compositions of a generation ago. At the same time they are more sincere and they exhibit a far more generous use of good techniques of English expression. This is as it should be. The period of elementary-school life is primarily one of development through experience and exploration. Crystallizing forms too soon only limits the possibilities of growth. Our object in story writing is to cultivate a sense of joy and power in the activity itself, and we feel that conscious evaluation and improvement of the creative products of this activity should wait for a later period of near-adulthood. Until the desire to write is firmly established, correction and criticism can but halt the whole process.

This explains why, in certain cases, a divergence of opinion between school and home poses a considerable problem. We have had some successes and some dreadful failures in trying to explain our point of view to parents. When discussing the English program in parents' meetings we mention how differently we approach the two types of writing. To show that we are not neglecting the tried-and-true English essentials, we send home evidences of practical writing which were required to be accurately and painstakingly done, but every effort is made to keep the carelessly written story papers in our own hands. As we watch the later records of children whom we have taught, we are more and more convinced that the stress we lay on respecting one's own thoughts and expressing them in one's own way pays far richer dividends than are gained through demanding that the clerical aspects of every paper be praiseworthy.

There are always a few children who rarely, if ever, seek the satisfactions to be found in imaginative writing. For them, we depend on practical writing, which is required of all children, to reveal their growing ability to put ideas into words. In reports and articles we take pains to commend any gleam of style or touch of unique expression that may appear. In this way we try to increase their desire to express themselves with vividness and individuality. Beyond this we feel an added obligation to search for and find other avenues for their imaginations to explore. It is essential that all children have some way of pouring out the ideas that are peculiarly theirs. Perhaps in music, rhythms, or dramatics, in sports, the arts, or the sciences, they will realize the delight of evolving something uniquely their own and will feel the spur to further effort that each attempt at creation brings.

Certainly to try to force children to "write for pleasure" dams the whole stream of writing, *both* practical and personal. However, once in a rare, rare while we do try to help even the laggards catch the excitement of storytelling. Our usual way is to take some day when the mood seems right to gossip about one of our familiar story characters. We all may invent funny things he did when he was little or propose possible future escapades. When ideas begin coming we may say, "Oh, these are good! For the next fifteen minutes let's write them down as fast as we can." Sometimes we write, too; sometimes we move about the room to give a needed lift to a fearful child. We may play secretary to a slow writer or stop to exclaim over some scrap of fresh invention. The literary results of such an experience are usually of small value but often some sluggish minds are stirred or a few of the diffident discover that they, too, have ideas. This kind of mass stimulation is charily used. For the most part we place no requirement of time or quantity upon personal writing.

How Children Write

The infinite variety of human nature is nowhere more apparent than in the strange and sometimes devious ways that children follow in putting thoughts on paper. Some can write in the midst of swirling activity, while others find the presence of even one other person a deterrent. Some love notebooks and the snugness of pages between covers; others choose the freeness of single sheets. Some think out all of a story in advance; others work from the most trivial starting point and know only what is going to happen next. Some write best in solitude; others like to write occasionally with a partner.

This desire to write a story with another child at first caused us real concern. Only reluctantly did we give permission for its trial, with many a pedagogical fear that each might not be learning as much as he should. After experimenting for more than a year, we became convinced that a child who sometimes wants to write with a friend, perhaps in a classroom corner or some other protected spot, is really freed and fortified by the experience. One child who had produced very little distinctive writing made up a complicated mystery with two other children. Afterwards he turned quite naturally to writing alone again, and his humorous account of the difficulties of moving from a house to a town apartment was a decided improvement over any previous solo writing.

The excellence that can be achieved by partner writing is clearly evident in the following story written in fifth grade. Two little girls worked so congenially that the product reflects the personal flavor of both and not the dominance of one, as we had feared it might.

* IN THE LAND OF RINGING BELLS

In the Land of Ringing Bells the Mayor was very worried because all of the time he would try to make a speech and the bells would ring. Whenever he would try to listen to the radio the bells would ring. Whenever he would try to talk with the chief of police the bells would ring. The Mayor grew disgusted; he grew mad until he grew *furious*. Now the Mayor could not think what to do about these bells so he went away to think without the bells ringing in his ears. While the Mayor of the town was away the people tried to think up a way to stop the bells from ringing but they did not succeed. When the Mayor came back he had thought of a way to stop the bells. He told his followers to tie the clappers with rope and take a bottle of glue to make them more secure. Now the pages got half way up to the bells when they started to ring as loudly as they could. The followers clapped their hands to their ears and ran to the Mayor. He had expected this so he gave his followers six inches of sealing wax to protect their ears from the sound. The followers put the wax in their ears. They went up to the bells again and succeeded in tying the clappers. Now all this happened on Sunday morning when everyone was in church. The priest was supposed to let the people out at twelve o'clock but it was now three. The priest feared that if he let the people out before the bells rang twelve he would be arrested by the chief of police. The cooks all came running down the street looking for their mistresses. When they heard that they were in church they reported it to the police. The police arrested the priest. The people went home to eat their cold dinner. Now this sort of thing went on all through the week until the people of the town complained to the Mayor. So finally the Mayor made a proposition to the bells to ring only when they were needed. And the bells kept their promise.

This is but one of many stories written by pairs or trios. Without exception we have been pleasantly surprised by their quality and sparkle. Our fear that in such combinations one worked and the other loafed has been completely dispelled. Indeed, it appears that here as elsewhere, ideas grow in the company of ideas.

Then again, some children work slowly, laboriously, choosing each word and achieving an economy of expression. Others write quickly and with a flourish, dashing off a story as fast as a pencil can go. Still other children write a bit, erase, rewrite, cross out, start over, and finally out of an assortment of scribbled scraps with arrows, erasures, and patches fashion an appealing story that delights the group.

There seems to be no limit to the ways of writing needed by different personalities. Each is uniquely appropriate to the person who thus expresses himself, and any inclination to change a child's own way of writing should be firmly checked.

The Unfinished Story

Not every story reaches the stage of completion necessary for reading aloud. Many times a child abandons a story half finished, and rightly so. Invention is at best a fickle power. A child may start a story in a fine burst of enthusiasm only to find that his idea does not work out and his invention dwindles; the adventure that had begun so gaily comes to a standstill, and he is heartily disappointed in it. An argument could be made that he be required to finish it before starting another. Upon a few fatal occasions we, with a puritanical eye on character building, have followed this policy. Almost without exception the children have tied trite conclusions to their often delightful beginnings. Nothing has been gained but a salute to perseverance, and much has been lost. The forced completion has made all storytelling such a disagreeable experience that only a singularly courageous child again attempts a venture that might so suddenly turn into painful drudgery. The teacher is left with a complete but woefully unbalanced story and the serious problem of overcoming a child's distaste for writing.

There are many times when a story is best left half-finished. Often the beginning is so engaging that it is difficult to accept the child's verdict, "I don't like it anymore." "I don't know how to end it." "I have a better idea now." Here, for example, is Ann's story. It starts in a pleasing manner, but it is easy to detect the spot where her invention faltered.

❋   ❋   ❋

Once upon a time there live a great big hen. She had laid some eggs. She was just going to sit on them when she saw a big fat worm. "Well," she thought, "this will be my last time I go off my nest. One little worm won't hurt."

But sly Mr. Fox was close by in the brambles. "My two dear children like eggs. I think I will get them some," he said. So he went home half-walking and half-running. He told his children how long it had been since they had some nice, soft-boiled eggs.

"May I have that ball, the little one you were playing with yesterday?"

"Here it is," said one of the foxes. "But you have spoiled our little ball."

"Do you want eggs?" said the fox. "Do you want to play a joke on Mrs. Hen?"

"Yes," was the reply.

"Now," he said, "which one of you wants to go to the beach with me?" They all did so Mr. Fox took them all.

When they got to the beach Mr. Fox told them to wait on the sand. Then he took the rubber ball and went down to the ocean and filled it with sea water. He then took his children home to bed. The next day he got up bright and early and again hid in the bushes near Mrs. Hen's house. Now Mrs. Hen saw . . .

Ann said, "I'm sick of this story—it's flopped." We agreed. Better to drop the story there, having had the fun of inventing Mrs. Hen and sly Fox than to drag it to a lifeless close. We accepted Ann's verdict quietly and read with enjoyment what she had written. Thus we kept the way open for future stories, many of which reached a conclusion satisfactory to Ann.

At other times it is obvious that a youngster has written a part of a story just for the fun of using a word or a phrase that has excited his imagination. Having used the bewitching phrase, he has no further interest in the story and is content to drop it. Here is a nine-year-old's unfinished tale plainly written just to use a fascinating word.

✿ ✿ ✿

The king was in an awful rage. "Where is my wise counsellor?" he shouted.

"Here I am, your majesty," said the wise counsellor, bowing until his beard touched the floor.

"Well, don't I have the biggest castle in all the world?" said the king.

"Indubitably, your majesty," said the wise counsellor, bowing until his beard touched the floor.

"And don't I have the largest army in the world?"

"Indubitably, your majesty."

"And don't I have the most golden treasure in all the world?"

"Indubitably, your majesty."

"Then why don't I have. . . ."

Again a story may be laid aside merely because a newly discovered idea is so tempting that a child loses interest in his current plot. We have found it wise to let him shift to the fresh idea since we know that the satisfaction of reading a whole story will help offset a tendency to skip endlessly from one unfinished tale to another. The child who regularly abandons his stories, almost without exception, fails to complete work of other kinds as well. The basic problem can be better handled in areas involving objective materials than in this realm of highly personal ideas.

We have learned to value that first quick surge of a story idea and to hide our disappointment when a promising beginning is forsaken for a new plan. Occasionally a child returns to an unfinished story and completes it, but more often he forgets it in the onrush of new ideas.

Probably one of the most common reasons for not completing a story is the simple and seemingly unavoidable factor of physical fatigue. Again and again we have seen a child tire of his story just because the labor of getting the words on paper was too onerous. When it is possible to relieve this impasse by writing for the child from dictation, his interest does not flag. But this course is seldom feasible.

We do not know to what extent this element of physical fatigue curbs a child's outpouring of ideas. We do know that Debby, who writes with average facility for a nine-year-old, spent five writing periods on a long but never-finished story and then turned to a shorter one. Obviously her loss of interest in the first was due to fatigue induced by the effort of trying to write in pace with her swift imagination. We have watched children who write slowly develop terse, telegraphic styles in order to transfer their ideas to paper without too great expenditure of energy. Others have said,

"Sure I have a story idea, but I just thought I would rest this period." Still others have written part of a story and then, as their hands grew weary, asked to tell the balance. Some have attached abrupt and trite endings to their tales, saying in explanation, "I know the ending's not so good but I got tired writing." This whole matter of fatigue is one aspect of writing about which we are especially curious for we feel it has not yet been adequately examined or dealt with.

Teaching Techniques

Abundance of writing is our initial goal. Only by writing and writing and writing do the channels of personal communication open for true thinking and feeling to come through. We make of our story writing a kind of playtime—play in the valid sense of doing something with one's whole heart—and we do all we can to keep alive the spirit of adventure and fun. As a result we get quantities of stories, many of which are poor and all of which could be improved. Yet we waste no time in remaking the poor ones nor in dwelling overlong on the few that hold promise. It is not the spirit of judgment, but that of spontaneous enjoyment we wish to maintain. Like the lumbermen around their campfire guffawing over a new Paul Bunyan yarn or the eager crowd transported by a minstrel into knightly feats of derring-do, we, too, ask only to be excited or amused. We feel no need to criticize. When attention is thus focused on the enchantment of the story and not upon its shortcomings, self-consciousness begins to drop away, and children come, more and more, to find satisfaction and release in the stories they create.

The more they write, the more they must bestir their minds for new ideas. Invention is indeed the primary activity of creative power. It is the *quality* in stories for which we watch most eagerly and are quick to acclaim: "That was a different idea." "What a surprise to have Mother Bear . . ." "You could have ended your story there, but instead you invented another happening. That's good." By question and comment we direct attention to the new, the individual, the unexpected. Such concern may not make for immediate story improvement; but we are working for awakened minds and at the same time we are trying to forestall a rehash of current radio and television fare. We want children to write out of their own musings and reactions, and when they do that, there is always at least a touch of the unique and the unusual.

During the reading periods we watch for such storytelling techniques as may appear, and we try, without seeming to teach, to make the children aware of them also. After a particularly tempting beginning we may stop the reader just long enough for the listeners to realize how much they want him to go on. We do not urge the use of such elements as good beginnings, details of characterization, moments of suspense. When children are writing with affectionate interest these things begin to appear of their own accord, and this is especially true if they have been mentioned approvingly in other stories. Naturally the effective techniques appear first in the stories of the more imaginative children, but in time others gradually absorb and use them. Each child seems to take over the elements that fit the maturity of his own thinking; hence they are part of the fabric of his story and not something superficially added because he was urged to do so.

Even in matters of vocabulary we no longer stress the use of colorful words. Instead our emphasis is on clear and true imagining; for when a child lives his story vividly in his mind, the fitting words seem miraculously to appear. We appreciate the words, to be sure, for the effect they have upon us. We see "the little bears squirming in their hot collars"; we hear Nig when he "growled in his toughest voice"; we feel the tactile sensation as did Mo when "hesitatingly he touched the baby's soft little paw." There is no special virtue in long words, new words, or bookish words. A word is good only if it tells exactly what the author had in mind.

But far more potent than our guidance, if what *follows* rather than *precedes* can be called guidance, is the subtle communication between the reader and his audience. The pleased sigh that follows a good beginning says more clearly than any words, "*Now we're off to a good start.*" The sharp intake of breath, the irrepressible giggle, the sudden stillness that comes from tense expectancy, all tell the reader what grips and moves his hearers. These flashes of success work powerfully to illuminate and foster sound narrative techniques because they are part and parcel of the moments when a story is working its magic in the hearts and minds of those who receive it. Thus against the natural reaction of responsive listeners the children shape and test their story-making power.

Sometimes it is possible to trace to the reading and appreciation of one story the adoption of a specific technique by many of the class. In an eight–nine-year-old group, three quarters of the stories ended with the comfortable and hackneyed assurance, "And they (he, she) lived happily ever after." The other quarter took the hero safely home, gave him his supper, and left him in bed. But Mary's story was different.

* A CAUGHT FISH

Once there was a little boy. His name was Bob. He was six years old. He decided to go fishing. So he dug some angleworms and got his pole, his fishing pole, and went to a lake. He fished and fished and fished. With angleworms. But he didn't catch anything and he got discouraged. Suddenly a gull flew over his head. The gull squawked and Bob looked up and the gull dropped a fish he was carrying home. Bob caught the fish in his hands. "Well," he said, "at least I can say I caught a fish."

When the teacher finished reading there was a quick outburst of enthusiasm for the swift and dramatic ending:

"Oh, Mary, you stopped right at the place for laughing."

"Well, he *did* catch a fish and that's that."

"In this story the last part is the best of all."

So the story was immediately reread with special emphasis given to the ending.

Although no further discussion of this technique took place, the stock endings soon began to disappear as the children experimented with other conclusions. Two or three wrote obvious imitations of Mary's tale in an effort to capture for themselves the warm approval that had been accorded her. And warm approval they received though not for the imitation, which the children dismissed with "The end sounds like Mary's story," but for some phrase or situation that was really fresh and genuine. Others adapted the technique to fit and strengthen their own styles. Here are the last bits of three stories written shortly after Mary's "A Caught Fish."

* * *

The prince came tiredly around the curve of the world back again to his own home and there in the garden with flowers all around it was the golden crown just where he had dropped it.

* * *

He went down a long black hall and came to a great door. He pushed and pushed. It finally creaked open. He found himself in *another* big room. "My," he thought, "I'll never get out of here." Just then he saw a window with a water pipe going by it. He quickly rushed to the window, slid down the pipe and was safe at last.

* * *

Buttercup Wilkins slowly licked the jam from her face and paws. She carefully closed the door of the jam closet and wearing a smile at the edge of her whiskers she slipped past all the mean chattering cats whose noses were so uppity they did not even see her.

Mary's story alone does not account for this development, but Mary's story *plus* the lively appreciation of it was directly responsible for the experimentation that followed. When children listen constructively to both story and comment, thus identifying themselves with the very warp and woof of the tale and its quality, they become increasingly imbued with what makes writing effective, and inevitably this learning is reflected in their own stories. Appreciative listening sharpens the urge for more writing and deepens the insight necessary for better writing. Indeed, listening, like writing and reading, is an indispensable arc of a productive circle.

Enriching Activities

Not only do we permit and encourage abundant writing, but we strive to enrich that inner consciousness from which personal expression springs. At odd moments we take time to savor the qualities of things: the stinging drive of rain, the first faint mist of green upon the trees, the muffled sound of footsteps upon a snowy day. We take time, too, to recognize the graphic truth of those spontaneous comments that children often make about what they touch or hear or see. We tell what we see in clouds or fog, what we hear in wind or rain, what we feel when walking on soft grass or crunchy pebbles. Often we note on the chalkboard the colorful or metaphoric phrases the children suggest. "Crunchy as potato chips" or "gossipy whispering" they may say about the sounds of walking in dry autumn leaves, for example. Then we erase these descriptive terms that so delighted us lest any child feel obliged to use them in a story or poem. The only residue we hope for from this exercise is the conviction that one searches for the word or phrase that says exactly what one sees or feels. Seeking to fit first-hand sensory experience into words so often results in vivid expression.

At times apart from writing periods we share with them some of the beauty, wonder, laughter, ruggedness, and vigor that we have found in literature. No medium is its equal for stretching and strengthening the imagination. The atmosphere of our reading is one of warmth and companionship. Here, too, when the action of a story grows lively, we may close our eyes to see it better; or we may say together some familiar lines of poetry because we like their meaning or their sound. Nowadays, when through movies, radio, comics, and television children are exposed to so much that is commonplace and artificial, we feel a double obligation to give them satisfying experiences in good literature; else how will many of them know the magic and the rhythm and the power of their mother tongue? Such reading is never consciously compared with the children's own efforts, but we are confident that through their rapt listening much good is absorbed—good that will add to the inner store from which the child creator draws.

Gaining Control of Skills

Would there be satisfactory improvement if children wrote just for the joy of creating a tale? This was a question that gave us considerable concern when we started our experiment. The answer is an unqualified affirmative. In both mechanics and style, the ability of these children at fifth- and sixth-grade levels definitely surpasses that of any other groups we have ever had. We had anticipated growth in the techniques of storytelling, but we were frankly surprised by the extent to which the mechanics taught through practical writing have transferred to personal writing.

Remember that there is no requirement of form in personal writing; no comment is ever made on correctness or the lack of it. No checking or copying is done except on those rare occasions when there is a good reason to put a story into form for others to see and read. Sometimes a class gets satisfaction from making a collection of their stories of the preceding months. "A Treasure Chest", "Ten Tall Tales," "Laughing Adventures" have appeared as titles on books of carefully edited and copied stories. Well-worn covers and much-handled pages attest their popularity. This revision of original stories is not commonplace. At most, it occurs only once in a year or two. Other than these rare instances of "publishing" stories for our own pleasure, we have limited the correction of mechanics and structure to practical writing and ignored them in personal writing. Yet after a lapse of weeks or even months, depending on the individual child, the items of punctuation, paragraphing, capitalization, and spelling taught through practical writing begin to appear in their stories. Even such stumbling blocks as apostrophes and quotation marks, first encountered in utilitarian writing and then explained and checked in that field over a period of time, begin to be used voluntarily in personal writing.

Here we have reproduced a story exactly as Claire wrote it in sixth grade. It is a fair illustration of the carry-over of forms learned in practical writing. Claire neither asked for nor received help of any sort. Indeed, there was nothing to be gained by correctness, for after the story was read to the class it was put immediately into her folder.

❂   ❂   ❂

It was Tuesday afternoon and a council was being held in Nig's room. It was being held because the new girl, Jean, who had come to school had invited Roy Bear to supper the night before.

"I say that Eenie's desk should be on one side of her and my desk should be on the other side of her," said Nig.

"But I always get people to like *me*," said Mo.

"You aren't quick enough about it," said Meinie, "it took you four years to get Alice Bear to like you and *she's* no good."

"Oh yes she is," said Mo. "As a matter of fact I'm taking her to the movies tonight."

"Well, *I'm* taking *Sue* Bear to the movies," said Eenie.

"I'm taking Nellie Bear," said Meenie.

"I'm taking Daisy Mae because Mommy said I could," said Meinie. Poor Nig wasn't taking anyone to the movies so he ran upstairs to his bedroom to hide. Soon he heard the others getting ready to go to the movies and after a while the house was quiet so Nig quietly opened the door and went downstairs to make sure nobody was home. Then he ran to the telephone and just as he got there it rang.

He lifted the receiver and said, "Hello, who is this?"

"It's Jean," said the voice, "could I speak to Nig?"

"This is Nig, what do you want?"

"I want to know if you can go to the movies with me?"

"S-s-s-*sure*," he said and hung up. He ran up stairs and quickly got dressed. Using some of Mother's perfume to fix his hair. He ran down stairs, out the door, and over to Jean's house.

Jean was waiting for him and had telephoned for a taxi. They rode to the movie house and were just ready to get their tickets when Nig realized that he didn't have any money. He started to apologize to Jean when up walked Meinie. He handed Daisy Mae to Nig, took Jean by the hand and got their tickets. Nig was so relieved he didn't mind having Meinie take Jean to the movies and the next day in school he changed his desk with Meinie's.

What has happened is that a reasonable degree of correctness has become a *natural* part of Claire's writing. It is paradoxical that although she corrected a mistake in punctuation in the fourth quotation by placing a period after "Mo" and a capital A in *As*, she has let the same type of error pass unnoticed in the preceding quotation. This irregularity is a characteristic step toward automatic control of items of mechanics. From the point of view of form the story is not perfect, but the consistently accurate use of apostrophes, the spelling of such words as "receiver, "apologize," and "relieved," the generally correct use of punctuation marks and capitals, all point to a real competence. We have, we believe, developed an acceptable degree of power over mechanics by teaching forms in practical writing, and waiting for their inevitable adoption in personal writing.

The illustrations that appear throughout this book give ample evidence of the growth in story-writing ability achieved by our children. What they cannot show is the children's keen delight in their stories, the carefully paced dramatic reading of each adventure, the sidewise glance to see if a special detail has caught the imagination of the audience, the quick lift of shining eyes at the end of the reading to measure the story's appeal. Writing is fun, and when it is fun one writes to renew his own pleasure.

chapter five

❀ ❀ ❀ ❀ ❀ ❀ ❀ ❀

CHILDREN'S VERSE

Tell me, where is fancy bred,
Or in the heart, or in the head?
How begot, how nourished?
—WILLIAM SHAKESPEARE, *The*
Merchant of Venice

To a young child life is new and full of flavor, and he reaches out to encompass it with all his senses. Because his acquaintance with language is new also, his use of it tends to be original. Frequently, too, his expression is so vivid and rhythmical that it verges on poetry.

Unfortunately, many adults seize upon such unusual remarks to quote them as amusing or quaint, or to make them over into a more familiar pattern by saying, "Oh, you mean . . ." All too soon a child begins to discount his natural, unique mode of expression and to substitute for it the empty, ready-made phrases that adults put into his mouth and mind. Thus he learns early that commonplace words and ideas protect him so that his own thoughts and feelings will not be laughed at or criticized. Perhaps, and we believe that this is true, they lead him into having commonplace thoughts and feelings as well. The fresh insight, the vivid emotion, the sensitive awareness wither away, and the original quality of language begins to disappear. So it is that children lose touch with the deep core of their own individuality. Happily, this contact can be restored— at least in part. They can be led again to savor experiences more poignantly, and to enjoy telling their reactions to them. Although their comments may not be poetry, for want of a better term we call them so, and undoubtedly they are the stuff of which poetry is made.

Stimulating Interest in Poetry

Nature phenomena seem to lend themselves readily to the adventure of poetry telling. We all are affected consciously or subconsciously by stars, night, changes in the seasons, the winter's cold, the color of autumn; but we forget that these experiences are not timeworn to children.

Perhaps, when there is a heavy fog or when the first frost covers the ground, we talk about it together, and the children are encouraged to put into words their awareness of the miracle. They react keenly to the quiet of fog, the sheen of a frost-covered lawn, the clink of icy branches, the sound of snow crunched under foot. Looking at these out-of-door happenings closely often establishes a mood in which they tap hidden resources of thought and feeling.

One windy morning the children came in drenched by an unexpected storm. They were so excited by the experience that they were talking breathlessly about what it was like. Each child seemed to be searching for the exact words to describe how it affected him. The teacher said, "Let me write down what you're saying about the storm. It may paint a picture or be a make-believe idea or tell something you wonder about. You don't have to say much—just a few words that really fit can do the trick. You'll have to keep very quiet inside so that you won't scare away your thoughts."

And then as they sat close to the teacher, there came a quiet, expectant waiting, which gradually gave place to open delight as they took turns telling their ideas. We wrote feverishly in an effort to capture them all. Of course, there was time afterward to read aloud what they had said, and to savor it. Here are some of their thoughts about the storm:

*   *   *

The wind has a shape like the waves.

It is pushing through the trees
It has holes in it so it can get by
          the branches.

The wind is rustling through the grasses
It is whistling down the valleys.

The wind is sweeping through the town
It is resting on the housetops.

The wind sounds like a boat
Leaving the dock.

It sounds like fairies
Whispering to each other.

It is raining needles
Because it pricks you—
It's like a porcupine
Rubbing against you.

Clouds open up
And swiftly little drops come down.

The rain touches the blades of grass
And they bend with the heavy load.
I think that the sky and ground
Look like they were twins—
The puddles look like the grey sky
And they look so much alike
That I think that it's hard
To tell them from each other.

Often we have stimulated our classes to poetic effort by reading to them from our collection of child-made poems. Through hearing the ideas of other children our pupils gain courage to tell their own thoughts and feelings. Of course, an abundance of adult-made poetry is read, too, for we want them to know and love great literature. However, much care is taken in selecting verse to read when the children are trying to express their own ideas; it is too easy for them to copy or to be overawed and to feel that their own thoughts are not good enough to share with others. We are apt to choose verse that is free in style rather than rhymed or strongly patterned. A child's ear often is so captured by the rhyming that he misses the meaning and the individual essence. When he tries to make poems of his own, he is likely to forget what he wanted to say and concentrate on the jingle.

Whether we read from our collection of children's poetic offerings or from the writings of accomplished poets, we keep the reading periods short. They take place when the class is relaxed and comfortable. During the reading we mention a part that "sounded different" or was "a new way of talking" about rain, or snow, or fog, or that used picture words. Only a little reading and talking are done. Ten minutes when the group is really listening are a better investment than a longer stretch when they are not so receptive.

Poetry and Make-Believe

In choosing poems, like the following, we take advantage of children's fresh and dramatic views of the natural world about them.

    ✿   ✿   ✿

Morning is when the sun
Wakes up.
He yawns
And turns his lantern on.
He wakes up all the birds
And other animals, too.
I surely would hate to be the sun
Getting up so early
In the morning.
I've never gotten up before him.
I wonder how he knows
What time it is.
I guess the moon comes in
And stops to wake him up
Before he goes on
To night again

    ✿   ✿   ✿

The moon must get tired
Of his business
Because on rainy nights
He never comes out.
That must mean

He's taking a snooze
Under the white clouds.
The stars crowd in with him—
He goes rolling out
Because he has no room.
After he rolls out
He mumbles to himself,
"How greedy those little stars are—
They can rest all the time
When I have to sit
Up in my throne
And shine upon the earth."

⁂   ⁂   ⁂

The wind comes down
In braids;
It comes down
Twirling around
On the clouds
When they're low.
The rain comes down
In splatters.

⁂   ⁂   ⁂

I like to watch the wind go by—
It must get out of breath.
I wonder how it floats
And ruffles
And makes all that noise
Many times at night
It wakes me up
With all its tumbling.

⁂   ⁂   ⁂

The cars are rolling along the snow-dressed road
Looking like black bugs—softly, softly
Horns honk in the grey mist—softly, softly
As the snow drifts down
Softly, softly.

✿   ✿   ✿

Darkness creeps along
As if it were going to pounce upon you.
On rainy days he steals the sun.
The clouds come floating by—
The darkness must run its fastest
To get to the other side of the world.

✿   ✿   ✿

When the silver raindrops
Softly patter on the earth
It sounds like small feet running along,
And the trees hold out their arms
To catch the gleaming.

Pictures in Poetry

Children also enjoy poems that paint vivid pictures. The following
have some intensity of feeling in their central idea or use language
with special color and pattern.

The first one balances the fate of the little grasshopper between
death by the sword or by poison—poison ivy in this case. In the
second the child tries to put wonder into familiar terms only to
return to his original question. All of the poems have some individuality of vision or play of language that lifts them above prose.

✿   ✿   ✿

The little grasshopper
Glides from one grass blade
To another
As though he were trying
To commit suicide
By falling on a sword.

He doesn't seem to have much luck
But he hasn't come
To poison ivy yet.

    *   *   *

Where does the dark go?
I don't know.
It may go down the well
And have the wind pull it up in buckets.
Or it may go down the chimney to hide,
And then when he thinks
The day has been enough
He creeps out.
All of a sudden
Before you know it,
It's dark.
I do wonder where the dark goes.

    *   *   *

Pansies nod their faces in the breeze,
Gossiping the news of a new little baby
That was born.
He has a velvet face, all yellow with violet,
And his mother is so proud.
That's the gossip that goes around
When a new pansy baby is born.

    *   *   *

We've got a Japanese cherry tree
That grows in our back yard.
It glows with pink
And makes a background
For all the other things—
Like a candle in the corner.

    *   *   *

April is a month when all the flowers
Come popping out of the ground.
It is just like a warning
That summer's coming.

All the flowers
Show their little buds
And so do the trees.
Even the grass
Shows happiness
By filling up your lawn
With its greenness
April is a special month
Just for loveliness.

❋   ❋   ❋

The wind is dashing
Through the trees;
It knocks the poor little leaves
Off their hinges
And chases them down
To the ground.
And then the mean old wind
Whisks them into the fire
Where they burn
Into black crumbly ashes.

Fears and Secret Longings

Some of the poems we read are those that little children tell when
they are not afraid of being laughed at or misunderstood. Even
though these expressions may have little intrinsic poetic worth, they
sometimes have therapeutic value. Often they are dictated by shy,
insecure children, who, through the telling, gain faith in themselves.
Many times, however, they express insights in forms quite tran-
scending in artistry the feelings that germinated the poems.

❋   ❋   ❋

Whenever I'm in trouble
And talk to myself out loud,
The trees nod their heads to and fro—
They know what is troubling me;
They hold out their arms
As if to make a bed for me.

I've always hated little children
Younger than me
Because they have
Such funny ideas.
They always want
To play with dolls and things.
That isn't a bit like me—
I always like to pretend
I'm a mother
And can drive a car.
I wish they were like me
Sometimes at least.

    ✿   ✿   ✿

Home's left behind when I go away traveling.
All my dolls as children may come with me,
But still my house is left behind.
My dogs and animals all may come,
But home is left behind.

    ✿   ✿   ✿

At night when I go to bed
You never would know
What's going inside my mind;
But it's nice to think
About all sorts of things
That nobody would know about
Except yourself.
I think and think
And when I wake up
In the morning
You would never know
That I thought about
Those things
And I even don't know;
But the next night
I try to remember
And keep the same adventure.

Wonder in Children's Verse

Children's poetic expression emerges from a variety of everyday things and from their looking at the familiar with fresh curiosity and wonder. Often they question what adults see as quite ordinary, and wonder what lies beneath the surface of life. Great size or strength as well as the diminutive and weak impress children. The affection of animals sustains them and humor often finds its way into their perception of the world around them. Feelings about these experiences come through in their attempts at poetry.

❁   ❁   ❁

I always wondered
If cocoons were butterflies,
I always wondered
How they creep out of their shells,
I always wondered
How they creep along
I never could see their feet.
I think they do very well
For their age and how small they are.
I wonder how they learned how to fly—
I think they taught themselves.
Sometimes I wonder if I could fly
As well as they could.

❁   ❁   ❁

Feathers tickle!
Why don't they tickle the hen?
They're on his back
So I think they should tickle him—
They tickle *me*.

❁   ❁   ❁

I often stay at the end of the beach
To look at the sea
The water comes in

And takes the tiny grains of sand
From my castle
And carries them all away.
Where do they go?
Do they see fish?
Or even a whale?
I wonder.

*　*　*

I wonder why birds
Sing so beautifully
Maybe it's because they practice
Or maybe it's because
They were born to know how.

Individual Dictation of Poetry

Sometime—early or late—during the reading of poems, children begin making poems of their own. Since the ideas are often fleeting, they may be lost before a child can write them down. Therefore, provision must be made for him to dictate them.

At the outset of a poetry-making period, time is taken to get the group in tune. A few carefully selected poems are read to create an appropriate mood, and a little talk helps to get them started. Something like this may be said: "Telling a poem is like painting a picture, only it's painting with words. It's as if you were standing by pots of paint and splashing the color on a paper with rapid strokes before the picture could leave your mind. A story comes more slowly. It has more words and often starts with 'Once upon a time.' But when you tell a poem you plunge right in, and with just a few words you give a picture, or a feeling, or a make-believe reason for something." Then, at another time, "Poems sometimes tell your hidden feelings. Try telling about your wonderings or your secret wishes."

For a few very shy youngsters the following comments seem to open the way: "Making up poems is like water flowing from a spring that has been choked up. First it is muddy, but after it has flowed for a while, the water bubbles forth clear and sparkling. You'll find that it's exciting to tell poems. You never know when you are going to get something you'll especially like. So you have to keep on letting them pour out."

We often suggest: "A good time to think of poetry ideas is at night just before you go to sleep when you have that comfortable drowsy feeling."

By stressing the fact that poetry is a quick way of saying something—"Poems don't need all the words that are put into stories; you just hit the high spots"—children are helped to make the transition from the detailed wordiness of a story to the essencelike quality of poetic expression.

The room setting is extremely important. The children and the teacher, too, should feel free from pressure. Quietness and a minimum of movement are two essentials. Before dictation begins, the children are helped to start activities on which they can work alone. Painting or crayoning a picture, modeling with clay, or weaving, keep the hands busy and at the same time permit the child's mind to follow any course it chooses. Not all are active. Some find that sitting in a quiet corner, or looking out of the window helps them to reach that dreamy state in which their thoughts take on the feeling of poetry.

The teacher usually sits at a low table beside the one who is dictating. The table is purposely low, for even the physical setup must not conspire to place the teacher in a dominating position. Because the presence of another is often confusing, each child comes up by himself to tell his poem. If, while he is dictating, others have poetry ideas, they raise their hands, and their names are jotted down. As soon as possible, they are called in turn.

At the close of a poetry dictation period at least one contribution from each child who has participated is read by the teacher in order to give the poems the best possible oral treatment. Thus every child has the satisfaction of hearing his ideas read aloud. At the same time his attention is directed toward the parts that have individual flavor; for example, when all of the poems have been read, the children tell which parts made them see pictures or were new ways of telling something that is true. Interestingly enough, it is the worthwhile things they mention. The mediocre expressions have not made enough impression to be remembered.

To free children so that they can reveal themselves is a matter that calls for patience and faith on the part of the teacher. She listens carefully for each hint of the individual voice and welcomes it warmly, no matter how crude it may be. Indeed, the crude expression often tells of superior things to come. The glib or sentimental phrases are a far cry from the honest, unaffected responses of the real child.

First feeble efforts must meet with reassurance if children are to learn to accept their own way of saying things. No child can have faith in himself unless he is confident all his attempts will be graciously received with no suggestions for changes or improvements, and no belittling comments by other members of the class.

Of course, the opening-up process takes time and at first yields only meager results. But slowly, as children gain the courage to be themselves, there is a deepening sensitivity coupled with a growing ease of communication, until eventually many attain the power to reveal their sincere reactions in language that is fitting and poetic.

From the beginning the emphasis is on letting children respond easily and naturally to experience. There has to be time for "moodling" if they are to discover that "down underneath" they have thoughts to surprise and please them. We avoid showing undue concern about the words they use, for we know that when ideas and feelings are welling up spontaneously the right words to express them will come. We may comment casually on the fact that such words as "pretty," "nice," "beautiful," "lovely" tell little; however, we never let a piece of real poetry pass by without taking pains to appreciate it. For example, we point out how clearly one can hear the sound of the wind when Lois says, "It wakes me up with all its tumbling"; or can see the blowing storm clouds when John says, "The clouds are mad, they are bursting with madness." We share our delight in Bob's vivid image of the Japanese cherry tree, which "glows with pink and makes a background for all the other things —like a candle in the corner."

Poetry with Young Children

It is fascinating to discover that even very young children take pleasure in dictating their poetry ideas. The following groups of poems, told by six- and seven-year-olds, illustrate the growth in self-expression that occurred over a two-year period. A few of their first attempts are given to show how very simple were the beginnings of this poetry dictation.

❀   ❀   ❀

Leaves, I love you
When you are colored.

❀   ❀   ❀

Sunshine, sunshine,
I wish you would sunshine
All through the spring.

❀   ❀   ❀

Come little snowflake,
Come little snowflake,
Soon it will be
Good time to play.

These were dictated later in the first and second grades:

❀   ❀   ❀

Little tree
Standing still
He sees everybody
Standing still.

❀   ❀   ❀

Oh, the sailboats
Floating down the river
And the steamboats and the freight boats
Puffing down the big, big lake
Puff—chug! Puff—chug!

❀   ❀   ❀

Sunshine, I like you.
Would you come for a big while

Because I want to make a picture of you?
I shall color the sky
Just as yellow as you are.

＊ ＊ ＊

Puff, puff—
The trains go
Up the tracks and down the tracks,
Carry people and baggage
Up the tracks and down the tracks,
All the day through—
Puff, puff.

＊ ＊ ＊

When I'm in New York
All I see is crowds—
Some going in theaters
Some going down the street
Some going in offices.
In the night
I see elevator lights:
The buildings light up,
They look like fireflies
Anchored in the air.

＊ ＊ ＊

Little birdie,
Every winter do you go down south?
'Cuz Mommie's going down
In the great big car;
If you stay on top of it
You can fly tomorrow morning.

Group Poetry Dictation

Many experiences lend themselves to group dictation of poetry ideas.
Sometimes they have to do with anticipation of a holiday such as
Thanksgiving or Christmas. Often an outdoor adventure—scuffling

through autumn leaves, catching the first snowflakes on mittened hands, examining the miracle of springtime during a walk in the park—inspires children to make observations and comments that are colorful and frequently poetic.

For children to give full expression to their ideas, the atmosphere must be one of quiet listening. Sometimes the teacher works with only a few individuals, sometimes with the entire class. When the children are in the appropriate mood, they stimulate each other to tell ideas in the very special way that reflects inner thinking and feeling. Sitting in a group near the teacher, one child at a time gives his thoughts or impressions about what he has seen or felt. In this welcoming environment, many volunteer to share their thoughts. The teacher records them as quickly as she can. At times she writes individuals' offerings directly on the chalkboard. Other times, she uses a note pad and transcribes the dictation to the chalkboard. Then she may work with the class or a small group selecting the thoughts that have true color and individual flavor, eliminating repetitions, and arranging ideas in a pleasing sequence.

Sometimes each child makes a copy of the group poem in his best handwriting, and with a suitable "decoration" it becomes a gift for a parent or a special friend. Frequently this type of poem lends itself to choral speaking, which the class or a small group can present to an audience.

* TOY MAKERS' CHANT

We are the toy makers
Tip, tap, tap!
We are the toy makers
Tip, tap, tap!

Hammering, cutting, painting, and inventing
We are the toy makers
Tip, tap, tap!

Sawing, sawing,—buzz, buzz, buzz
Polishing, polishing—smooth, smooth, smooth
Snipping, sewing—pricking our thumbs
OUCH!

Shaping and shining
We make our toys
There will be happy faces with big broad smiles
When children get our toys for Christmas.

* A CHISTMAS POEM

This is Christmas
Stars light up the heavens,
Snow fairies dance on the window sills,
Snowmen greet us in our gardens,
Children stand before shop windows, longing and hoping.

This is Christmas
People carol merry songs
Church bells harmonize their tunes
Sleigh bells talk of happiness,
Bells tinkle as they sway
Among the green arms of the trees.

This is Christmas
Pies and cookies send their fragrant messages,
The crackling fire scents the air as the Yule log glows,
The Christmas pudding fills the kitchen
With its promising sweetness.

This is Christmas
In the happiness of the dark, cold evening
Children say goodnight with excitement in their hearts,
They fall asleep dreaming of the first Christmas
And a starlit night in Bethlehem.

Transition from Dictating to Writing Verse

In the primary grades the teacher must act as the recorder to catch
children's philosophical musings and poetry ideas. As children grow
older, a transition period allows many to spell and write well enough
to capture at least some of the highlights of their individual reactions in written form. Armed with these notes, a child may refer to
them when he has his turn to dictate to the teacher. Always we

encourage the individual to enlarge upon what he has written if he wishes. His paper, with its cryptic and often fragmentary and misspelled jottings, serves an important purpose: it helps him to remember thoughts that came in a rush or expressions that sprang from deep and very personal feelings.

As the teacher writes from dictation, the child's rhythm of talking indicates what should be included in each line. It is gratifying to hear the way children's poetic language falls naturally into patterns that fit the individual and what he wants to convey.

The examples presented illustrate the combination of a child's writing and dictating. In the first, the girl wrote only two lines, but the rest poured out so fast the teacher used many abbreviations in her recording, as the reproduction shows. The printed version is presented also to facilitate reading. The second example of combined writing and dictation shows that the author was intent upon getting words down to hold his powerful imagery; it shows also the sharp contrast between a total lack of alignment when he wrote and a very effective line division when he dictated. Curiously enough, Jack was an excellent speller generally, but in the tumult of this composing experience he misspelled some words he could spell correctly and yet handled successfully words like "molten" and "lava" that he rarely had occasion to write.

Independent Writing of Poetry in Later Grades

Some of our pupils continue to write poetry throughout the elementary grades and on into high-school years. By far the majority, however, seem to have greater needs for other kinds of outlet and to increase their writing of stories and reports rather than verse in the late elementary school.

Even with a great deal of stimulation to write their own, most of our older children did very little, though they maintained their zest for listening to adult-made verse. Rather than require attempts at verse writing, we continued to hold open the door to poetic experimentation, to welcome it when it came, and to search for reasons for an apparently natural diminution of lyrical expression. Causes lie, we have come to believe, in the hastening tempo of pressures from areas of subject matter and skill mastery, from an

The wind is blowing
A breeze across
    the summer air

The leaves rust—
+ " lovely sum— mist
Comes a glorious feel—
To the world around.
The sum— feel— is always here
For those who want it,
The glory of the summer
Will never go away.

The wind is blowing a breeze
Across the summer air;
The leaves rustle
And the lovely summer mist
Gives a glorious feeling
To the world around.
The summer feeling is always here
For those who want it;
The glory of the summer
Will never go away.

A Sowrd

A sowrd has a master
that swings the sowrd
on so high the bllold
drips like red drops of molten lava
Poring down like a waterfull
and when a sowrd win's
a victory you see
a slight smile on the
glittering gems. of the shining
handle

A Sword
A sword has a master
That swings the sword on so high
The blood drips
Like red drops of molten lava
Pouring down like a waterfall
And when a sword wins a victory
You see a slight smile
On the glittering gems
Of the shining handle.

overweening concern for living up to adult standards in all the arts, from a heightening interest in the overt and factual standards that seem a normal part of children's orientation in the years of preadolescence. Perhaps, too, there is a deep-seated need to protect oneself from exposing the more intensely subjective facets of personality, a period for gathering of inner strength for the later demands of adolescence when, given a conducive environment, the writing of verse again appears to flower.

The children who continued to write poetry, for the most part, have shown the more mature control of imagery and form that one would expect from individuals with so strong a commitment to their own subjective responses. Note the greater maturity of "The Haunted House" as compared with "Me" (See Joanne, Chapter 6) written about two years earlier. Here in a delightful play of imagery a little girl contrasts her own thumping of the piano "like a giant" with her mother's playing which she likens to that of the fairies or "fireflies dancing at night." The verse has effectiveness both in picture and in rhythm. However, "The Haunted House" does more than provide imagery appropriate to the mood; it does this, but it also sweeps along in a crescendo from an initial rhythmic repetition to a dramatic conclusion.

Group dictation in upper grades often sprang from the incentive of celebrating some special occasion. Exhilarated by an approaching holiday or school program, the children responded with many appropriate contributions. For such ventures into group composition our technique has generally been to set the stage by talking apparently quite casually about the subject at hand, while inviting comments that would give unique and true impressions sensed by individuals. We have not expected, nor have we gotten, universally productive responses, but we have always had a majority of children contribute actively. Many others participated quietly though not passively. We have made it possible for those few who could not become honestly involved to turn to other quiet work.

Usually a session of this kind of dictation of verse has resulted in the chalkboard's being filled, with more lines spilling over to chart paper or a convenient notebook. Then came the task of selection and arrangement by a committee. Ordinarily this has been better when left until next day, but at times it has been imperative to clear the boards the same day. One plan has the advantage of perspective; the other of momentum. In either case, the committee has always found some alternatives about which to consult the teacher and the class. At times, oddly enough, the very children who could not get into the current of expression when ideas were flowing richly were the most helpful at the editing-polishing stage.

From one such cooperative experiment in group dictation—and this sort of writing is always experimental and tentative—the following litany emerged. It shows both the unevenness that usually char-

acterizes group poetry as well as a rich variety of ideas woven into
a common and sustaining theme and form.

* OUR LITANY

For the earth we live on and all it holds for us
For a heaven and stars to dream about,
For the fertile ground which gives us food,
And for the changing seasons with their beauty and their joy,
    We thank thee, God.

In the Fall

For the whistling winds that blow so strong,
For piles of red and yellow leaves in which we jump and tumble,
For bare trees strung with shining drops of rain,
We thank thee, God.

In winter

For the coat of white that covers the land,
For soft drifts to wade through,
For delicate frost pictures on our window panes,
For the glow of street lights in the falling snow,
And for the joy and fun of Christmas
We thank thee, God.

In spring

For the sparkling freshness of our world,
For the sun shining on the new green grass,
For old trees bursting into beautiful patterns of leaves,
For soft rains and the misty fogs that sometimes follow,
We thank thee, God.

In summer

For long lazy summer days
For shining birds and humming bees and all wild life
For the clean smell of foliage after rain
We thank thee, God.

For good food and clothes and healthiness
For warm homes and pleasant schools
For our mothers and fathers, our sisters and brothers, and our friends,

We thank thee, God.
For the fun and excitement I've had with my mom and dad
For horseback rides on paths of beauty
For the dog that meets me in the dark when I am coming home
And makes me feel safe and warm inside
For jolly play times with the other fellows
And quiet times alone
We thank thee, God.
For the freedom and the peace our country has
And for the brave men and women who gave us our America
We thank Thee, God.

Poetry in the Perspective of the Classroom

In a busy schoolroom poetry making does not go on without inter-
ruption. Because it requires an atmosphere singularly free from
pressures it usually cannot flourish when children are engrossed in
other types of class activity, such as preparing a play or following
a strong science or social studies interest. But in the unhurried
periods that afford a sense of leisure and repose, poetry making can
come into its own. After dictation gets under way it ought to be continued for at least a week or two even at the cost of considerable
readjustment of the daily schedule. Poetry-making is essentially an
uncovering process, and the truly personal thoughts and feelings are
often slow to emerge. However, as children begin to realize the
satisfaction that comes from voicing their own ideas, they unconsciously permit more and more of their deeper selves to be revealed.
Often they become so captivated by the experience that they appear
before school begins in the morning or stay on after dismissal to
have their poems written down or to show what they have written.

Even the best child poems contain only a line or two of unusual
beauty or individual sparkle, and in an effort to create a more perfect whole a teacher may feel tempted to weed out ordinary expressions or to build up worthwhile bits. It is well to remember that
it is just as dishonest for an adult to change a child's utterances
as it is for a child to copy the work of another and call it his own.
Moreover, a child is bound to suffer loss of confidence when a
teacher makes suggestions for the improvement of a poem, or adds

a few words to smooth over what she considers to be the rough spots.

Much of the satisfaction that children derive from poetry-making comes when their offerings are read aloud to the class. It is this sharing that seems to insure the continuance of the experience. When a poem is especially colorful or original in its expression of truth, it receives appreciative comments from the others, but it is never unduly featured. Once it has been shared with the group, its maker seems to forget about it. Instead of mulling over what has been done, he turns instinctively to new effort. The publishing of an unusual poem in the school magazine or newspaper so focuses the spotlight of attention on it that it takes on the characteristics of a model. Often the child who created it no longer feels free to express his ideas as naturally and joyfully as he did before. It is as though he cannot compete with what he considers to be his own best self. And in many instances the creative effort of the other children is snuffed out because they sense that their work is unworthy by comparison.

The poem is never the all-important thing. The satisfactions that children gain from expressing their innermost thoughts are what really count. This is the reason we want children to become acquainted with the power of original expression. We want them to know that this power is theirs and to have faith to use it. We want them to dig beneath clichés and accepted patterns of thought to find out what they really think and feel.

chapter six

❀ ❀ ❀ ❀ ❀ ❀ ❀ ❀

INDIVIDUAL DIFFERENCES
IN WRITING—CASE STUDIES

*If we are to achieve a richer culture, rich in human
potentialities, we must recognize the whole gamut of human personalities and so weave a less arbitrary social
fabric, one in which each human gift will find a fitting
place.—*MARGARET MEADE, *From the South Seas.*

Cases studies of ten children, ranging in ability from average to highly gifted, present a clearer picture of growth than any
amount of description can portray. Selections of their writing, both
personal and practical, reveal some of the basic trends of matura-
tion and learning that take place in the elementary school years.
From these samplings it is evident that each child lends his unique
quality to his writing when he is allowed to do so, and that this
uniqueness is effective style. The obligation to learn correct forms
in practical writing and the manner in which children can and do
apply these forms in personal writing are shown as each child develops. And conversely, it appears that children color their utilitarian writing with that delightful individuality fostered by their
free and copious expression of imagination and invention.

Ten cases reveal the growth of ten different personalities. Could
we present a hundred of those we have worked with, the result
would be a hundred personalities, each as different as those presented here. We have sought, therefore, to select the ones that give
an honest cross section of the children we have studied. All these
children were of average or superior ability, for we have felt it un-
fair to describe so personally those of inferior power because of

141

the possibility of identification. But even weaker children showed visible growth.

In some cases we have included only one year's work; in others we have sampled a larger spectrum of four years of effort and development. A more exact picture could, of course, be sketched if more cases appeared, since each child grows in his own particular way. The children were different at the beginning of our study; naturally they were more different as time went on, for age always increases divergences of ability. Moreover they wrote with a feeling of satisfaction and security in the undertaking, with eagerness, and with courage. No groups with whom we have used more conventional methods have approached the degree of control shown by these children over accepted English essentials of form, structure, and organization. It has become our sure conviction that every writing experience, lived joyfully and richly, contributes to the maximum development of writing power.

Katie in Second Grade

Katie arrived in our second grade with a report from her previous school describing her as "cheerful, willing and well-behaved, an average student." This was, indeed, a reasonably accurate picture of Katie who would be picked out of the group not because she had any special ability or disability, but because she was so pleasantly "average." She did what was asked of her without comment but with a cheerful concentration of her competence. She rarely compared her achievement with that of other children, seeming to be satisfied with the knowledge that she had done her best. Although she did not volunteer for classroom responsibilities, she was always ready to do her share of whatever the class was undertaking and, because she was a careful worker, she was often chosen a member of a small group to work on a special project. In class discussions, she listened attentively, responding with her eyes rather than her voice, although here, too, if a specific response were asked, she would have an opinion to express. She moved through her days cheerfully and capably, but one had to seek ways to give Katie the joy of being important.

Early in the fall when Katie wore a new dress, the teacher took time to make her the center of attention while all admired the lovely colors of the dress and its gay trimming. Perhaps because she had thus been brought to the attention of the children, at story-telling time that afternoon the class asked Katie to tell a story. She had previously been only an appreciative listener but, urged by the children, she told, with some reluctance her first story which is here reconstructed from notes the teacher made of this important first step.

* * *

Once there was a little girl and her mother. They didn't have any money. So they had to go out and look everywhere, but they couldn't find any. Then the little girl saw a box under a bush, and she looked in and there was a *lot* of money—one thousand sixty-seven gold dollars! So they took it to the store and got all the things they wanted.

It bothered neither Katie nor her audience that this tale was almost a duplication of the story told by the child who preceded her. The one new element she had introduced, "one thousand sixty-seven gold dollars," caught the children's fancy and Katie squirmed with delight as they talked about this fantastic sum.

A few days later when someone recalled the massive sum of money, a child asked Katie if she had another story. As in other situations Katie responded to a request. This time the story was her own and gave the first indication of the slightly impish humor that was to mark many of her tales.

* * *

Once there was a little kitten named White Paws because, of course, he *had* white paws. Well, one day he jumped on the desk and knocked a bottle of ink on the floor. And he walked all around in the ink and all over the carpet. So they had to call him Black Paws, and he had to stay outside after that.

Katie just glowed when appreciative laughter acknowledged the "good joke" about the kitten's name, and at the end of the period asked when the next storytelling time would be. She no longer needed the prod of a request to start off on a story. Sometimes what she told was merely a new variation of a story told by another, but at other times she drew entirely on her own invention. Usually there was the mark of her own special light humor.

The practical writing required in the early months of second grade (lists, memos, brief notes) Katie did both amiably and capably. This sort of writing, which requires coordination of mind and muscle just to produce the necessary words, often finds its individual distinction only in the decoration children love to add. Katie's embellishments were simple and neat. As the physical act of handwriting became less arduous and children could be concerned with what they were saying, Katie's writing began to reflect something of the special touch which marked her stories.

Her note of appreciation to a mother who provided a Halloween party for the class follows:

Dear Mrs. Burns,
    Thank you for giving us a party. You tricked us with a yummy treat.
                                              Love, Katie

Some time after Halloween when children were dictating stories, Katie, pulling her chair beside the teacher, listened to two or three stories. When the teacher asked if she would like to dictate, too, Katie immediately began her tale of an orange jack-o'-lantern. It is interesting to observe that each time Katie was ready to take a new step forward, the way had to be opened for her with a request or suggestion.

❀   ❀   ❀

Once upon a time there was a little orange who lived in a store with lots and lots of other oranges. Right then it was Halloween and this little orange saw all the children and their mothers coming in that store and buying pumpkins for Halloween, for jack-o'-lanterns, of course. Well, this little orange wished someone would buy HIM for a jack-o'-lantern. He was very little and didn't know any better. So, well, the other oranges told him he was silly but he didn't care except that he cried because no one bought him for a jack-o'-lantern. Well, when Halloween night came, all the pumpkins had been sold, but *still* the little orange wanted to be a jack-o'-lantern. And you know what happened? A fairy came in that store looking for a jack-o'-lantern to scare baby ghosts with and she saw this little orange crying so she said, "Why do you cry like that?"

And this little orange said he wanted to be a jack-o'-lantern and you know what? That fairy said, "You are the very thing I have been wanting. I'll make you into a jack-o'-lantern just my size, and we will scare baby ghosts and everything." So she took him home and they lived happy ever after.

This tale, with its well-maintained story line is so far removed from Katie's first feeble attempt at storytelling, that one might anticipate continued accelerated growth. However, it represented a high level of achievement, which Katie did not attain again for some time. Although she continued to tell stories, many were similar to her earlier efforts and when at Christmas, the class became interested in giving plays, a general lull in storytelling took place.

After Christmas, there were occasions for short notes that Katie particularly enjoyed since she could write just what she wanted. Her pleasure in this writing is quite obvious.

Dear Miss Moore's Class,
    Thank you for inviting us to your machine program. I enjoyed it very much. I liked the pulley and the song you sang. The mural of the machines was really something to see.
                                        Your friend,
                                        Katie

Dear Sarah Lou,
    Too bad you are sick. We got our goldfish. They look pretty surprised to be here.
                                        Love,
                                        Katie

Later when the class was studying weather, several children dictated poetry ideas about wind, rain, or snow. Although this activity was not uncommon in the class, Katie had never taken part in it, but once again she edged herself near the teacher, listened to others dictate, and then responded quickly to the teacher's asking if she had a poem to dictate. It was something of a surprise that her first effort should prove to be so effective.

❋ ❋ ❋

Lightning
Who made you?
Did some great giant
Write you with a flashing pen?
Did he?

Once again Katie seemed astonished she had produced something that could enchant the other children. She quickly announced that she had "lots more poetry ideas" and in the next days dictated several. Some of these were as trite as this:

❋ ❋ ❋

The wind blows through the trees
It makes a good breeze

But another really sounded like Katie at her best:

❋ ❋ ❋

The world is like a bakery shop window.
Soft white frosting
Is on top of everything.
Don't try to eat the cake, though!

However, she seemed disinterested in poetry after this brief period and dictated nothing until late spring when she came in from the playground early one morning to ask the teacher to write down her poem.

＊　＊　＊

Run little squirrel, run.
Run across the yard.
Don't look back
At the big black dog.
He can't *ever* catch you.
But run, little squirrel,
Run, run, run!

At Easter time, storytelling became again an important activity of the class. When Katie joined in, it was obvious she had only the start of a story in mind, but she began with a sparkling assurance that had been lacking in the fall. Her tales were marked by long repetitious dialogues but usually she managed to stick to her story line and bring about some sort of logical conclusion.

＊　＊　＊

Once upon a time the Easter Bunny and his helpers were dyeing eggs and they ran out of pink dye. Now, of course, every Easter basket has to have some pink eggs but the Bunny didn't know what to do. He sent his helpers to the store to get more dye, but there wasn't any.

"Well, get some," said the Bunny.
"We can't. There isn't any."
"Well get some anyway."
"We can't."
"Yes, you can."
"No, we can't."
"Yes, you can."
(This was repeated several times while children laughed.)
"Well," said the Bunny, "I know one thing we can do. We can take our red socks and cook them up in some water and that will make a good red dye and then we can put more water in and make it pink."
"Good idea."
"O.K. Take off your socks."
So they made some red sock soup and then dyed the eggs.

and every Easter basket had some pink eggs in it and no one knew that they were really dyed with red socks.

During the spring the amount of practical writing done by the children increased slowly as their mastery of handwriting and spelling skills made them more independent. However, only two children in this class attempted to write stories although several asked to finish in secret a story which they had dictated in large part. Katie used this technique in order to surprise her teacher with the end of this story.

   ✿   ✿   ✿

Once there was a squinch bug which can squinch down so small that human people can't even see it. That's why it is called a Squinch Bug. Well, one day this little squinch bug was walking along the edge of the teacher's desk and it saw her glasses so it tugged and pulled and pushed and shoved those glasses until they were right *under* a paper. The teacher wanted to read to the children, but she can't find her glasses anywhere. So everyone starts to look and the squinch bug sits and laughs because no one looks under the paper because the teacher keeps patting the corner of the desk and saying, "I *know* I put them right here."

Well, after a while the teacher *accidentally* happens to knock off the paper and she said, "There are my glasses. My goodness, how did they get *under* that paper?"

The squinch bug laughed and the teacher heard and she said, "Did you do that?"

The squinch bug said, "Yes. Ha. Ha! Joke on you."

And the teacher said, "Just wait till I get you," and she was going to swat that bug but . . .

(The balance of the story was written by Katie. Spelling and punctuation have been corrrected to make for easier reading.)

   ✿   ✿   ✿

. . . the squinch bug quickly made himself very small. First the teacher could hardly see him even with her glasses and then she couldn't see him at all. So she swatted the place where she thought he was, but he had gone away to think up other tricks for her.

When the teacher read the story to the group and the children had fun identifying the teacher in the tale, Katie announced that the story had a name, "Too Small To See But Not Too Small To Play Tricks" and added that it was her best story—so far.

For Katie second grade had been a year of sampling various activities. She had felt a happy satisfaction in her adequacy in practical writing, and in the field of personal expression she had experienced a warm reception for everything she offered. She had also known the special delight of finding just the right words for a fleeting "poetry idea" and of telling a story that charmed her listeners. Katie, one of the great number of so-called "average children," upon occasion moved from her limited but adequate way of working into vivid expression of her own ideas. Her explorations led her to a road to be traveled with happy expectations and new courage.

George in Fourth Grade

*For the thoughts of youth are long, long thoughts.**

George entered our school in fourth grade, a sensitive, slightly built lad whose need of friendship was apparent from the first day. With keen interests in science that he was overready to express, he frequently irritated some of the less intellectual children who felt that he was trying to show off. Actually, this was not the case. It was only that George's enthusiasm for precise knowledge spilled over along with his eagerness to be a part of class discussions. In contrast to this strength, he was weak in the play skills where most of the boys excelled. This shortage of George's exaggerated his lack of ease in getting on with the other children.

The lack of rapport between George and the rest of the class was epitomized in their calling him "Old Georgie," a name they used for him with obvious overtones of opprobrium. During these early months of the school year he was often on the defensive, unable to make casual responses to the normal aggressiveness of nine-

* Henry Wadsworth Longfellow, *My Lost Youth.*

year-olds. But there was courage in the boy for often a hurt look on his face was the only outward token of his feelings. And after a while he found ways of proving himself. Naturally he overdid this, often running the risk of fighting much bigger boys when his reactions—like his feelings—were out of proportion to the provoking incident.

At the beginning of the school year, while he was trying to become "one of the boys," George took advantage of all opportunities to write stories since this was one way of getting some much needed satisfactions. His stories revealed that a very tense little boy could not relate to other children easily in imagination any more than he could in the casual give-and-take of playing with his classmates. George made his story characters do what he himself longed to do but did not dare; but having done this he had to get back to his safe, familiar pattern of correct behavior. This he did by stressing the moral at the end of every story.

During the first of October, in less than a week, he wrote six short stories that illustrated this pattern. Several weeks later his Halloween story, although somewhat longer, was still highly moralistic. His first story and the one about Halloween follow. Spelling has been corrected as well as a few errors of agreement of subject and verb. Though some punctuation was omitted in the original, George ended each sentence appropriately as he read aloud to the class.

* * *

Once there were some bears. Their names were Moe, Goe, Soe. They always were bad. Once Goe ran into the street and broke his leg. Moe and Soe gave him a gift. It was big. But it got smaller and smaller. Then he found a card. It said, "It is not big but remember—don't run out in the street."

The End

* HALLOWEEN NIGHT

Once there were two boys named Joe and Larry. They were bad. On Halloween they went trick-or-treating. When they got to 8 Maple Terrace, they rang the bell. When the lady came, they said, "Trick or treat."

The lady said, "I'm not giving candy to kids."

The boys hit the lady. The lady took off her shoe and threw it at them. The boys ran and they never played a trick again.

Don't play a trick on Halloween either.

By Christmas time, however, George no longer needed to emphasize the moral in a story that his title indicated would be a humorous one. How far it missed that mark is immediately apparent to the adult reader.

° A FUNNY CHRISTMAS

This story is about a boy named Lou. He always had funny dreams. It was Christmas Eve when he dreamed it was Christmas morning. He went downstairs. First he looked in his stocking and what did he see? Was it a chicken foot! Then his mother came downstairs. She said, "What did you find?"

Lou said sadly, "A chicken foot."

His mother said chuckling, "That's because you've been a bad boy."

Then he opened a big box. He found a card in it. It said, "To the best boy in the world."

He turned around and said, "Grandma doesn't think I'm a bad boy."

Having gotten a reasonable amount of satisfaction from inventing these tales, however meager, George began to try his hand at informational writing. During the first half of the fourth-grade year, most of the factual reporting was done orally because of the lessened likelihood of copying. In mid-January the class was ready to put into written form their month-long study of the Vikings. It was surprising to discover that George, who had been so inhibited in imagining fanciful stories, showed a much more creative approach in expository writing. Confidence in his ability to convey knowledge resulted in considerable fluency and originality. What was even more important at this time was his complete delight in the task itself.

The following excerpts from his report entitled "Explorers from the North Sea" are but a few of the many topics included in the complete report. Besides those given here, he also wrote about shelter, clothing, food, boats, travel, geography, skills, tools, and weapons.

* FAMOUS PEOPLE

One famous person was Eric the Red. He was known for his red-hot temper. He was thrown out of Norway and Iceland for killing some men. Then he sailed farther west and discoverd Greenland. It really wasn't green. Eric just said it was green to get people to go to it and live there with him.

* CUSTOMS

The Vikings would raid islands to get thralls, food, clothes and women. Some of these islands were the Shetlands, the Faroes, and others near England. They would raid Ireland and other big countries, too, such as England and France.

P.S. Thralls are slaves that they had captured.

* NORSE GODS

When Vikings roamed there were beliefs that there were a lot of gods. One was the god of thunder called Thor. He had a big hammer that he would throw into a cloud and the hammer would make thunder and the hammer would come back to him eager to go again. Another god was Odin. He was king of the gods. There was a belief that if the god of the land saw a dragon's head on a boat there would be bad luck. Another belief was that the dragon's head protected the Norsemen from the dangers of the sea.

° SAGAS

One saga is about Leif Ericson. He found North America. There are two sagas about how he found this continent. One is that he was caught in a storm and discovered it by accident. Another is that he heard of this land and set out to explore it.

P.S. A saga is a story passed down from father to son by telling it.

The finished copy of this quite lengthy report was carefully proofread, illustrated, bound in heavy colored paper, and taken home for a present. George's account of his parents' enthusiasm for the gift reinforced the deep satisfaction that had attended the completion of this book.

Writing reports of factual data continued to delight George. Quite on his own responsibility, he wrote a report on the John Glenn orbit, catching the dramatic flavor of much that was going on at that time on television and radio. One day when the children were asked what work they would choose for a "choice period" George replied, "I'm going to write some more on my report about John Glenn. I've got him as far as the third orbit now." The spontaneity of his comment was evidence of the pleasure he derived from thus recording his own knowledge.

In early spring, the class was actively engaged in a study of the solar system. Again, during group discussions, George showed delight in sharing newly found facts. After several weeks of class work, each child selected a planet about which he was to become an "expert." George was the first to say he wanted to start writing his report. His enthusiasm for the work had been manifested for days in his choosing to read more reference material than was generally required. The impulse to gather accurate data and to write it in a manner that others would enjoy carried him through six closely written pages of rough-draft writing. For a nine-year-old, his finished report showed a considerable knowledge of the facts then known about Mars, and a sense of personal concern that gives vitality ot style to his writing.

The following excerpts from a few of George's topics indicate this range and accuracy of information as well as clarity in presenting it. The form is often childlike, but the extent of his mastery shows through the occasional immaturities of expression.

* MARS

Introduction

I would like to tell you about the planet Mars, the planet of mystery, the planet of colors. I think that Mars is one of the planets that causes a lot of interesting questions. Mars is the mystery planet in our solar system—even though it is a close neighbor we don't know much about it yet. Now I have the pleasure of introducing Mars.

Some people think that there is life on Mars because they think the lines on Mars are canals full of water. But most people think the lines are plants and there are no people on Mars.

Tycho Brahe in the sixteenth century made the first observations of Mars. Tycho was a Danish astronomer who liked astronomy very much . . . Astronomers think that there are great sandy waste lands on Mars. One mystery is what causes the color to change. Scientists think it's because of the seasons but we can't be sure. The reason we have so many mysteries about Mars is because we can't get a good picture of it. The air around the earth blurs our seeing it clearly.

George did not return to story writing. He was content to put his individual stamp on the practical writing he enjoyed so much. However, there was one exception. When a wave of enthusiasm for poetry writing caught the fancy of most of the children in the spring of fourth grade, George had a try at that, too.

* THE UNIVERSE

The universe, the universe
Full of gases
Full of meteors
Would you like to be going
In a rocket

From planet to planet?
I would!
Would you?

This effort is not rich either in imagery or individual flavor. Even though attempting a poetic form, George dealt with an intellectual idea somewhat as he might have in report writing. Apparently he still needed to feel that he was in complete control of facts, but at least he showed a willingness to play with words and to permit some of his wishes to shine through.

In practical writing George gained the confidence that released his superior powers and brought increasing satisfactions and enrichment into his life. Not only in writing was this evident, but also in his relationship with his classmates. George had come into his own. Now the give-and-take of play and lighthearted teasing fell into perspective. Fortified by his success in holding his classmates' interest when he read his distinctive informational reports, he took recourse less frequently in hurt feelings or excessive retaliation. And now the nickname "Old Georgie" used hurtfully in the fall, had changed to one of affection for "good old Georgie."

Ellen in Third Grade

Kind hearts are more than coronets.*

Whereas a few children in third grade begin early in the year to write stories in a richly fanciful manner, in our experience a much larger number delay this stage of writing until they have achieved considerable assurance in spelling and handwriting. Not until January of her third-grade year did Ellen volunteer a story on paper, although before this time she had done the practical writing tasks generally required of her class.

Whatever the origin of this postponement in Ellen's case, she quite made up for it in the volume of material she wrote in the latter half of third grade. Both practical and personal writing showed a spurt of growth in this five-month period. Much of her writing was mediocre in quality, but a gradual progression in imaginative detail and in mood can be observed. As she gained confidence in

* Alfred Lord Tennyson, *Lady Clara Vere do Vere.*

projecting her own feelings in her stories, they took on some of the characteristics for which Ellen herself was so much loved by her classmates. She had a gift for unobtrusively setting things right for other people. When tensions mounted in some conflict among the children, perhaps over a lost hat or over a decision as to who should start a new game, it was Ellen who would quietly suggest a way out of the impasse. Her desire to forestall people's getting hurt amounted to a real compassion seldom observed in children. Ellen not only felt good will toward her companions; she took time to express it even in the hurry and pressure of everyday classroom life. Yet little hint of this inner loveliness comes through in the first story she wrote. In it the hero takes care of his little sister throughout; otherwise it is a rather familiar tale of apprehending robbers and bringing them to justice.

* THE SECRET COP

Once there was a boy named Peter, but everybody called him Pete. One day, Pete was playing with his little sister, Sue. Mother said that he had to take care of his little sister while she was going to see a lady. Sue wanted to play dolls so *he* had to play.

All of a sudden he heard a big noise at the museum. So he ran to see what it was. He grabbed his little sister's hand and ran. He saw some men coming out of the building with some guns, so he hid behind a tree. He wanted to go after them because he was a secret cop. So he hid. He walked and walked. Soon he saw the men go into a cave. His little sister stumbled on a gun that one of the men had dropped, so he picked it up and went in. He told him to drop his guns and he picked them up. Then he called the police when he got home with the men.

Two days after this first experiment in controlling characters on paper, Ellen wrote another story. Sustained by the friendly reception accorded her tale of capturing the museum thief, she wrote a pleasant little story in which she personified two cars who found good drivers and friendly homes. Note the light touch given to the attraction between the cars and the balance effected in the parting between Speedy and the "lady car." Ellen illustrated this story with a crayoned drawing in which the two cars actually seemed to smile even though they had no facial features. Her picture showed both cars standing in front of a blue house, facing each other in a driveway surrounded by sunny green fields, bright flowers, and strong green trees.

Speedy

Jan. 6, 1960

This took place in a small ~~tome~~ town named smallville were cars were made. One day the men were, a little Speedy ~~car~~ *working on* the the next day ~~it was~~ *they were* all throw it was a beautiful day the sun was out. then a man came a rowd to ~~so~~ *see* all of the beautiful new ~~cares~~ he saw Speedy then the man went ~~over~~ over to the other man and gave hem something Speedy did not know what ~~he~~ was ~~doing~~ going on then the *man* got in I Speedy. Speedy did not like the man to get ≠ in hem. He ture on the morter

° SPEEDY

This took place in a small town named Smallville where cars were made. One day the men were working on little Speedy. The next day they were all through. It was a beautiful day. The sun was out. Then a man came around to see all of the beautiful new cars. He saw Speedy. Then the man went over to the other man and gave him something. Speedy did not know what was going on. Then he got in Speedy. Speedy did not like the man to get in him.

He turned on the motor, Brr--rr-rr. Brr--rr-rr, and off he went, out into the world. On the way at a red light, he met a truck. Speedy started to talk to the truck. The truck said, "Don't bother me, Little Car. I have work to do. Run along." The light was now green. He somehow turned the corner. He saw a beautiful lady car. The man parked near the lady car. They said, "Hi." Then the man came. Speedy did not [know] what to do. Also a lady came out. The lady got in the other car and the man got in Speedy. Soon the two cars went off. Then Speedy put on his blinker and went into a beautiful driveway.

It must be pointed out that the mechanics of written English offered Ellen many hurdles. Although she read the above story aloud with proper deference to sentence endings and in an altogether clear and understandable manner, her punctuation and spelling were full of errors. Apparently her major concern was with getting the action to start. Note the difficulties presented in the first few lines of the original, part of which is reproduced. With the urgency of getting the plot started, Ellen's precarious handling of mechanics suffered badly. It was not until much more writing of stories gave her the necessary confidence in her own imagination, not until purposeful correction of rough drafts of reports and letters resulted in correct practical writing of which she was justly proud, that she asserted control over spelling and punctuation. In later grades she attained a very creditable balance between ideas and correctness, but throughout third grade her accuracy in matters of form remained very low.

Five days after writing "Speedy" and reading it to the class, Ellen wrote a pedestrian account of a pig who heard some men say that she should go on a diet. The pig did not know what the word "diet" meant, so she asked a lamb who told her "it meant not to eat a lot." Ellen concluded firmly: ". . . so she did not eat for five whole days and she got thinner and thinner, and one day she won a prize in a pig contest." Characterization was very weak in this story. The main value that this sort of account holds for children may well be the sense of power in manipulating character and situation. There is also a second value of which they are quite unaware: the growth toward fluency and rhythm of phraseology, an important by-product even though the story itself lacks color and individuality.

The very next day Ellen wrote a story about a crocodile that reflects the age-old interest in the person who cries too much or who cannot cry or laugh at all. Ellen's handling of this theme is characteristically immature, but she shows courage in trying a new kind of invention where feelings are not quite so sunny as in the story of Speedy.

° CROCODILE

Once there was a crocodile who had the "crying giddies." His name was Tye. He was always crying. Tye never stopped crying. One day he was going to the lake. When he looked into the lake in two minutes the lake would overflow. One day he went to the doctor. He gave him medicine and some pills. Now Tye could never cry, and when he felt sad he still could not cry.

Ellen typed all but the last two sentences of the crocodile story herself. The last two she wrote by hand and here she gave noticeably less attention to punctuation and capitalization. Whether fatigue caused this slump or whether the typed form demanded a product that looked more like book print, we cannot tell. The crocodile story brought to a close the cycle of story writing that had so pleased Ellen during January. It had been her first venture into the realm of written expression and it had provided her with rich satisfaction. In the weeks that followed, Ellen continued steady progress in academic areas. She was a good little mathematician with a sure sense of how to go about the work and with obvious pleasure in being sure she was right.

In the late winter the class carried out a science study of the human body. Ellen chose to report on "The Heart, The Eye, and The Bones." Her carefully finished copies of these brief papers appropriately illustrated and mounted in final good form give little indication to the casual observer of the labor that shows so eloquently in the rough draft. Note the struggle with spelling and

The Heart

¶ The ~~hart~~ heart is ~~an~~ important~~bt~~ ~~they~~ ~~p~~organ
in your body. It pumps blood
through blood vessels.
~~thought~~ your ~~body~~ The
~~hart~~ heart is one big muscle. #
When it's quiet you can
hear your ~~hart~~ heart beat.

~~every body hart beat at the~~
~~same time see if it so was~~
~~very quiet you coud hear~~
~~one ta beat of two peoples~~
~~there if~~ Your ~~hart~~ heart is almost
the same size ~~of~~ as ~~your~~ ~~~~

Page 2
fist ~~~~ The
~~hart~~ heart isn't ~~is like~~ a valentine ~~hart~~ heart.
~~but~~ It is ~~the~~ tilted at the
bottom. It ~~goes~~ tilts toward the
left so many people ~~think~~ think the
~~hart~~ heart is on the left side.
It really is in the
center.

sentence formulation. Note also the clarity of wording: "The heart isn't like a Valentine heart," and "Your heart is almost the same size as your fist." Ellen's own efforts show here as well as the editing done with her teacher. What does not show in the rough draft (p. 160), is the willing spirit which she continued throughout the whole laborious task.

The treatment of the eye and the bones is in much the same hard-working vein, showing an honest attempt to be clear and accurate.

The pride engendered by this experience provided a firm foundation for the beginning of Ellen's next big step in practical writing. The report that follows was the culmination of a long-term study of Indian life in which the class had its first systematic individual guidance in gathering data, selecting important matter to include, writing a rough draft, and editing it with the teacher. Many facets of this process had been learned during the preceding few months, as for example, in planning and writing letters and editing them before copying and mailing them. But the longer task of gathering information, reading and rereading for specific information, plus the sequential steps of organizing material around important topics was a big stretch for these children nearing the end of the third grade. Intensity of effort is clearly apparent in this first page of Ellen's first draft. Note how much she corrected herself in the process of formulating her thoughts on paper. Note also how much she and her teacher found to correct when they read aloud in the editing conference.

The following topics were included in the class outline, and Ellen wrote copiously on each one. She arranged her topics in a sequence that pleased her, beginning with the lively one of telling her own feelings about Indian food, and following in this order:

Indian food
Education
Weapons and utensils
Clothing
Indian homes

Excerpts from only the first, second, and last topics are included here.

Indian Food

¶If I ~~was~~ were ~~and~~ an
Indian I ~~share~~ sure would
not ~~it~~ ~~like~~ like all the
things ~~I~~ ~~I~~ they ~~Indian~~
~~Li.~~ had to eat. It must have been very
hard to ~~I~~ ~~coke~~ cook
things in the ~~old~~ ~~Indian~~ Indian days.
In the ~~Indian~~ "wilden" times the
men ~~would~~ would ~~go~~ go ~~huan~~ hunting and
~~I~~ ~~shout~~ shoot a deer. They ~~How~~ would.
~~the~~ ~~Indian~~ ~~would be~~
~~to~~ have an Indian in the ~~front~~ front

* INDIAN FOOD

In the Indian times the men would go hunting and shoot a deer. They would have an Indian in the front and the man in back would chase the animal to the other hunter. The men carried the deer on the limb of a tree.

Like our eating bread, the Indians used corn cakes. The women took mortars and pestles and ground the corn into meal. Then they made it into cakes and cooked them in the fire. I bet the children's stomachs got hungry when they saw those very good cakes.

I think you know that the Redskins had fish. The name of the fish was shad. I have not tasted but I think it is good. When the fish were caught, the Indians put some of them on racks and smoked them so they would keep and not decay. You see the "wilden" did not have refrigerators then.

* EDUCATION

Education for the Indians is much different than ours. Ours is going to school, but the Indians had to learn to cook if you were a girl and make grass mats. Boys have to learn to hunt and make dug-out canoes and houses. And if they did not, how could he or she live?

* HOMES

The Lenni-Lenapes' wigwams were like upside down bowls. First the Indians bent over trees called saplings and made a frame. These they covered with bark. Then the women made grass mats to put over the wigwams so that when it rained the water would roll right off the house. For the door, usually a skin of an animal was used.

Inside for beds, the "wilden" would have furs. In the top of the wigwam would be a hole for the smoke so that they could have a fire in the house.

Ellen concluded this account so rich in visual details with some mention of how she would feel about smoke in a wigwam. The complete report totaled five rather closely written pages. The length as well as the content were a matter of pride to Ellen. Copied from corrected first drafts in "best handwriting," mounted on heavy paper, copiously illustrated, and bound in book form, the report became a worthy gift to her family. After completing this long writing job, Ellen enjoyed other pursuits for a time—and then in May she again turned to the pleasures of story writing.

The first in this group concerns a boy who on his way home from school found a motor that he could use in a rocket he was building. Ellen's rather lengthy introduction casts the story in the familiar framework of a dream and then starts the action.

* * *

So that night he had a dream about the moon. He went up, up, up. Zoom, up more he went. Now he saw the little, little earth. Soon he was on the moon. It was summer on the moon. Little people were running all around putting little moon cakes in one big bag. Now Pat was standing on a big moon cake. Two little moon men went up to Pat and were squeaking and pushed at Pat's feet. Pat was a little afraid so he jumped off the moon cake. The little men ran back to the bag and put it in and ten little people had guns and were all ready to shoot him when he woke up. He ran to the rocket and threw it out the window and went back to bed and that was the end of his rocket.

The class enjoyed the novel idea of "moon cakes," the vigor of the action including the disposal of the rocket, and even the return to quiet sleep. Though a story of limited imagination, it did show a bit of originality. Ellen had the satisfaction of manipulating characters and shaping events as she chose. Curiously, the leading role never becomes quite real in this fast-moving tale. It is obvious that Ellen is experimenting with plot, not with characterization.

A direct contrast to this earlier emphasis on action is to be seen in the next story, which Ellen wrote later the very same day. Although the plot here is slim, there is a clear effort to build more of a person in Mr. Pink-Eyes. It is here that Ellen's kindliness shines through again as it did in some of her earlier stories. Both characters achieve the cozy living arrangements that seemed so meaningful to Ellen herself.

*   *   *

Once there was a man named Pink-Eyes. He always said he was seeing pink elephants. One day, the circus came to town. It passed by Mr. Pink-Eyes' house. In the parade were three pink elephants. Mr. Pink-Eyes' eyes popped out of his head and fell on the floor. He picked up his eyes and put them in his head. One of the elephants came to the window. Mr. Pink-Eyes was afraid, but he patted the elephant and said, "Go away." But the elephant did not go away. He liked Mr. Pink-Eyes, so the two lived together and Mr. Pink-Eyes was never afraid of an elephant again.

End

Three weeks later, Ellen wrote her last story of the year, fittingly entitled, "How Nice Are You?" A more fluent style and more rhythmic phrasing are at once apparent. So, too, was the much better handwriting on the original. Although it was devoid of punctuation, Ellen read it aloud with appropriate terminal inflections, showing that she had fashioned it with her "inner ear" alert to accustomed patterns of English sentence melody. Perhaps of even greater significance, is the fact that this last story of the year is better rounded as to plot and lacks such unattractive, though admittedly childlike, elements as Mr. Pink-Eyes' dropping his eyes on the floor! Here we have characterization and incident moving along in proportion to each other and playing complementary roles.

* HOW NICE ARE YOU?

Once upon a time there was a little dog named Pups. Poor little Pups had no home to stay in. No home at all! One day, Pups was walking around. Soon he saw five little mice running around him.

"Hello," said Pups.

"Hello. Do you know who we are?"

"No."

"We are mice."

"Oh!"

"And we are here to help you because you are so nice to mice. And we want to help very much. Will you give us a piece of your hair?"

So Pups pulled out a piece of hair.

"Thank you. Now say, 'one-two-three.' "

So Pups said "One-two-three" and [there was] a big house in front of Pups' eyes.

"For me?"

"Yes," said the five mice together. "For you."

"Thank you very much," said Pups.

"Thank you," said the biggest mouse, "for all the things you have done for mice."

And all five mice went away and Pups never saw the mice again.

The End

It is obvious that in this last story in third grade Ellen projected much of herself through her generous little characters. Her freedom in revealing their kindness through fast-moving conversation rather than just generalizing about their good intent is admirable. The children loved the "mouse talk" and both storyteller and audience enjoyed the novelty of a dog's being nice to mice. Though the faint echo of an old fable is to be heard, the theme is handled with some originality. It was the bigger animal who started the cycle of kindness which returned eventually to him, just as Ellen herself was often a moving spirit in a cycle of generous behavior that encircled her and her many good friends.

Ruth, Grades Three through Six

*All children under nine or ten years of age are poets and philosophers.**

Ruth entered our school at third grade and came into a group notable for its *esprit de corps.* The children welcomed her warmly, but were at the same time abashed by her shyness. She was naturally a bit awkward because of being strange to a group that had known one another for at least two years. There was a kind of glow about her, however, that made her easily accepted without the teacher's needing to promote friendships, as one so frequently must do for newcomers. Coupled with this friendliness was an unusual timidity, to which a number of circumstances had contributed. This diffidence limited the effectiveness of her abilities, which, though not at all outstanding, were adequate for normal growth. She needed constant assurance of her power to enter into the various activities of the group and even to cope with routine tasks.

During the first half of the third grade the children continued storytelling and dictating. Though she had always been an appreciative listener, it was not until after Christmas that Ruth ventured to tell a short story. When, near the end of the year, a few of the children began to write stories, Ruth, after frequent assurances that it "would be all right," wrote the following stiff and meager tale. This reproduction of her own handwriting shows the strain

* E. Dimnet, *Art of Thinking.*

Tale of a Monkey

Once upon a time in a jungle lived a monkey. He had a lot of friends. This little monkey always played tricks. One day all the little monkeys were playing under a palm tree but one. He threw down a coconut. All the little monkeys looked up and ran away.

under which she worked. A printed copy is included under the illustration for easier reading.

Even a sympathetic and hopeful teacher can find nothing promising in this story. But it was Ruth's first and was therefore important. Indeed, all first stories are important and this one especially so because of the timidity that had held the child. This feeble attempt was courteously accepted by the group. Appreciative reception, along with her delight in actually seeing her own story on paper, proved so tempting that in spite of her fear of failure Ruth was eager to try again.

Because writing had once been fun, her practical writing also began to show improvement. She now worked with zest at most of the tasks that up to this time had been burdensome. Another year of growth, continued building of self-confidence, and further experience in writing with satisfaction began to free her from her earlier fears. The following story written at nine years gives evidence of a developing ease and fluency in marked contrast to the stiffness and poverty of the "Tale of a Monkey." In her typically uncertain way Ruth asked for many corrections while writing. Hence, in this corrected version, only quotation marks and a few changes in spelling were needed.

* WHEN I WAS A LITTLE GIRL

When I was a little girl I didn't like to go to bed. One night Mother had a dinner party. I thought I would listen to what they said. So when they went into dinner, I sneaked into the living room and hid behind the couch. I waited and waited till finally they came in. Some people sat on the couch and talked. They had long dresses on. Pretty soon they started dancing. I had never seen anything so funny in my life. Pretty soon I started laughing. Everybody got scared. I felt awfully bad and crouched down. Everybody asked where the sound came from. Someone said, "Over there." Daddy looked behind the couch and saw me. He yelled, "You bad girl, don't you do that any more." And I never did.

By reading the story with all the dramatic power she could summon, the teacher saw to it that Ruth had the satisfaction of an audience's spontaneous approval. Even though the story had not sufficient merit to be read again to the class, it had served its purpose in keeping alive Ruth's desire to write. At the same time the experience in telling a story had done much for Ruth's growth in fluency of expression. Obviously the first sentence sets the stage quite directly for the action of the story. Compare the use of the beginning complex sentence with the jerky beginning of "Tale of a Monkey." Note also the use of such graphic verbs as "sneaked" and "crouched," as well as the use of conversation in an effective climax. Though this story does not compare with those written by other children in the group, either in imagination or in style, it

does show for Ruth a real growth in conception of plot and supple-
ness of phrasing.

During the next year, experience with uncriticized personal writing helped considerably in freeing Ruth's imagination. Greater control of mechanics resulting from further practical writing gave her
an increased confidence. She developed some power of invention,
but still needed the comfort of an adult's approval. She asked if
each detail of her story "would be all right." Given needed support, she was able without further help to carry out her plan
effectively.

In the sixth grade she wrote with comparative ease in both the
utilitarian and imaginative fields, though she occasionally asked for
help that she did not really need but which gave her the assurance
she still wanted. She accepted for herself high standards of clarity
in informational writing, as can be seen in the following excerpts
from a comprehensive report on tobacco. Ruth divided her material,
culled from reading and conversations with a recent visitor to Cuba,
into five sections: Growing, Curing, Tobacco Uses, Statistics, and,
of course, References. "This is getting much too long," she complained on the seventh page of handwriting, "but it's all part of the
report, and I don't see how I can leave any of it out." Only parts
of each section can be included here, since the final report was
four full typewritten pages.

° T O B A C C O

Growing

   Tobacco grows mostly anywhere in the earth except where
it does not rain often enough for the soil to be moistened. It
takes a great amount of patience to take care of tobacco from
when it is first planted in a seed bed. (The farmer has to plant
the tobacco in a bed first because the tiny black seeds are so
small that 60,000 of them make one tablespoon, enough to sow
100 square yards of seed bed.) . . .

Curing

   Curing is done when the tobacco leaves are fully grown and
they are taken to a barn or put under a cheesecloth to be dried
in the sun. Tobacco cured in a closed barn by means of hot air

is called "flue cured." Tobacco cured in a curing shed is called
"air cured." After tobacco is all cured sometimes the cured leaves
are shriveled up half their size and many times one third their
regular size. . . .

Tobacco Uses

Tobacco is used for five or six purposes. They are snuff,
smoking, cigarettes, cigars, and chewing tobacco. . . .

° SNUFF

There is a certain kind of tobacco grown for snuff. It has a
very strong flavor. Snuff tobacco is ground up to a very fine
powder. It is then used by people who like to sneeze. They take
a pinch and place it in their nose and then sneeze. In the olden
days the men used to carry the snuff under their cuffs. They had
very small boxes and very elaborate ones. . . .

° CIGARS

(Note: The following is a description of how cigars are made
in Cuba, as described by a person who saw them made.)

There are four things that people do in a cigar factory. There
are girls that wear white gloves who take the largest tobacco leaves
and split them down the center vein. Then the split leaves are
given to a man who does the first step in sorting the tobacco.
He takes the split leaves and sorts them into about twelve different
piles according to their color. This man has to have excellent
eyesight. He must have the light coming from the north. There
are about 100 different colors and there is a very slight difference
between them. The lightest cigars are the mildest. . . .

The scope of information treated here and the detail included
indicate the thoroughness of Ruth's preparation before writing. She
listed questions before she started her reading of references and
added to them in our conferences. These questions shaped the
general organization of her paper, which seems to us admirably
carried out for an eleven-year-old. The detailed background, along

with the control gained by frequently talking over her ideas and findings with the whole group, enabled Ruth to write with greater power.

Of course, increased maturity also accounts in part for her use of more involved sentence structure. Elsewhere in her report she wrote, "After the cigars are made they are taken to a man who sorts them into piles according to their color." This complex sentence with two dependent clauses was used naturally by a child who understood the relationships existing before she tried to verbalize them. Note also that the sentences vary in length, construction, and order. One cannot help but note the frequent bridging over from near-adult constructions to quite delightfully childlike expressions, as for example, "It is then used by people who like to sneeze." It suggests the amusement felt by Ruth and others of the group at what seemed to them phenomenal. Sneezing meant having a cold and having to stay in bed. Just imagine liking that! In contrast to this juvenile reaction to the use of snuff, the transitional sentences introducing the uses of tobacco are remarkable. Ruth presents a new phase of her subject and indicates five subordinate but pertinent topics in clean-cut fashion. Control of the subject matter is evident in her organization.

In the sixth grade the group was studying medieval life. Following several weeks of group study and building a common background, each child selected one phase of the study for individual pursuit. Ruth chose the daily life in the monasteries and, after general reading and discussion, made the following plan for her report: Daily Religious Life, The Rule, Work, Writing, and Clothing.

Only the first two paragraphs of her report are included here, but these are enough to indicate the increasing smoothness of phraseology and more dignified style appropriate to her subject.

❊ ❊ ❊

Six times a day the monks gather for prayer and singing of psalms in the chapel. Again at midnight the bell called them from their hard couches to services. The monks who cultivated the field did not come to the chapel for every service but they would kneel on the ground and pray till the service was over.

The "Rule" of the monastery at all times ordered that they should "speak slowly without laughter, humbly with gravity, with few and sensible words." At meals they sat silently while one monk (who was allowed to eat earlier) read from some religious book.

Monks did more than just pray and have services all day. Each monk had his own task. Some worked in the kitchen, some in the monastery garden, some would tend to the cattle and sheep. Some gathered fuel, others tilled the fields, some cobbled shoes, others wove baskets until in a short time there came to be a thousand and one different occupations. The monks were assigned to different jobs by the head of the monastery to which they were best suited.

In spite of the misplaced clause in the final sentence of this excerpt, this is an excellent piece of paragraph construction for an eleven-year-old child. Note the transition sentence "Monks did more than just pray and have services all day," taking the reader from the first two paragraphs about religious services to the specialized tasks each monk performed for his monastery. Note also the variety of sentence length, the repetition for emphasis, and the economy with which the concluding idea is presented. Growing confidence is evident in content, phrase, and form.

By this time Ruth thoroughly enjoyed writing and wove her own friendly sense of humor into her stories in a truly effective manner. It seems scarcely possible that the same child who wrote with obvious fear and strain the stiff, meager "Tale of a Monkey" could, less than three years later, write with keen enjoyment this gay and well-constructed story. Ruth laughed as wholeheartedly as any of the other children over the events of Mr. Martin's evening. Her first draft, shown in part, displays her growth in mechanics and coordination.

* COOKING DIFFICULTIES

Mr. Martin, I must tell you was not an expert cook. His wife and children had been invited to a dinner party but *of course* he wouldn't be invited. He sat perched in an easy chair with the

Cooking Difficulties

Mr. Martain I must tell you was not an expert cook. His wife and children had been invited to a dinner party but of course he wouldn't be invited. He sat perched in an easy chair with the evening paper in his hand, cigar in his mouth and radio on. The clock hands ran around till Mr. Martin became hungry He strolled out to the kitchen wondering what to eat that was different; by this I mean besides mashed potatos, lamb chops, and lima beans. He hastily pulled out the cook book. Finally his eyes sighted a picture that made his mouth water. The picture was of Devil's Food Cake. He started putting sugar and eggs in a bowl and began mixing them. The draft blew in from the window and the old wind puffed at the cook book and a few pages flopped over. Mr. Martin was too busily beating the eggs and sugar to notice the pages turn over. As his eye glanced back to see what was next to go in the

evening paper in his hand, cigar in his mouth and radio on. The clock hands ran around till Mr. Martin became hungry. He strolled out to the kitchen wondering what to eat that was different; by this I mean besides mashed potatoes, lamb chops, and lima beans. He hastily pulled out the cook book. Finally his eyes sighted a picture that made his mouth water. The picture was of Devils' Food Cake. He started putting sugar and eggs in a bowl and began mixing them. The draft blew in from the window and the old wind puffed at the cook book and a few pages flopped over. Mr. Martin was too busily beating the eggs and sugar to notice the pages turn over. As his eye glanced back to see what was next to go in the bowl the next thing his eye saw was two cups of vinegar so in went the vinegar, wesson oil, salt, pepper. Then he put it all in a pan and put it in the oven. Mr. Martin turned the temperature gadget up to 520°. He then began to hear a funny noise. He hastened over to the oven; and there right before his eyes his supposedly devil's food cake was bubbling, fizzling, popling and doing everything. Mr. Martin got thoroughly disgusted; he stamped his foot, shut off the oven, turned off the lights. Mr. Martin then went down town to eat dinner at a restaurant, bought a box of cigars and went to a Mae West picture show.

What more typically human anticlimax could be imagined? The warm and humorous appreciation of simple, homey situations is as much a part of Ruth as of her story. Her perception of adult foibles and frustrations is both amazing and disconcerting. She maneuvered Mr. Martin into a ridiculous situation but with no cruelty in her treatment. Through graphic detail Ruth achieved a climax in which the oven's sound effects are exceeded only by Mr. Martin's noisy activities of retreat. Ruth has maintained her characterization of a comfort-loving person from the first sentence to the last.

Danny, Grades Two through Six

. . . yet, even like an ocean, you cannot hasten your tides. *

Danny was the middle child in a lively, capable household. Shy and frail, he very early built for himself a protecting cocoon of silence and docility, within which he lived an exciting life of his own devising. Out of the abundance of interests to which he was constantly exposed, he took for himself only the things he wanted and moved along untouched by the rest. Thus with an intuitive wisdom he preserved and nurtured his unique self, although by the same process he developed an indifference to directed learning that made his academic progress slow.

When Danny first came to school, he rarely talked. If he had to

* Kahlil Gibran, *The Prophet.*

communicate with adults, he hid his face in his hands, and mumbled so thickly that his words were scarcely intelligible. Fortunately he found release in doing things. He was a busy child, cluttering up his room at home with roughly made toys or "inventions," and following at school some engrossing interest that was usually quite unlike what any other child was doing. It was not that Danny was uncooperative with children. On the contrary he displayed a friendly eagerness to help, but his vital activity—the kind that engaged his power—followed an independent course. And it was only as we examined his self-designed experiments that we began to appreciate his potential strength.

Through the early school years Danny continued to be a diffident, inarticulate child. Toward the close of the second grade, however, after he had been with the same teacher for almost two years, he felt enough confidence to dictate a few stories—some at home and others at school. One of these follows. In it he tells the story of his own craving. He is the weak and puny little rabbit that longs so passionately to be big and strong like the older ones in his family.

* THE RABBIT WHO LIKED CARROTS

Once there was a little rabbit who liked carrots so much he ate them every day. One day he had some lettuce, but he wanted some carrots and he said he didn't have any for a long time. One day his mother kept on giving him more carrots and more carrots and more carrots until he got sick. When he was well again he still wanted carrots so his mother told him where he could find them because she was tired of picking them for him. So he went there and ate up all the carrots and he didn't have any more. He wondered what to do.

One day he decided to go out and hunt for some more. On he went, and on and on and on till he came to another city where everything was very big and where he came upon some carrots and the carrots were very, very big. They were as tall as trees to him. Then he saw a man coming. The man, who was a very big man, asked him what he wanted. The rabbit told him he wanted the carrots so the man took out his knife and cut the littlest piece he could, but still it was bigger than the rabbit. So the rabbit said, "Give me the littlest knife you have in the city and maybe I can cut it." So the man gave him the knife, but when the rabbit got it he could hardly lift it. So the man helped him till he got the piece he wanted. He ate on and on till he grew very big like the other rabbits in the city.

He went home, but when he got to his house, he was too big to get in. So he went where the carrots were, but the carrots seemed so little to him that he could scarcely see them. Then he heard a voice. It was a fairy. He looked around a bit till he saw the fairy, who was very hard to see because it was so tiny. The fairy said he'd have to live in her house six weeks before he'd be small again. He couldn't fit in the castle so he stayed outside. The fairy took her wand and touched a place in the ground and there grew a big castle, big enough for him to get into. So he stayed in that castle six weeks and then went home where he lived happily ever after.

Over and over again we have had from young children similar stories or rhythmic chantings that were vigorous and sincere because they had been prompted by deep-seated personal impulses and desires. However, many forces operate to close the channels through which this original self emerges. With Danny, language expression was curtailed because his third year began with a new teacher. Again afraid, he slipped back into his sheltering cocoon. He followed what went on in the group as though he were an outsider, and in a detached, dutiful way did only what seemed to be required. Nothing broke through his defense until small groups began giving playlets. These he watched with obvious enjoyment. Gradually, very gradually, he began to take part. At first he was only a mover of scenery; later he performed small bits in pantomime, and, finally, by the spring of his fourth year he was doing very short speaking parts with some degree of confidence. During this time he had told no stories, although in the last months of the fourth year he wrote two short ones.

This early history scarcely prepared us for what Danny did in his fifth year. Again he had a new teacher, and again he assumed his uncommunicative role. That fall the teacher began the writing periods by reading a variety of things, some from her files of fifth- and sixth-grade work and others from adult authors. The children were invited, though not urged, to contribute anything they had written. At first the offerings were disheartening. Little came and that little was lifeless and dull. Nevertheless, the contributions were read with as much enthusiasm as the teacher could muster. One morning she chanced to give them Sterling North's "Five Little Bears and the Milkman." The next day Danny handed in a tale of his own about the same characters. Eyes lighted up as the teacher read the new version, and there was a clamor to know who had written it. The hearty approval his story received worked a magical change in Danny. From that moment he began to grow visibly in poise and power. Although writing cost him great effort, every few days he produced a new story for our enjoyment. At length he persuaded his father to be his scribe, and the stories laboriously written at school were supplemented by those dictated at home. Experiences of the Five Bears were continued, and other series were invented. For many readings Danny held the class enthralled by the adventures of the Great Chimino, the second chapter of which follows. Even at this early stage he had learned, when ending one chapter, how to whet the appetite for the next. In this and the next story, appropriate changes in mechanics have been made to facilitate reading.

* THE ADVENTURES OF CHIMINO, CHAPTER II

It was not long before Chimino met his first adventure. He came to the edge of a canyon completely made of glass. The sides were smooth so that he could not climb down and at the bottom there was a fiery dragon.

Chimino scratched his head and wondered how he could climb down. Finally he had an idea. He took one of his pills and then he let himself over the side of the canyon slowly. Then he kicked the glass with his foot and made a foothold. He did this several times until he finally came to the bottom. Then he traveled the best he could on the glass, but often slipped. Before long a fierce growl met him. He looked up and there was a fiery dragon.

Chimino took out his sword and hit the dragon with it. The

dragon was very angry at this so at once he jumped around, but slid on the glass and fell flat on his back. Then Chimino jumped on him, but the dragon jumped up and kicked Chimino. Before long it was a regular mix-up. Chimino and the dragon were slipping all around the canyon. The dragon shot fire on one side while Chimino sprang around to the other. Then the dragon would quickly jump around, while Chimino sprang over to the other side and the dragon slipped on his back. Then Chimino jumped on him and lashed him with his sword.

Before long Chimino won and at once continued his travels. In a short time he came to the other side. He climbed up in the same manner in which he had climbed down, although he slipped a few times and nearly lost his life.

When he got to the top he came to the same kind of forest that he did at first. Finally he got through to the other side, where he saw the wildest land he had ever seen in his life. It was all swamp and mushy, and there were a few trees that were very high and bigger than ordinary. All across the sky were black blotches. One seemed to get bigger and bigger. Suddenly an enormous black monster blotted out the whole sun. His huge hand quickly grapsed Chimino and carried him away.

Although the Chimino stories gave full scope for Danny's love of invention, his bear stories were more revealing. The one that follows has an imagined setting—the old-fashioned school with the dunce cap, the answer book, the whippings—but it is peopled with characters from his own environment: the absent-minded teacher, the boy who hid the chalk, the fair-minded, energetic mother, and even Danny himself. In the character of Mo he exposes his own reactions to life—his experimental attitude, his childlike way of reasoning, his immunity to punishment, and his open delight in getting ahead of adults.

❀   ❀   ❀

It was Mo's second day at school. He had lately tried out some experiments, and he had found out that if you pushed pencils off people's desks, they got sent down to the principal to be whipped. And also he had found out that there was no school on Saturday or Sunday.

Now it happened that Mo was in school or rather in the dunce chair admiring the dunce hat that he was wearing. He had just lately tried to get out of school another way. Then he said to himself, "What good is it to get Roy sent down to the principal if I don't see him whipped?"

So while he was waiting he grabbed the chalk that the teacher had put down on the desk when she wasn't looking. The teacher, without noticing this action, got another piece of chalk. Then she said,

"Roy Bear, what is three times two times six times eight?"

"It's the same as eight times six times two times three," Roy answered.

"That's no answer," said the teacher.

"It's fifty-four," whispered Meinie into Roy Bear's ear.

The teacher gave Meinie a severe look. "What's the answer, Roy Bear?" repeated the teacher.

"Fifty-four," said Roy Bear.

"Wrong," said the teacher.

"Then what is the answer?" said Roy Bear.

"I don't know," said the teacher. "I'll have to look it up in my answer book.'"

By this time Mo had taken a full box of chalk from the teacher, and the teacher was looking in the cupboard for another one. So Mo grabbed the pointer and hit Roy Bear over the head with it.

"Ow-w-w!" yelled Roy Bear.

The teacher jumped ten feet in the air. She was so startled.

"What do you mean by making such a noise?" she asked. "You ought to be whipped. In fact you will be. Go down to the principal at once."

So Roy Bear walked out of the room. While Eenie was giggling to himself, Mo calmly took off his dunce cap, put it on a chair, and then walked toward the door.

"Where are you going, Mo?" asked the teacher.

"To see Roy Bear whipped," said Mo.

"Why do you want to see Roy Bear whipped?" asked the teacher.

"Because I banged him over the head so he would yell and get whipped. So it is only fair that I should see it."

"There is something in what you say," said the teacher, "but I was the one that sent him down, and so I should go down and see him get whipped too."

"The only one who has seen him get whipped so far is the principal," said Mo.

"Then I shall go down and watch him get whipped and I think that I will fire the principal and take her place."

"I don't think I need you along," said Mo quickly.

"Oh, yes, you do," said the teacher. "Come here."

"Goodbye," said Mo. "Hope you have a nice time," and he ran out slamming the door in the teacher's face.

Now the principal didn't have as much pleasure as the teacher thought she did for the principal was blind. Mo was running down the hall with the teacher right at his heels. He could hear the yowls and shrieks of Roy Bear, but this was not unusual because he heard them every day. The principal was just reaching out for Roy Bear, but Roy ducked and she accidentally grabbed the teacher and began whipping her. Roy Bear and Mo laughed and laughed. Then Mo climbed out the window and ran all the way home and said to Mother Bear in an excited voice:

"Do you know what I did, Mother? I banged Roy Bear over the head so he got sent down to the principal and by mistake the principal whipped our teacher. And oh, it was funny," he said, wiping a tear out of his eye. "And do you know what Meinie did? He told Roy Bear the wrong answer to a problem and Roy Bear got heck."

"Oh, he did, did he?" said Mother Bear who was very angry. So she put on her coat and went all the way down to school. When she got there she saw the teacher crawling back to her room. So she helped the teacher up, and then she went in and pulled the other four bears out by their ears. She took them home and put them to bed with Mo.

In bed Nig said to Mo, "Gosh, Mo, what did you squeal for? You always are a big tattletale."

"Oh, I couldn't help it," said Mo. "I was just telling Mother Bear how funny you were," and he began to laugh.

So Nig tried to go to sleep, while Eenie and Meenie played rock, stone, and paper, and Meinie tried to figure out what three times six times two times eight was.

The heartwarming success of his bear stories seemed to vanquish Danny's fears. From the day he read the first one, he gained confidence steadily and soon became an energizing influence in the class. Longer than most children he had stayed on in the inquisitive, seeking stage. He felt a naive and serious wonder in everything he did, so that learning retained for him the fresh excitement of personal discovery. Whatever ideas he chose to consider were not passive abstractions to be stored away or verbally rehearsed; they were dynamic suggestions to be tried out at once. When he saw his brother enlarging a map at home, he found out how it was done. The next morning he came to school early, asked for a big piece of paper and set to work on the floor making a large map of Greece, the country we were then studying. When the opportunity came to work on the auditorium lighting, he not only learned how to manipulate the switches, but he equipped his home puppet stage with as elaborate a system as he could manage. When the family got a new automobile, Danny, who so short a while before had sidestepped all speaking in public, begged for a chance to talk to the group. He told in detail how a gasoline engine works, and later came to school with an excellent illustrative model made from tin cans. These are but a few of the interests that his active curiosity followed and with which he infected others in the group. His quiet but wholehearted enthusiasm spread a contagion that few of the boys could resist.

Because Danny put so much feeling and tireless effort into his work, one would naturally expect his craftsmanship to be of superior quality, but that was not the case. Apparently he was so stirred by doing and discovering that he failed to see his results apart from his dreams. As a consequence he exhibited with proud satisfaction work that to us was distressingly crude and untidy. The glaring defects were not due to lack of interest or exertion; they were the reflection of Danny's immaturity. Until he had developed more manual skill and had gained the power to view his work more objectively, overemphasis on points of correctness could only confuse him. Therefore, in practical mechanics, we held him to standards as high as we thought he could reasonably accomplish, and we did not urge him beyond those. We believed that if we could preserve that deep personal concern in what he did, he would master the necessary skills when he came to see the need and had acquired sufficient muscular control.

Undoubtedly the fifth grade was the turning point in Danny's school history, for it was then that he broke free from the fears that had restrained him. The early years of stubborn struggle had strengthened his courage, but the success of his storytelling gave the needed spur. During the sixth grade, he continued to develop along the lines already begun. So it is that whenever we think of Danny, our faith in the force of personal expression is renewed. To remember him literally sweating over his smudgy papers tells us how important creative effort was to him. To realize the change that was worked in Danny himself reveals how potent such effort can be in establishing self-faith and in releasing pent-up power.

Joanne, Grades Three through Six

No bird soars too high if he soars with his own wings.*

On the playground Joanne was such a rough-and-tumble little harum-scarum that one would scarcely suspect the sensitive, fanciful nature her writing revealed. In the classroom she was the teacher's delight—and her despair. Her poetic imagination, her humor, her feeling for the dramatic, and her eager aliveness gave color and joy to the school day; but her spelling, her arithmetic, her penmanship, and her housekeeping refused to conform to accepted standards. Her whole nature intuitively resisted set pattern and routine. Even though she well knew that six times two are twelve, she disliked having it be that *every* time. She could invent freely, abundantly, joyously; but she could not imitate. Copying was almost impossible for her to do correctly, and even a finished picture bore little resemblance to the initial sketch. Attempts to direct her creative work were fruitless. She promptly lost interest in the thing discussed and turned to something else. In this simple, effective way she maintained her creative integrity.

---

* William Blake, *Poems and Prophecies.*

In the third-year group Joanne was the first to express herself poetically, and from the beginning her individual expression was fresh, rhythmical, and strong. The fun she had in voicing her ideas was so genuine that the desire to do likewise quickly infected others. Her childish ponderings were transmuted into lyrics. "Me," dictated late in that third year, expressed in its rhythmic pattern, as clearly as in its words, the inadequacy a little girl can feel.

* M E

When my mother plays on the piano
Her fingers dance like fairies
In the summer on the grass
Or like fireflies dancing at night.
But when I try to play
I put my fingers down on the keys
And the piano goes
Thump, bang, thump, ping.
It's like a giant stamping all over the land.

"Paper White Narcissus," dictated a year later, tells that there are fairy children, too, who cannot remember the practical and the mundane.

* PAPER WHITE NARCISSUS

You know that flower called Paper White Narcissus?
Well, the fairies use it for paper
To write their letters on,
And for their children who can't remember
What they have to get from the store—
A dozen ant eggs, or a pound of dandelion leaves,
That's what Paper White Narcissus are used for.

In the fifth year there was for Joanne, as well as for the rest of the group, a decided dropping off in poetical expression. The teacher, though sympathetic, was new, and so there was a slight constraint. There was more drive on academic work, and less op-

The Haunted House
Once there was a house on the grey still ground;
Once there was a house all misty with fog.
Once there was a house and ghosts lived in it.
Once there was a house all boards a-shaking.
Once there was a house; nine grey old men lived in it.
(Fast, lightly) Down by the wayside, there's that house.
(Slowly) Witches are in it, but DON'T go there.

portunity for the teacher to be the scribe for the children's ideas. Perhaps, too, there were changes in the children themselves that led to different kinds of expression. The compact lyrical form may be more natural to the younger age. We do not know. Whatever the reason, Joanne turned to stories and to playing with the sounds of words. Often a tempting title was made up first, such as "Why Witches are Waterproof," or "The Short, Short Sink That Went to Heaven," and then a fitting story concocted. She struggled earnestly to be her own amanuensis, with results that were untidy, inaccurate, and often half-finished. Her clerical power could not keep pace with her flashing mind. But even under such difficulties she continued to experiment, to find joy in the doing, and to produce a few things that were truly good. Sometimes sound and rhythm engrossed her, quite to the exclusion of sense. In "The Haunted House" there are music and mood, but there is little logical meaning. Note in the reproduction of the original the indicated improvement she made in the last line, and the directions she gave for the reading.

Consistently, everything that Joanne did revealed her as a free, intuitive worker. Her arithmetic, after the first few examples, never went in orderly rows, and her writing jumped from pigmy to giant in a single line. Her art work was distinguished by its spontaneity and its rhythmic movement and even her factual reports were transformed by her imagination into episodes that were vivid and alive. During her fifth year she made a study of ants, at the end of which she submitted the following resumé. It is not a report at all, but a fanciful incident focused dramatically on the queen and the royal eggs. In it, however, an abundance of information is evident, information that she had made truly her own. Since it was to be part of a class book, Joanne, with her teacher, edited her report to this extent.

* MY TRIP THROUGH THE ANT HILL

"Oh, Mr. Guide," I said, "what is that tunnel and why is it so long?" "Well," said the guide, "it's this way. The queen of this state is laying eggs there and does not want to be disturbed." "Do you think she would mind me seeing her?" I said. "Well, I'll see," said the guide; so he went to the door. "Knock, knock." "Yes," came a voice. "What do you want?" "Well," said the guide,

"I have a visitor and she wants to see you." "Show her in," said the voice again. The guide led me through many passages till he came to a door. "Knock, knock." "Come in. I am expecting you." The guide opened the door and bowed. "Your—your—Majesty," blushed the guide, "here is your visitor." I had seen many things, but none so beautifully made. The walls were solid and hard and shining dirt. All were even with no faults anywhere. After awhile the queen said, "Do you know I make my kingdom?" and she laughed, "I should say queendom. Well," she went on, "I lay eggs and every once in a while I lay a royal egg which is a male or prince or queen. The male and queen are rare; but princes quite common." "Oh," I said, "that's interesting. I always thought . . . Well I don't know what I thought." "Well," she said, "you had better be going because I have to lay my eggs." The guide took me out and said, "Would you like to see our workers? You know," he said as he went along, "we only have a few men and women to mate. Most of our people are workers which are neither males or females." "Oh," I said, "that seems impossible." "Well, it isn't," he said.

By this time we had reached a tunnel. An ant was guarding it. "No one allowed!" he said excitedly. "No one allowed! Danger of falling pebbles. No one allowed. It is a newly made tunnel and we are making room for the royal eggs. No one allowed!" And I saw a pile of white eggs or cocoons. I looked closely and a black head peeked out of one. Then came the body. Then we went on. Suddenly a great commotion fell over the ant hill. All subjects were running to and fro. The new tunnel was finished and eggs were being stored away. I asked my guide what was happening and he said, "There is a war and we are against the red ants. Most of our workers are fighting and not many are left to do the storing of eggs." Soon the war was over and it was victory for the Black Ants. "Well," I must be going now," I said. And that ends my chapter and I hope you enjoyed it.

The End

This is not a true story.

The same spring, caught up in the class enthusiasm for "The Five Bears," Joanne wrote a story strongly marked by her individual traits. It has little plot, but is rather a series of lively pictures with touches of fun and with shrewd observations of human behavior.

* THE FIVE BEARS HAVE A SPRING FESTIVAL WITH SURPRISING RESULTS

PART I

"Ma!" called Mo as he came down the path, "we're having a Spring what-cha-ma-call-it, and I dress up as the Big Bad Wolf. Eenie, Meenie, and Meinie are the three pigs and Nig's the announcer. Sue's the Mother Pig. She has to fasten two pillows in front of her to make her fat and some string on for a tail, and you," he added, crossing his arms, "have to make us jackets."

"Well," said Mrs. Bear for the first time that she was able to speak, "well, that's nice."

"Ma! Ma! got to tell you sumpin'," yelled Meenie, dashing down the path with the other three bears at his heels.

Then Mo said calmly, "I told it all."

"Oh!" Meenie's jaw dropped, "you would."

"No, he didn't," said Mother, "what is it?"

"Well," Meenie brightened up, "it's a festival—a spring festival. Nice?"

PART II

The time had come. All the mother bears were chattering in the classroom, sitting in the children's chairs. Now and then a bear's face would peek out, or rather a pig's face or Red Riding Hood. Then Nig stepped out.

"Ladies and perfume bottles," said Nig—he was so confused by the smell of perfume. "We are having a May—rather a fest— oh! no, no, we're having a play."

He disappeared through the curtains amid the titters and giggles of the mothers. The curtains opened with a jerk.

"Hey, it's not ready," said a voice, and then the curtains closed again. This statement was greeted by a roar of laughter.

Five minutes later the curtains opened again. This time Eenie was sitting by a paper hut. He began to sing, "I build my house of horsehair—I mean hay. I build my house of hay, hay, hay. Oh, here comes Mo—I mean the wolf," he said as he ran off the stage. The wolf paused only to push the house down and then he ran off. All went well until the wolf was supposed to come down the chimney. The pot had a pillow in it so as not to hurt Mo, but just then Eenie yelled, "The pot's not there!" But it was too late. The wolf had fallen and that started a fight. The curtain closed on the unpleasant scene. The class acted a play "Red Riding Hood," but the bears did not see it for the night found all five bears tenderly rubbing their seats in bed.

Although Joanne revealed originality and distinction in her writing, she was woefully inadequate in the skills. Through the fifth grade she evaded all our efforts to teach her as persistently as a boy escapes washing the back of his neck—and for the same reasons. In her eyes, to spell and write correctly were hard work and were useless. She was having fun playing with her mind, and she wasn't caring at all about appearances. Of course, we could have been insistent and perhaps thereby have made Joanne a better speller, but we might have stopped all spontaneous outpouring. So, instead, we lowered the usual demands made in practical writing to match her undeveloped power, and we watched to commend her slightest effort to improve her use of the prescribed skills. In her sixth school year our faith and forbearance were justified. Joanne was eleven when suddenly she came to care about her use of tool techniques, and she exerted enough well-directed effort to accomplish reasonable mastery of them. She always found it difficult to conform to set patterns, to discipline that pixie spirit within her. But she managed to write with acceptable correctness and with unabated satisfaction and joy.

Arthur, Grades Three through Six

*With the exercise of self-trust new powers shall appear.**

Because Arthur appeared to be always sweet-tempered and at ease, few people realized how much he was haunted by the fear

* Ralph Waldo Emerson, *Essays.*

of being inadequate. Lacking all inner assurance of power, he leaned heavily on the approval of others and worked as earnestly as he knew how to deserve that approval. On the playground his athletic ability combined with his strong desire to keep everybody happy made him a popular leader, but in the classroom satisfaction did not come so easily. In his eagerness to do the expected thing he seized upon the forms, rather than the substance, of learning. Whatever the task, he set at it quickly and worked with dogged determination, though usually to the wrong purpose. In reading he aimed to call words and cover ground, in arithmetic to keep farthest ahead in assignments, and in practical writing to produce numbers of correct papers limited in vocabulary to his own scant spelling power. His workmanship was tidy and he was always among the first to finish because neatness and speed were to him evidence of success.

For a long time we believed he could do no better. We respected his gallant though misdirected effort and accepted gratefully such meager accounts as the following:

* AN EXPERIENCE

One time my Mother and brother and I was walking by a lake in California and I thought I saw a fish but it was a crab. I jumped in and I nearly drowned, but my brother got a stick and pulled me out.

Then one day when the class enthusiasm for telling "poetry ideas" ran high, Arthur's feeling was so stirred that it broke through the mask that had effectually concealed him. This time he had a real experience to tell, one that had touched him intimately. Without fear or hesitation he dictated:

* ORCHESTRA

When I blow the bugle
It's such a funny noise
And when I blow it for my father
He laughs at me.

> And then when I grew up
> I was in a big orchestra
> And my father came to watch me
> And he DIDN'T laugh.

This and other dictations that followed exposed a sensitive, proud little boy who wanted too much to please people—not the dull, unimaginative child we had thought him to be.

Arthur began the next year by writing an impressive number of letters to all of the friends he had made at camp—the counsellors and caretakers as well as the boys. The following immature note is a fair sample of them all:

> Dear Robert Dixon:
> I hope you are not sick. And I hope you are feeling well because I am. Please write soon and tell me what grade you are in. I am in the fifth grade. I guess you are in the fourth grade.
> Love from
> Arthur

This was the only kind of voluntary writing he did for weeks and weeks. Eventually, however, he too began having such fun over the adventures of "The Five Bears" that again he forgot himself and made up a story called "The Pond," which surprised us by its length as well as its merit. It is strongly reminiscent of his happy life at camp, but his memories of the woods, the pond, and the games in the water have been converted by his imagination into a new story. In it he showed a power to handle language that we had never suspected. Note the effectiveness of the opening sentence, the suggestion of character, the movement, the action, and the graphic quality of the whole. Some errors in form have been corrected for easier reading in this publication.

* THE POND

On the steps of a shack on the edge of the woods were the five little bears. Their names were Eenie, Meenie, Meinie, Mo, and Nig. Meenie said, "Let's go swimming at the pond."

Mo said, "Where it is?"

Eenie said, "Don't you remember? It is about a half mile away."

"Come on," said Meenie.

"Let's go. What are we waiting for?" said Mo. So they started down the woods without telling their mother or anyone.

Meenie said, "Don't you think we better tell Father or Mother?"

"No," said Nig, who was very bad. "Why do Mother and Father Bear always have to know where we go?"

"Oh, well, let's go," said Mo, so off they went. Soon they came to the pond.

"Here it is," said Nig, "I will beat you in."

"Oh, yeah," said Meenie.

"You wait and see," said Nig. Off went Nig's pants and shirt and off went Meenie's dress and bonnet and there was a splash and then another.

"I beat you," said Meenie.

"So what?" said Nig. And then came three more splashes.

"Let's play tag," said Eenie.

"No," said Meenie, "let's play leap frog."

"O.K.," said the rest of the bears. The pond was four feet deep.

"I am scared," said Mo, "I want to be the first one because it is too deep in the middle."

"I am not scared," said Nig. "I will be the last one to be jumped over. Eenie, you be second. And Meenie, you be third; Meinie, you be fourth. And I will be last. Mo, you jump over Eenie and then over Meenie and then over Meinie. Last of all jump over me."

Over the first he went, then the second, then the third, and then the fourth, but where was Nig? Then they saw a lot of bubbles forming on top of the pond.

Mo said, "I bet he has drowned. How will we get him?"

"Eenie, you can swim under water. You get him," said Meinie. So under he went and brought Nig up.

"My, he looks fat," said Mo.

"He isn't fat," said Meinie.

"He drank a lot of water and he got blown up and can't talk," said Eenie.

"Let's sit up in the tree and put him under it to dry," said Meinie. So they did and while they were up there Eenie fell and landed right on Nig's stomach and all the water squirted out and he woke up.

"What happened?" said Nig.

"You blew up," said Meenie.

"WHAT?" said Nig.

"You blew up," said Mo.

"Let's go home," said Meinie.

The End

Arthur was so lacking in self-faith that he dared not reach down into himself to discover and express his own thoughts and feelings. Therefore he fed his hunger for satisfaction with the social approval he received. All of his work was necessarily shallow and stereotyped. Only on these few occasions when a wave of feeling swept him out of his usual narrow channel of behavior did he reveal his potential power.

This case was especially meaningful to us because it indicated that we frequently may underestimate children's abilities. The customary school procedures seem to freeze them in the limiting patterns that they have already established. Undoubtedly, more learning experiences that are not set in conventional molds are needed to stimulate genuine personal interest. Only through such experiences can children free themselves so that they can begin to express their own possibilities.

Lucy, Grades Two through Six

*Now it appears to me that almost any Man may, like the spider, spin from his own innards his own Citadel—the points of leaves and twigs on which the spider begins her work are few, and she fills the air with a beautiful circuiting.**

It is often surprising to see how clearly a child reveals himself in

* John Keats, *Letters of John Keats to His Family and Friends.*

writing. An adult might have known Lucy for some time without being aware of her unique qualities. She was an unobstrusive child, sensitive and shy without being aloof, and capable with none of the aggressive or irritating characteristics frequently implied by that word. But no one could have read what Lucy wrote and remained ignorant of the nature of her personality. Even her earliest stories exposed a power of sustained logical thinking, a love of fun, a rich, but realistic imagination, and an ability to lose herself in what that imagination created. Probably the fact that she was an only child kept at home frequently by slight illnesses fostered the development of these traits. Warmhearted and lonely, she found companionship in stories—usually stories she read, but sometimes those she invented. When she was working upon one of her own, she lingered over the fun of making it up, savoring each personality, each bit of adventure, each possibility for laughter. She never created rapidly in spontaneous outbursts. Stories did not pour forth from her as they did from Joanne or Danny. Instead, they were fashioned with leisurely and affectionate care. The ideas emerged slowly and lay for some time in her mind taking on shape and depth and color. Eventually she wrote them down. There was no need for haste because the story had been completely possessed and patterned before the writing began. Consequently her first drafts were reasonably correct and tidy. But they were still work sheets to Lucy, and she went over them thoughtfully, substituting a more exact word here or adding an enriching detail there. Such capacity for long-continued and painstaking effort is not usual for a child. It was, however, an essential feature of Lucy's personality and was evident in all that she did. Once in clay modeling she had worked for several successive periods on the figure of a dwarf. To the teacher it looked finished and so it was set on the shelf to dry, where Lucy found it, next art period. "Oh," she demurred, "I wasn't through. There were some little things I wanted to do to it." Thus she followed her own deliberate rhythm of working toward the high standards that she herself had set.

In the second grade Lucy wrote "The Story of a Car." It is long as second-grade stories go, and it shows thoughtful planning. Moreover, in spite of all the magical happenings, it is at heart a realistic story. Upon getting its wings the car does not go adventuring in the air, as a more fanciful child might have had it do, but instead it lands "plunk" in its own garage.

° THE STORY OF A CAR

Once there was a doctor and he had a very nice car. One day the doctor had to see a sick person, so he jumped into the car and off he went. While he was inside the car drove off. It went on and on. While the car was going down the road it met a kangaroo. The car stopped and asked the kangaroo to give him a pair of his hind legs. So he gave him a pair and the car went hopping off. Pretty soon it met a leopard. The car asked the leopard if he would give him some spots and he said "Yes." So the car said "Thank you" and went on. Pretty soon he met a bird. He asked the bird to give a pair of wings. The bird said he would so the car tried to fly but the car was too heavy that the wings could not hold it up. So down the car came and *plunk* it was in its own garage.

All of Lucy's free writing was narrative. During the next two years, when most of the children in her group were interested in reporting their "poetry thoughts," she made no contribution. Finally, toward the close of the fourth grade, she wrote "Indians," which was clearly an outgrowth of her reading. The idea, the phrases, perhaps even the design were unconsciously borrowed, but the power to imagine vividly was Lucy's own. In the picture of Fleetfoot battling the storm she succeeded in transferring her rich imagery to paper, but it was beyond her ability to continue writing in such full detail. The story grows increasingly sketchy until the climax is reduced to "a sigh of relief."

° INDIANS

A cloud of silvery dust rose up behind the black hoofs of Fleetfoot now tan with dust. As the mare battled her way through a sand storm her black mane was sprinkled with sand. Her black coat was tan with sand. Her head low, Fleetfoot faced the storm. Her rider, Don Barton, would occasionally put his head close to

Fleetfoot's ear and whisper, "We have got to warn the settlers. Indians, hear me, Fleetfoot, Indians." Don ducked as an arrow grazed his head. Another hour of hard riding and through the sand storm Don saw a ranch. At the gate Don leaped from the saddle. "Indians," he shouted. In the saddle Don warned the neighboring ranches of the attack. At the last ranch Don stopped to rest and then to fight with the rest of the men. In an hour many guns were being cleaned and bullets found. Soon an army of arrows fell upon them. Men went flying to their posts while women and children huddled together. After two hours of fighting a sigh of relief ran through the settlers. The red men had been defeated, a victory for the white men.

Less than a year later Lucy wrote "The Five Bears and William Whiskers," which shows a remarkable gain in the patience and the power necessary to record the complete story as she saw and felt it in her mind. In it there is a warm human quality and a sense of completeness that could come only with slow ripening. This was her single offering during the time that Danny produced thirty or more. While his active mind was bent on creating adventure after adventure for rather puppetlike characters, Lucy was cultivating such an intimacy with the people about whom she wrote that what happened grew naturally out of the kind of folks they were. Undoubtedly it was Danny's unflagging and sometimes strange invention that did most to maintain the lively interest in the story-reading period during the fifth year, but it was Lucy's single story that sharpened the group's awareness for the more subtle qualities of characterization and style. A few corrections in punctuation have been added.

* THE FIVE LITTLE BEARS AND WILLIAM WHISKERS

One sunny afternoon the five little bears were walking the ridge pole of their roof. Their cousin, Nellie Bear, had come over to visit them. She was such a golden brown little bear that even baby Mo admired her. Nig just loved to show Nellie how far he could walk on the ridge pole without tottering too much. He was just doing that now. His arms were wide apart and the leg he wasn't standing on was always swinging. The other five bears were sitting on chimneys swinging their short fluffy legs. But Nellie didn't look very happy. She kept glancing down at the ground and holding the edge of the chimney so tight that her knuckles showed white. Just then Mo said in his small voice:

"I'm hungry," and he began to whimper.

"Oh, all right," answered Nig. "We can take some fruit home from William Whiskers, the old billy goat gardener. He won't mind."

"You hope," put in Eenie.

"Let's go down the drainpipe," said Nig.

"O.K.," said Eenie. So the six little bears whizzed down the drainpipe. Splash!

"Oh, dear," said Nellie. All six little bears had landed in the rain barrel. "Oh, dear," said Nellie again, "I'm wet."

"I think," said Eenie, who was always making wise cracks, "I think we slid down the wrong drainpipe."

"I wouldn't doubt it," said Meinie.

"Well," said Nig, "let's go to the orchard. We're men. We won't let a little water stop us, will we?"

"No," said Eenie, Meenie, Meinie, and Nellie together.

"No," said Mo last of all in his weak little voice.

So they all started out for the orchard single file, Mo taking up the rear as usual. They got to the orchard, but just as they were coming out with the fruit, down the path came old William Whiskers whistling a sailor tune. He had been a sailor a long time ago, and he had beautiful red and blue tattoos up and down his arms. The little bears dashed down the path past him and into the road still holding the apples and pears. William Whiskers stopped short and then ran after them, calling, "Ahoy, there—Ahoy, there! To the starboard! Port! Drop the anchor! Blast ye!"

"There's Father's car," yelled Nig. "Jump in!"

They did. Then Nig stepped on the starter. He thought he could drive, but five minutes' driving brought them to the brink of a lake. Plunk! The car was in it. Luckily it was an open car, and in a minute up popped Nig sitting on a cushion, and last of all Nellie and Mo clinging to each other.

"What do we do now?" said Eenie, blowing the water out of his nose.

"Nothing but wait," said Nig, hitting the side of his head to get the water out of his ears.

All of a sudden apples and pears began to pop up on every side.

"They look very nice in the water, don't they?" said Meinie.

"They'd look better in my stomach," said Mo.

"I could get them if I had my butterfly net," said Meenie. You see he was very interested in insects.

"My stomach doesn't feel good," said Nellie. "Boating never did agree with it."

"Mine doesn't feel top hole either," broke in Mo weakly.

Just then William Whiskers appeared. He began to laugh. He laughed and he laughed and he laughed.

"Oh, please get us out," said Nellie.

"On one condition," said William Whiskers.

"What is it?" said Nig.

"It is," said William Whiskers, "that you stay out of my orchard."

"We will," said Mo.

"Oh, sure we will," said the rest of the little bears. Then William Whiskers got a rope and threw it out to the bears. Then he put the other end around his horse and pulled. Soon they were on the bank of the lake.

"Oh, what a relief," said Nellie, with a deep sigh.

"And we promise we won't take any more fruit," said Nig.

Everybody was happy, especially William Whiskers. But one week after if you had looked at the spikes on top of the orchard gate, you would have seen little pieces of brown fur and little pieces of blue trousers that can come off nothing but little bears.

When Lucy had finished reading "William Whiskers," the response of the class was unique. Instead of the restless, excited approval that usually greeted the stories they liked, there was a pause and then a fervent, "Oh, that was good!" We talked a little then —a very little—about how clearly we had seen the funny, moving pictures. We spoke, too, of how the ending had pleased us because it was exactly what might be expected of those mischievous little bears. Besides, it tempted us to go on imagining what happened the next time they got caught.

This experience illustrates how we did most of our teaching of story writing. Lessons were never worked out in advance. Instead, we seized upon an effective use of a technique when it appeared. Then by appreciation—not by precept—we focused attention upon it, hoping thereby to infect the children with its worth. This does not mean that after the single instance of talking over "William Whiskers" the next crop of stories all had excellent endings and a wealth of concrete detail. Well-rooted growth comes slowly; hence we neither expected nor desired such miracles. Our purpose was, through repeated exposure, to lead the children to recognize and to appreciate some of the factors of good writing. We knew that each child would gradually appropriate the techniques for which he was ready and would use them in sincere ways.

In the early stages we chose basics in story structure, such as beginnings that evoked curiosity quickly, interesting inventions or surprise turnings, the sense of movement, and satisfying closings. Later we watched for the more mature techniques of lucid and convincing style. Natural audience reactions fortified our praise. In fact we believe that it was the audience situation—the age-old pleasure of telling one's tale directly to eager listeners—that inevitably drew forth the story qualities that grip and stir the imagination. Each child, being listener and writer in turn, became increasingly aware of what to do to hold his hearers in expectant attention to the end. It was out of their successes that story form naturally grew.

In the sixth grade Lucy wrote much more freely and abundantly. Her stories though perhaps not so compactly organized as the one about William Whiskers, grew richer in human insight and significant detail, as evidenced by the following excerpt from "The Hero." Through them all, too, ran an undercurrent of fun, as though she herself were highly amused by the way her characters behaved.

* THE HERO

Nig was on his bed pulling his shoes on and thinking very hard. "Gosh," he whispered, "I wonder what she's like. Maybe she's like Neillie's baby calf, but gee, I don't think I'd like that," he added, "or maybe like the puppies Roland Bear's dog had." Nig was thinking like this because his very own mother had had a baby. It was a girl. All he knew was that the five bears had to be very quiet, and he was very curious. Nig could hear Father Bear tiptoeing up the stairs. Father was trying to keep house. He pushed open Nig's door softly.

"Come down to breakfast," he hissed, and tiptoed out again. Nig slid off the bed and followed the other bears downstairs. They had named the baby Daisy Mae. Father was doing the cooking. He had on a big checked apron and his hands were dripping with something. "Oh, can't someone help me?" he whispered almost in tears. "This is killing me. I hope we don't have any more children. Isn't six children enough?"

"I'll help," said Nig weakly. He brought in the food. The five bears grunted softly. Father Bear did not know how to cook.

"I don't think we're so hungry," hissed Mo.

Nig walked to school with half the school around him. "And," he continued, "I'm going to see her this afternoon."

"Gosh," said Roy Bear, "do you think she's real?"

"Well," answered Nig doubtfully, "I'm not so sure."

Nig was the center of attention at school. No one had ever had a baby sister before. Even the teacher was interested although Nig couldn't keep his mind on his work. "How's your mother?" she asked.

"O.K.," answered Nig. He was dreaming of little babies with wings on their backs.

The five little bears were standing outside Mother Bear's door. They were all very nervous although they tried not to show it. Nig was thinking, "What if she's awful funny looking after all I've told the kids at school."

"I'm not so sure I want to see her," hissed Mo.

"Oh, don't be so dumb!" whispered Nig, whose knees felt like water. Then the door opened. Nig said, "Hello," to his mother hastily, looking the other way at a crib in a dim corner of the room. He walked over to it and peeked in. There was the sweetest little brown ball that Nig had ever seen. "Oh—gee—gosh—oh my," he whispered. He was overcome with surprise. The other bears were watching the baby too. "Gee, could I touch her?" Nig asked. Mother Bear nodded. Hesitatingly Nig touched the soft little paw. He smiled down at the baby. The baby smiled back. Nig just stood there a while looking at the baby. Then he began to recover himself. He thought he must look very silly. Before he hadn't cared. Now he did. He saw Mother Bear smiling at him. "Pretty nice brat," he said, hastily trying to break the silence.

"I think she likes you best," Mother Bear answered. "She's smiling at you." Mother Bear tried to keep the amusement out of her voice. Nig blushed a deep red. Mother Bear could see his ears turning red.

"I think she's swell," cooed Mo. "Don't you, Meinie?"

"Uh, huh," answered Meinie, turning pink. He knew he was in bad with Nig for saying it.

"I agree," chorused the other two bears. They were a little scared too.

After they had gone outside Nig called a conference. "Now listen," he growled in his toughest voice, "I don't think I like her so much, but I'm older and I'm more careful so when she gets old enough and can go out I'm going to take her out, see! And understand first I don't like her. I just want to take her out."

Eenie murmured something like, "Oh, yeah," but nobody heard him, which was lucky for him.

About the time she wrote "The Hero," Lucy prepared an article in connection with a study of weather. The children had chosen to record their findings in booklets, an idea that the classroom teacher encouraged because she knew the problems in expression that they would encounter. After the science teacher demonstrated the making of a mercury barometer, they set to work readily enough, thinking it would be easy to write down what had happened. Soon, however, brows began to pucker, and one after another found himself unable to go on. Much of the difficulty lay, they concluded, in their lack of exact observation and understanding. So the demonstration was performed again, and points that had been vague were talked over. A second time they set to work at their writing, but they still found it an onerous task. Some gathered in small groups to read to one another and to ask for help on the parts that were not yet clear. At length the teacher put Lucy's account on the board as an example of a lucid and complete explanation.

* MAKING A MERCURY BAROMETER

Mr. Allen filled a tube with mercury. The tube was about 36 inches long. One end of the tube was sealed as in picture A. No air was in the tube. Next Mr. Allen put some mercury in a bowl. The bowl was about ⅓ full. Next he put his finger over the open end of the tube, turned it upside down, and put the open end into the bowl. It was quite difficult because the mercury tried to escape. No air got in because the end of the tube was in the mercury. Then the mercury escaped into the bowl as far as it could against the pressure of the air, as in picture B. No air could have gotten into the space at the top. So all that was in there was a vacuum. Mercury is very heavy. Vacuum has no power. When the tube was full, it was heavier than air. But when the four inches of mercury escaped, it was no longer heavier. The air and the mercury in the tube went down as far as it could against the pressure of the air. The air was pushing all around as in picture C, trying to get into the vacuum. In pushing down on the mercury in the bowl it held up the mercury in the tube.

Each child was allowed to check his own against it to see if he had included all of the essential information. The whole emphasis was on making the report as accurate as possible. Nothing was said about the abrupt beginning or the short, jerky sentences. Such awkward expression invariably occurs when children start writing in a new field. They feel the same lack of sureness that an artist feels when he undertakes a new medium. Fluency of expression comes only after much experience in this different way of thinking, and writing at this point can serve best by revealing the inadequacies in that thinking. As the ideas and relationships become more familiar, sentence structure improves. This we know from experience.

Through six years we watched Lucy's growth with justifiable delight. From a shy little girl who flamed with embarrassment at the slightest provocation, she developed into a poised and able child. Many factors contributed to this wholesome change, not the least of which was the satisfaction and approval that came to her through her story writing. Because the stories she wrote were so intimate a creation, she felt their warm reception was a reception of herself. Slowly but steadily she grew in assurance and self-esteem. Furthermore, the rich quality of her writing was a quickening force that gave impulse and direction to her group's writing improvement. We frankly admit that workers like Lucy do our most fruitful teaching.

Pat, Grades Three through Six

But I did see this—that like a carpenter who makes a table, a man who has written a poem has written it like that on purpose.

From the beginning a certain neat directness was characteristic of Pat and all his work. In science and arithmetic he showed remarkable precision even at eight years. Interestingly enough, his art work was definitely superior and characterized by the counterpart of this precision. His painting and clay modeling were distinguished by a strong sense of design and a dramatic use of color. In contrast to Ruth's uncertainty and fearfulness were Pat's clean-cut sense of direction and economical route to achievement. Though not outstanding in ability, his sureness of approach and his selection of significant detail gave power to everything he wrote. His thrifty style is evident in the following story, written at eight.

⁕ LITTLE RABBIT

Once there was a little rabbit. One day he went down to the river to get a drink. On the way he met a fox. Now this was a very wicked fox. He had tried to catch little rabbit and now he had him. The fox sprang. Little rabbit tried to run, but the fox was too quick for him. The fox took little rabbit to his den. Then the fox tried to eat little rabbit. But when he had his hands on him little rabbit bit him. Then the fox screamed. So at last the fox let him go and never tried to catch him again.

This story had several errors in sentence structure and in spelling, which was Pat's Waterloo. However, the tale served its immediate purpose: the group was entertained, and Pat was pleased.

During the following year increasing experience in the practical

⁕ Walter de la Mare, *Come Hither.*

phases of writing provided both the necessity and the opportunity for correcting mechanics. It was characteristic of Pat's whole make-up that he should assimilate most of these skills quickly and thoroughly. He did all the required writing with ease, but never produced an abundance of personal writing. Perhaps this was due in part to his ability to express himself effectively in the field of art.

Pat was nine when he wrote "Mr. Ghost's Night Out." This story shows a decided growth in his particular narrative style and increased facility in the mechanics of writing. Several errors in spelling have been corrected.

* MR. GHOST'S NIGHT OUT

One night Mr. Ghost sneaked out to play poker with the other ghosts. They played about two hours. Then Mr. Ghost looked at the clock. He snatched his hat from the post and ran home. But meanwhile Mrs. Ghost had found out he had gone and grabbed her rolling pin and started out to look for him. About halfway between the two houses they met. And in the dim light Mrs. Ghost saw a dark figure of Mr. Ghost. But she did not know who it was. A terrified look came over her face. She let out a scream and threw up her hands. The rolling pin went sailing into the bushes and away she went yelling and screaming blue murder. However she got home. Mr. Ghost ran home a different way. They got home at the same time. When Mr. Ghost came in Mrs. Ghost told all about what had happened and Mr. Ghost patted her on the back and said, "Don't worry. I'll protect you," and he took her off to bed.

Even though "Mr. Ghost's Night Out" is a much more ample tale than "Little Rabbit," its greater length is due to a larger concept of plot and not to superfluous detail. Note the incident in which "Mr. Ghost looked at the clock." Pat left interpretation to his audience but chose significant detail from which the reader can sketch the rest of the picture. Again, in the ending, Pat avoided the trivial, which clutters up much of children's writing.

Naturally in this class there were many occasions for letter writing. Pat was especially adept at this for he enjoyed addressing his ideas to a particular audience. His letters were characterized by a precision that in time became the essence of his style in other writing, too.

Here is a letter written when Pat was ten. Note the choice in telling detail and the richness of implication in its placement.

> 7 Corning Road
> Bronxville, N.Y.
> May 19, 1937

Dear Uncle John,

We had an art exhibit in school. We hung all our pictures we had made this year in our classroom or in the halls. Most of the children made clay models, too. These we put in glass cases in the halls or laid them on the ledges in our room. All the children in my class made a picture of either an imaginary or a real flower. The day after our mothers came we went around to the different groups to see the other classes' pictures. The sixth grade in my opinion had the best ideas but they didn't always have the best painting.

I hope that you are much better now and that you will soon be able to be out again.

> Love,
> Pat

Of course, this is a real letter of which the second draft was actually sent to Uncle John.

Writing, both practical and personal, increased rapidly in amount throughout the fifth and sixth grades. The following report is one of several that Pat wrote, but is reproduced here because it shows a danger signal. Pat's power of selection when confronted with a wide and somewhat confusing array of material produced this inadequate and telescopic report.

* AUTOMOBILES

One of the first attempts to drive a carriage by steam was made by Captain Nicholas Joseph Cughot in 1769. By 1830 England had developed a steam carriage that could travel at ten miles per hour and safely ascend and descend hills.

Two-thirds of the automobiles made in America are produced

in Michigan, Ohio, and Indiana. Great centers are Detroit, Lansing, Pontiac, Cleveland, South Bend, and Connersville. The reason Detroit is a great manufacturing city is because it has cheap lake transportation, plenty of iron and steel, and good hardwood forests near by. In recent years there were 25,000,000 automobiles in the United States which is over four-fifths of the automobiles in the world. Our motor vehicles include 25,500,000 passenger cars and 3,500,000 motor trucks. In Michigan in 1933, there were twenty-four establishments manufacturing automobiles, having 59,725 employees earning in wages $66,675,000, and having an output valued at $588,302,000. Not all factories make the same part of an automobile: for instance, some factories make only batteries. Then we say that they specialize in making batteries.

In a factory there are many workers. Each worker has his own job in manufacturing an automobile. If he does not get it done on time, the car goes on to the next worker for him to do his job. When the car reaches the end of the assembly line a man drives it out to test it. Then it goes to the dealer who sells the car.

References

Automobiles From Start to Finish, pp. 3–56.
The United States in the Modern World, pp. 186, 187.
Our World, p. 145.
Living in the Age of Machines, p. 262.
Economic and Social Geography, pp. 563, 567, 569.

Pat did not need much help either from his class or from his teacher to see that his report left too much to an uninformed audience. He sensed, also, that he had not sufficiently understood and digested his material to use it in following his plan of sequence. This was due in part to his use of too difficult reference material. A later report on armor, for which appropriate references were available, shows a reasonably thorough assimilation of facts and a more adequate presentation. A portion of this report is quoted here:

❋ ❋ ❋

An armorer also made suits for knights to wear under their armor. To make a suit of mail the armorer took a small iron bar. This he heated and pounded until it was like a fine wire. Then he wound it around a small stake so that it took the shape of a circle. At that point he cut the wire into a link the ends of which he flattened and pierced and fastened together with a tiny nail. Often the nail was not larger than the head of a pin. When one link was fastened another was put through it and fastened in the same way. A shirt in a museum was estimated to have a hundred thousand links in it.

This paragraph contains facts garnered from three references, but Pat's increasing skill in selecting detail plus his realization of the dangers of telescoping material produced a clear and interesting picture.

One of the last stories Pat wrote in the sixth grade may well be contrasted with "Little Rabbit," for in it one can mark the same qualities, though strengthened and expanded, that were lightly indicated in that early story. Spelling errors have been corrected; otherwise it is exactly as Pat wrote it.

   ❋   ❋   ❋

One day on the beach of Plome Island a white speck was sighted not far from land. As it came closer the bathers realized that it was a sea monster. From the water, women's screams pierced the air. For days no one ventured near the water until one day when there was no speck in sight, two men went in and swam out quite far. Then one of the men whose name was Joshua felt something very slimy against his legs. Now he was quite a show-off on shore with his loud bathing suit but in the water with this thing around his feet he sang a different tune. "Help," spluttered the unfortunate man, at the same time floundering wildly. His companion, seeing the antics of his friend, thought he was crazy and started swimming for shore as fast as he could. Meanwhile Joshua saw that the thing was slowly but surely coming to the surface of the water. When it came up far enough for him to see it plainly he found it was a dead shark. Seeing that it could do him no harm he turned it toward shore and was highly praised for his work. It was later found out that the "sea monster" was this dead shark because when a fish is dead it floats with its stomach up so that the white speck that was supposed to be the sea monster was the dead shark Joshua found floating around beyond the breakers.

Pat's own neat way of telling a story remained unchanged during the three years since "Little Rabbit," but time brought growth and refinement of his style. Contrast, for instance, the characterizations "a very wicked fox" and "He was quite a show-off on shore with his loud bathing suit . . ." Both are quick, but the latter is subtle as well. The same direct, economical narration, the thrifty choice of detail, the same quick characterization that we have noted will no doubt always distinguish Pat's writing, for they are as much a part of Pat as his straight back and steady blue eyes.

Sarah, Grades Three through Six

For out of the abundance of the heart the mouth speaketh.*

Sarah was indeed a rare child. Seldom does one meet a person of so many dimensions. Physically large, often clumsy, interested and able in almost every field, whether artistic or academic, Sarah radiated a generous warmth that permeated all she did and fairly engulfed her friends and associates. She wrote copiously and, as you will see, well. She was gifted in music, studied both piano and violin, sang well, and had an unusually acute ear. Sarah's greatest love was for dramatics. She had an amazing insight into human nature and unusual power to create and interpret a wide variety of characters. Superior ability in art was but another part of this extraordinary constellation.

Intellectually Sarah was also richly endowed, and she explored each new world of ideas as zestfully as she hurled herself into a game. This verve was coupled with almost irrepressible high spirits, which made Sarah an unusually delightful person. But sometimes her joyous headlong pace, joined with a complete disregard for the value of material things, wearied her teacher and companions. Sarah, for instance, had great difficulty learning to take care of her belongings or even to put her desk in order. Nevertheless, she welcomed severe correction with the same generous spirit that prompted her to

* Matt. XII:34.

give away her best automatic pencil. Quick to sense a dramatic situation and eager to be a part of it, Sarah got into and out of an unusual number of childish scrapes. Her abundant sympathies were at once a strength and a potential danger.

Though absent more than half of her third school year, Sarah was one of the first to turn from story telling to story writing. Even at this early age she showed keen invention and a flair for the dramatic, as can be seen in the following story. We have added some of the quotation marks and corrected the paragraphing.

* A STORY

Once there was a poor little boy. His name was Bobby. Bobby wanted to go to the circus. But he didn't have any money. His father was dead, he lived all alone with his mother. The circus had come to town that day and Bobby's heart was set on going. He had never been to one before. The boys on the block said it was wonderful. He asked his mother whether she would give him twenty-five cents to go to the circus.

"My son," she would say, weeping, "you ought to be glad you have bread and butter."

The next day Bobby went near the tents. He was just going to go in when a rough hand grabbed him. "Give me your money," said the man. And before Bobby could say "Jack Robinson" he landed neatly on the hard ground.

That night Bobby asked his mother whether he could get a job at the circus.

"Yes," was her reply.

The next morning Bobby got dressed and ran down to the circus grounds. Again the gruff man asked what he wanted there. "I want a job," Bobby replied.

"All right, what's your name?"

"My name is Bobby. What's yours?"

"My name is Bill. The manager is over there."

That afternoon Bobby White, for that was his name, came rushing home.

"Mother," he said, jumping and shouting, "I got a job at the circus and I can see the show free."

"But what do you do? How much pay do you get?" his puzzled mother asked.

"I carry water for the animals and I get twenty dollars a week."

Bobby went to the circus.

The dramatic quality of this situation and the method of its resolution are too obvious to need pointing out. Even at eight, Sarah enjoyed a cleverly turned phrase and graphic word, such as: "his puzzled mother asked" and " 'My son,' she would say weeping, 'you ought to be glad you have bread and butter.' "

At nine Sarah was writing copiously. But in addition to rich invention and dramatic quality other essentials of good writing began to appear. For example, contrast the structure of the first three sentences of Sarah's circus story with the first three sentences of "The Wormy Snake." Sarah was already alert to balance of sentence arrangement and quite unconsciously made use of a delightful cadence or euphonious quality in her choice of word and phrase. Note also Sarah's sly observation in the instance of Snapper's confession of what had not even been noticed by the unobservant school marm. Only two minor corrections in mechanics have been made.

* THE WORMY SNAKE

High in the tree-tops Miss Songster called all her pupils to singing class. One by one they came, Jenny Wren, Bob White, Jr., Cluck Cluck, Peep Peep, and many others. After all the rest were there, in walked Snapper.

"Snapper," said Miss Songster's sharp voice. "Why are you so late?"

"I—er—fell down."

"Well, never mind. I am going to call the cards."

Nobody liked singing lessons, especially the boys. But they couldn't play hookie because if anyone was absent Miss Songster would call up their mothers and ask them if their child was sick. If the mother said no, then when the children came home they would get a spanking.

But Snapper had a little scheme of his own. After the roll was called Miss Songster didn't pay any attention to the children.

He sneaked out while she wasn't looking. When he was out of sight he thought he'd dig a worm. He did not have to dig because there was one right on the ground in front of him. It was a great big one, too. He tried to pick it up. It was too heavy. The animal turned around. Snapper saw what a mistake he had made. It was a Rattlesnake. Snapper had been strictly warned about snakes.

He flew back to the schoolhouse with unusual speed. Snapper confessed everything. Miss Songster was a bit puzzled. She had not yet noticed Snapper's absence and she was surprised he confessed.

Snapper is now the best singer in Birdland and he doesn't mistake snakes for worms.

During fifth grade when the group was hit by an epidemic of mystery stories, Sarah produced one as bloodcurdling and stereotyped as all the others, but still marked by a rich flow of language and by varied techniques of characterization.

Sarah, like many other children, got a positive glee from inventing preposterous names, as indicated in the following excerpt from a fifth-grade story:

❁   ❁   ❁

Oscar (Oscar Aloysius Wurtelstein) being the ambitious type of brat suggested that we try a few of Timothy's (Timothy Potomus Bethybotom) father's precious fifteen-cent cigars.

Oscar, I take it, was not accustomed to this form of a delightful afternoon.

Cuspert and I lighted our cigars together. Cuspert took a terrific draw, (this is the first time he ever tried it) but managed to live through it. We sat for a few minutes calmly puffing while Oscar, Jedzercuss, and Timothy were half asleep in the lubber's hole. I was sitting there smoking and looking at the river when there was a terrific BANG!

The world was dead to all. . . .

Now this is, of course, a very poor tale. And the whole story is no better than the excerpt indicates. But even a superior child seldom travels an unbroken course from triumph to greater triumph.

Moreover, it becomes increasingly obvious to us that children do gain something worthwhile from writing even such a yarn as that of Aloysius. Fluency, flexibility, a certain abandon seem to be achieved only from quantities of writing. Sarah, like others in her group, wrote increasingly in the fifth grade, and much of what she wrote was distinguished by nothing more outstanding than an ever-widening vocabulary.

At the end of fifth grade, Sarah's group was asked to try doing personal editions of an old and well-known fable. Though this is an experiment that must be used infrequently, it provides opportunity to see individual style. Sarah's wealth of imagination and dramatic sympathy began to take on a certain subtlety of expression and a rather mature quality of implication, which can be seen particularly in the conversation in the following story. This story also shows superior control of form. No changes have been made.

* TOADS AND DIAMONDS

Once upon a time there was a widow with two daughters. One of these was just like her mother, ugly not only in facial expression but in temper also. The youngest however was just like her dead father, pretty, generous and had a good temper. Since the eldest was the very image of her mother naturally she was the favorite of the two. The mother made the youngest daughter do all the hard work and worst of all sent her to a well one and a half miles away twice a day with a tankard. One day when she was getting water she saw a beggar boy trying to get a drink with his cap but it all leaked out and the poor boy couldn't get any. The girl (whose name was Janice) being very courteous offered him some water out of the tankard. The boy accepted the drink readily. But as she held the tankard for the boy it grew heavier and it burned her fingers but she still hung on to it.

"May I have another drink?" asked the boy.

"You drink a lot for a boy your size. You may have another drink," replied the girl.

As you know by now, the boy was a fairy trying to find if the girl was really courteous. This time the tankard was very heavy and it burned more than ever. When the boy finished he threw down the tankard and he turned into a glamorous lady with a wand in her hand.

"Janice," she said, "you gave me water when you thought I was thirsty even if it was heavy and it burned you. I shall reward you with a lovely gift. Whenever you speak either jewels or flowers will come out of your mouth."

Janice was so bewildered that she ran all the way home without the water or the tankard. When she got home her mother yelled at her and said, "Stupid! Why have you been so long and where is the water? And the tankard?"

"I'm so sorry," said Janice, And three roses and four diamonds came out of her mouth.

"My dear child, how did this happen?" (This was the first time she had called her 'My dear child.') "Fannie, my little pet, see what has happened to your sister because she went to the well to draw water. Janice, how did this befall you, darling?"

Janice told the story simply and truthfully.

"Fannie," cried her mother, "take a pail and if you see that boy, treat him civilly."

"I'll look like a fine how-do-you-do drawing water," answered Fannie and after much grumbling she departed with a golden pitcher.

When she got to the well she saw a tall thin lady with a crown on her head, undoubtedly of some high rank. But it was really the fairy trying to find out how far the girl's ugliness would go. Fannie started to draw water when the tall lady asked for a drink of it.

"Did your Grace think that this pitcher was for the use of every person who comes along? However, here is some," Fannie threw the whole vaseful at the lady and dropped the golden pitcher which broke instantly. The princess suddenly turned into the fairy.

"For your meanness, I shall give you a gift. Whenever you speak a snake or a viper will come out of your mouth."

"Humph," said Fannie. A snake came out of her mouth and she went home. When she got there her mother said:

"Tell me what happened, sweet, and I'll count the jewels that come out of your mouth."

"It's all that miserable creature's fault," said Fannie (a lizard and a viper came out of her mouth), "and that horrible witch's!" And she told the whole story.

By the time she was through the kitchen floor was full of snakes and toads and lizards. The widow gave Janice a beating and turned her out of the house. Janice wandered into the woods and lay down and cried. Now the sovereign of the country who happened to be coming back from a fox hunt, saw this fair girl weeping on the ground and asked her what was wrong. Janice told him how her mother had turned her out (not sparing the jewels and flowers). The king was very angry and wanted the wicked mother and daughter executed but Janice, being very kind, would not have it. The king took her to his palace and there they were married and lived happily ever after.

Space prohibits the inclusion of any other fifth-grade writing, personal or practical. But Sarah, of course, did the expected amount of writing of letters, records, brief reports, and shared in the preparation of a science book about trees for a second grade in her school. The latter offered an excellent opportunity to practice simple, clear writing. And considerable practice was needed! The entire group profited much from the discipline of exact expression and continuity of organization.

During the sixth grade momentum increased tremendously, partly because the prewriting stages of development had been richly explored. Though Sarah wrote frequently with a partner or two, only a few examples of her individual writing are shown here. When the sixth-grade group was making a series of industrial studies in geography, Sarah chose to study oranges and wrote an extended report noteworthy for its improvement in organization.

Another piece of work done by Sarah during her sixth year was entirely self-chosen. She had visited Austria at one time and had heard much about the days of the "dual monarchy," a phrase in which she took delight. With the class she keenly enjoyed hearing Kate Seredy's *White Stag*, and brought her own copy to school to hold and look at while the teacher finished reading the last chapters. When the class was studying medieval life, any reference to the Huns was sure to evoke some special response from Sarah. Her report was heartily enjoyed by the class, and Sarah was so excited that she had twisted herself from one side of the classroom to the other by the time she had finished reading it aloud. An excerpt follows:

* THE HUNS

There are few certain facts known about the early Huns. In medieval books (which are very few) they were only spoken of unfavorably.

The Huns were very small in stature but their bones were strong. They also were very quick on their feet. These small men often had to endure unimaginable hardships. A Hun sometimes lived on his horse for days. This made him bow-legged. His broad face, large ears and slit-eyes half scared people out of their wits. He had no hair on his face except perhaps for a fierce mustache. When they were babies hot irons were applied to their faces and all the hair on cheek and chin was burned out. That accounts for all the scars on their faces in later years. Another custom of the Huns was to wash each new born babe out in the open air (regardless of winter or summer) and give it a bath every day for forty-two days (six weeks). These were to last it for the rest of its life. Cattle could not stand the rough life the Hun led so he had to keep sheep and horses. Sometimes he had camels. His food consisted of milk products (preferably mares' milk) and sometimes horses' blood. They also ate half raw meat which they warmed by putting it between their and their horse's body. . . .

References are duly quoted by pages so that notes can be rechecked if necessary, a technique highly respected by Sarah and the whole group.

The last story written by Sarah in the sixth grade follows:

❀   ❀   ❀

"I can't see," muttered Johnny Elephant, as he strutted before the reflecting walls of the mill-pond, "why all the girls of this village aren't in love with me. I being such a handsome young fellow."

So saying he reached into his back pocket, brought out his red bandana handkerchief and wiped his tusks. He then picked a white flower at the edge of the mill-pond and put it into the lapel of his little blue jacket. Then looking very important he put his hands into his pockets, held his head high and strutted down the road to Suzie May's house.

Splash! He had unexpectedly landed in a mudpuddle and a thin high-pitched voice was giggling from the house.

"Ha, ha! You—are funny," giggled Suzie May. . . .

In the rest of the story, Sarah developed the adventures of the young show-off elephant who finally ran away from home to make his fortune. She ended the story thus:

It must have been around twelve o'clock when he woke up and found two shining eyes staring at him out of the darkness.

"Oh," he moaned, as he cuddled closer to the tree. "I want my mother."

"Booo-o-oo," went the voice of the owl, who was the owner of the two staring eyes.

Johnny did not hesitate for a moment. He leaped up and ran as fast as he could.

The next day Johnny ate off the mantlepiece.

The discernment of human frailties so whimsically treated in the adventures of Johnny Elephant is another evidence of the flowering of unusual gifts. Furthermore, one sees real growth in ease and flexibility of structure, in economy and subtlety of implication. It is also obvious that the needed discipline in skills and techniques had in no wise crippled the free play of an active imagination. It seems essential to preserve in any child that spontaneity so necessary for later development. Therefore, it is a matter of signal importance that Sarah, like less able children in her group, retained a delightful unself-consciousness and a genuine zest to write simply for the joy of writing.

chapter seven

❖ ❖ ❖ ❖ ❖ ❖ ❖ ❖ ❖

WRITING AND GROWTH

The art of life consists in creating an individual and a unique self.—POWYS, A Philosophy of Solitude

The complete freedom necessary for the life of the creative spirit has always stood opposed to the methodical acquisition of skills and techniques. Correctness has appeared the antithesis of spontaneity. Many persons dealing with young children have felt a real need for a more careful analysis of these antagonisms. Our guiding premise has been that a more constructive synthesis could be made of these apparently disparate elements. To this end we have recorded our experience.

Long dissatisfied with the results of our teaching of writing, we had through trial and error discarded at least a little of the empty ritual. A nucleus of common belief incited four of us to experiment more definitely along the lines of our emerging understanding. So with the happy accident of continuity of pupil groups we proceeded to test and to clarify our beliefs. These years of experience and study have led us to believe that we have found ways to nurture the creative spirit and at the same time to effect power in the use of writing skills. Gratifying results have come from what we believe is a clear understanding of the essential functions of written expression and of the natural tendencies of children's growth in relation to writing. It appears that the utilitarian and artistic phases of writing are not mutually antagonistic when the reality of the one and the freedom of the other are zealously guarded.

Basic Beliefs

Writing, we believe, serves at least two needs for writer and audience: that of artistic self-expression and that of communicating functional ideas. One is personal, individual, imaginative, and highly perishable. The other is utilitarian, realistic, or intellectual, and needs the discipline of correct mechanics to be socially acceptable. The former seems to be kept alive best by complete freedom to experiment and complete assurance of a respectful reception of the product regardless of its nature. In contrast to this the acquisition of form seems intrinsically a function of realistic writing in which other people are practically concerned. Writing of this nature springs from relatively constant sources; the need or the authority remains as a point of reference against which the product can be checked. The author works more as a reproducer of known facts, conditions, or ideas, presented, of course, in his unique fashion. But the material recorded exists outside himself. Hence the writing is not so intimately personal. Correction and verification can be required without injuring the individual and without the loss of ideas. Moreover, these operations take time, and only where the material is more nearly objective and the needs or the data are rather permanent can the teacher and pupil work over and improve expression to say *exactly* what the writer needs to say. Not so in personal writing where the sources lie almost wholly within the individual and where there is no final authority other than personal taste. Time out to revamp independent clauses may mean loss of the whole idea. Or of even more serious import, editing story after story may so curb the swift imagination or so fatigue the uncertain and immature young writer that desire to write turns all too often to dread of writing. Confusion that arises from trying to shape a child's ideas to an adult's conception or pattern has resulted in mimicry or even in obvious plagiarism.

Furthermore, the same literary designs that conscientious teachers would imprint, usually with deadening consequences, develop more vividly from inner necessity. When children write with the definite idea of enlisting the attention of an audience from the beginning to the end of an engaging tale, they learn in time to select what gives vigor and spirit to their writing. To hold even a tolerant and friendly audience in gratifying suspense, a writer must really tell a story. Beginning with a propelling idea or suggestion, implying just enough probability of outcome to start the listeners' curiosity, opening several possible ways of working out a solution, holding the suspense to the very end—these and other elements are found by actual, personal trial to be effective techniques of story construction. Design thus emerges from the same storyteller-to-audience situations that have been the beginnings of our literary heritage. Writer, storyteller, and audience form an organic whole that operates naturally to strengthen and vitalize written expression. Indeed, rules of literary structure have come from just such reality, but they have been crystallized into academic principles that usually leave the young quite ignorant of their functional origin. The real situations that first produced those principles of structure need to be relived again and again by young writers. Continued experience in being sometimes a writer and frequently an avid listener can make an individual so sensitive to elements of story design that he naturally appropriates some of them for his own use. The delight of entertaining an audience with the magic of his own creation is a pleasure to be sought again and again. And satisfaction from such success begets even greater zest for writing.

Practical writing, too, makes its contribution to the balanced growth of writing power. When a child's first contacts with the art of writing have been truly meaningful to him, an effective beginning has been made. Situations so realistic that the results of a written communication are readily observable kindle a merited respect for writing as a means to action. This feeling of reality is essential; otherwise learning to write can become the merest muscular performance. But a skill that is significant in a child's important affairs has a far different future. For the person-to-person directness of most utilitarian writing necessitates clarity—the hallmark of fine exposition. Continued experience leads naturally from the most practical and necessary communication to the recording of worthwhile discovery and experience. Striving for clarity and order in purposeful written expression fosters further respect for the effective economies and obligations of good utilitarian writing. In this more objective expression some success is possible for nearly all children. Many a youngster feels his first, perhaps his only, power over elusive words by producing an informational record he is proud to call a book. Some children who cannot lose themselves in flights of invention find their greatest satisfaction in the graciously worded social letter or in the unmistakably clear report. For them, this is a real outlet, no less worthwhile than lyric, phantasy, or enchanting story. Individuality is just as likely to find expression here and to be further cultivated by such experience.

Standards of attainment, too, are more easily applied in the fields of practical writing than in those imaginative areas where the individual must be his own authority. A child can be more certain that his product is good in the usual, conventional sense. Direct teaching of some of the accepted forms of punctuation, arrangement, and structure make children sure that what they have written will meet established standards. For some uncertain souls this assurance is necessary and productive of further strength in writing as well as further self-confidence and security. And for all, pride in workmanship, so often lacking in our age of ready-made commodities, can be a wholesome experience.

The Teacher's Role

As we became aware of children's potentialities for growth in writing, we came to see our own responsibilities more clearly. The more we saw power emerging from the complementary experiences of practical and personal writing, the less we felt the need for pressing children to write. Children's response to their own purposes spurred them to more and better writing. Individual projection to an understanding audience was the basis of wholesome self-realization and a means to stronger, clearer written expression. Our role was to establish those situations that not only allowed for writing but that also fostered it and at times required it. Most important of all, we found ourselves responsible for the emotional climate in which creative insight deepened.

A second aspect of our teaching function came into sharper focus as we worked longer in the valuable discipline of practical writing and the joyous expansion of personal writing. We could not adopt a laissez-faire attitude of letting children grow. Rather, we had to sense when and how to introduce fresh experiences, to open new vistas in keeping with the children's developing capacities. This timing of new ventures was not easy. Depth of experience was more productive than a surfeit of experiences, for the latter course resulted only in superficiality and indifference. Children need adults to bring them into effective relationship with new materials. Left to themselves their explorations lead to a thinning of content and a dulling of perception. Shared with a knowing adult, their efforts achieve a status that empowers them to reach out to greater maturity. The direction of children's growth from dependence to independence is based in large part on adult dynamics.

Principles of Composition

In the years since the publication of our first statement, we have continued to seek new insights and greater clarification for our original understandings. In a variety of situations that we have seen, the roles of practical and personal writing demonstrate their complementary nature. Other teachers likewise, have found the techniques herein described gratifyingly productive both for the enhancement of creativity and the control of correct form.

Our own teaching and observation and the experience of a considerable number of teachers have led us to believe that the measures we have reported proceed best under certain productive conditions. These we attempt to predicate as guiding principles.

• Personal writing should not be expected until a child has had a wealth of satisfying experience with oral expression and has gained sufficient physical skill to prevent undue fatigue.

• Each child's ability to express his ideas is distinctly unique and personal. The rate at which this ability grows is likewise individual. Only harm can come from trying to force more mature forms of expression than children show themselves ready to use.

• From the beginning, practical writing must meet high standards of form and organization, which most children accept willingly because their writing serves a genuine use.

• Personal writing needs to fulfill only the child's desires, except upon those extremely rare occasions when correct form is necessary out of consideration for others or when the product is to be permanently preserved.

• It is equally important to accept a child's own form for his personal expression and to help him learn conventional forms for practical writing. Each experience contributes to the other, leading to a natural integration of style and technique as the writer matures.

• Every child writes himself into his product. Style, tempo, phrasing, characterization, choice of subject are exponents of individual personality.

• Since the child can write honestly only what is truly his, time to assimilate experience and information is vitally necessary.

• Involvement in literature contributes immeasurably to a rich, adequate expression. Conversely, the effort of trying to write one's own ideas effectively and colorfully heightens sensitivity to good literature.

• Direct sensory experience promotes lively observation and precise, vivid expression. Putting firsthand experience into one's own words helps to avoid the dangers of plagiarism.

• Children's writing reflects the impact of such mass media as television, radio, comics, and movies, not only in vocabulary but also in tempo and characterization.

• Personal writing serves the need for the release of tensions and for the draining of aggressions, fears, and destructive emotions.

Of Personal and Practical Writing

If personal writing is to be kept a joyous and genuine outlet, it cannot be strait jacketed in subject and form. When written expression is truly free and spontaneous, all sorts of ideas and shades of feeling emerge. Stimulation or suggestion may give direction to some pupils at some times. But the human mind seems much too wayward to be confined in its artistic experimentation to a prescribed or given content. Even the child's mind—perhaps even more certainly the child's mind—is not likely to be spontaneous in verse or prose about a particular unit of study. Only rarely does the elementary-school child so thoroughly identify himself with a portion of the curriculum as to draw upon that experience in his personal writing. Individual impressions of the adult world, concealed desires well-cloaked behind natural or fantastic figures, naive reactions to what is taken for granted by adults—these and many other strange avenues are likely to be taken with perfect freedom. Truly there can be no bounds in children's personal writing, for each individual must speak from and for himself.

On the other hand, the immediate activities of the elementary school offer abundant opportunities for exercising utilitarian language. Clear structure, sound organization, and correct techniques are necessary aspects of a product to be shared with others. These elements learned in action become part of a child's working equipment. Teaching them in functional settings increases the efficiency with which they are learned.

Probably everyone who has experimented with children's creative enterprises has been amazed and deeply gratified to witness the tremendous energy and concentration that characterize such activity. This absorption with an idea, a dance, a picture, a story, a play, is too important an aspect of child life to be lightly treated. An activity that so genuinely engages the whole person and either thrills him with his success and prowess or frustrates him with his failure leaves almost visible changes in that person, who for a while lost himself in his adventure. For a time, at least, the adventure is all-important; the product with which he struggles banishes all self-consciousness. The creator is objectified in what he has produced. Perhaps because of this important quality of personal absorption in the job, such creative outlet builds anew the child who, but a brief hour before, has been the builder. Where children are concerned, the rewards of creative action to the individual are more important than the excellence of the product. Seldom will even our most gifted children produce lasting works of art, and then only after considerable fumbling and mediocre output. But the growth of the personal entity, though immeasurable as yet by scientific procedures, defies negation. Those who have watched the process *know*. Those who have seen energy kindled and honest pride effected by creative effort with music, or poetry, or dance, or well-delivered research, have seen also a new and stronger person quicken into being.

This process of growth and creation remains as mysterious as any original creation upon which mankind has ever speculated. But the manifestations of growth from the limitations of childhood to the full maturity of the articulate adult are discernible though infinitely subtle and delicate. Children come slowly into their heritage of that most significant cultural tool by which man has recorded much of his intellectual and esthetic achievement. We have been privileged to study a process at once intriguing and elusive.

☼ ☼ ☼ ☼ ☼ ☼ ☼ ✿

STORY
SUPPLEMENT

We have found it helpful to have on hand a stockpile of children's stories to be used for various purposes. Such a collection is not an accumulation of the best stories but rather a full cross section, including some that are meager, some that are full of active aggression, and some that start with verve but are unfinished. We have found we could never have too many stories on hand, for what catches on with one group may fail to stir another.

From this collection we draw stories to read during the warming-up process with a new group, or when a class is caught on a plateau of writing and needs a lift to a new level, or just for fun because children take such delight in them. Always we read for stimulation and enjoyment, *never* to make overt comparison or to present models to be copied.

The stories that follow are kinds we have found useful; they may serve as the beginning of a working collection. To facilitate reading, spelling has been corrected and punctuation added. A few obviously omitted words have been inserted in brackets.

° A MONKEY WITHOUT A TAIL

There was once a monkey that had no tail. His name was Burk and he lived in a forest.

He asked his mother, "Where can I get a tail?"

His mother said, "Go to Mr. Owl. He will tell you where to get one."

"Thank you," said Burk, and he went to Mr. Owl as fast as he could go.

225

Mr. Owl said, "Go to the Wishing Well and wish."

So Burk went to the Wishing Well. When Burk got there he wished. Then he waited and waited. Then Burk began to worry, but a low voice said, "What you are supposed to do now is to go home."

So Burk went home. He wanted to have a tail so he obeyed the voice. That night a litttle fairy came and gave Burk a tail.

In the morning Burk didn't see his tail, but his mother said, "Burk, I told you Mr. Owl would tell you where to get a tail."

Burk said, "Where is it? I didn't see it."

"Here it is.'"

Burk was so happy he forgot where he got his tail. He began to ask his mother, but then he remembered that Mr. Owl had told him to go to the Wishing Well. Then he stopped thinking. He went to Mr. Owl and said, "THANK YOU".

So Burk lived happily ever after.

A second-grade girl

* A GIRL THAT MAKES MEN INTO FOXES

Once there was a mean old girl. She liked to make men into foxes. Every man she sees she makes into foxes. She saw the biggest man and she made him into a little fox. Then she saw another man, and she made him into a fox. Then she met a boy and he killed the old girl and all the men came back to be men again.

A second-grade boy

* THE CAVE

Once there was a cave. It was a big one. It looks like some-one has been living in it. Somebody like a bear could live in it. Maybe a lion could live in it. Maybe one of those could live in the cave in the woods.

Then one day a little boy came to the cave. He walked right into the cave, and he was never seen again. Then one day a man looked all over for the cave but he could not find the cave.

Then the next day a man was taking a walk, and right before him was the cave. So the next day he went to the newspaper place. He told the newspaper people that he had found a lost cave. The newspaper people had the story in the newspaper.

The next day hundreds of people got around the cave. Then the cave disappeared just like that. Then all the people sued the man. The man did not have enough money to give everyone. Each day the man got a penny he had to give it to someone. Every day he got any money he had to give it to someone. Two weeks from then his aunt sent him some money but he had to give that money away, too. The next day he wrote a letter to send him some more money, so his aunt did send him some more money and he had to give that away, too, to some people. Soon he had enough money to pay all the people. And he could buy food for himself. He had so much money that he was rich and he never was poor again.

The End

A second-grade girl

* THE LION THAT TOOK OVER THE TOWN

One time there was a town that was quiet. Then the zoo bought a lion. He was king of the beasts. Then the lion broke loose. Everyone hid.

Then one man said to another, "What should we do? The police have hidden, so we should hide, too. So they did.

The lion saw where the two men hid. Then the lion went to the place where the two men hid. Then the lion opened his mouth. The two men thought they were dead ducks, and they were right. The lion did eat them up.

The town did not want to see the men die. A man said, "We should fire a cannon ball."

So they did, but they missed the lion and hit a tree.

Then a man said, "Let's get a machine gun." And so they did. And this time they got him, but the people did not believe he was dead. But a man went by the lion, and the lion did not

do anything. Then the people believed he was dead. Then everyone got out of their hiding places and went home.

A second-grade boy

* JIMMIE'S STICK

Jimmie had a little stick that was magic. And one day Jimmie
wanted a dime.

He said, "Hocus pocus, let me have a dime."

And that second he had a dime. And he said it over and
over again. And he got more and more money so that he can
have ice cream and soda and candy and cake and all good things
to eat. And he lived happy ever after.

A third-grade boy

*   *   *

There was a little bear. He did not have a name. People called
him names, and he punched them and sometimes he cried. And
he tried and tried to get a name. But he cannot. So he sat down
and he was thinking for days and soon he came to a name. It was
"Fire."

And a fox asked him, "What is your name?"

He said, "Fire."

The fox said, "I can't hear you."

So he called out, "FIRE."

So all the animals in the jungle came and wanted to put out
the fire.

His mother told four animals to come to the house. So they
came. They sat down thinking. The four of them had a name
and all of them had the same. The mother bear said to one, "Have
you got a name?"

He said, "Bee."

"No, no," said the mother bear. "That ain't a name." So little
bear started to cry.

Mother Bear said, "Little bear, do not cry. You can go out
if you like."

"I do not want to go out. All the animals will call me names."
So he named himself "Monkey."

So the same fox asked him, "Have you got a name?"

He said, "Yes, I have."

So the fox said, "What is it?"

He said, "Monkey."

So the fox called out, "Foxes, come here. This little bear's name is 'Monkey.'"

So all the foxes called out, "Oh, look at the monkey."

So he went home and told his mother and she named him "Tim" and he lived happy ever after.

*An eight-year-old boy**

❋   ❋   ❋

Buttercup Wilkins was a yellow cat, a really nice cat, but no one liked her. The other cats felt very uppity about her and never asked her to play with them. But Buttercup Wilkins didn't mind. She had fun by herself.

One day Priscilla Moore, a black cat with white paws, made some duckleberry jam. Duckleberry jam is a very extra-special good and she decided to have a party about it.

She said to the other cats, "Will you come to my house and play cards and have some of my duckleberry jam?"

They said, "Yes, but don't ask that Buttercup Wilkins."

"I won't," said Priscilla. "Come tomorrow at three."

But they didn't know that Buttercup Wilkins was hiding in the bushes beside them.

So the next afternoon Buttercup Wilkins watched the other cats go into the party. Then she slipped gently through the door into the pantry where the jam was. Without making a sound she quietly pawed out and ate every bit of that jam. She even put her nose in each jar and licked it shining.

Then Buttercup Wilkins slowly licked the jam from her face

* The boy who wrote this at the end of the third grade was burdened with the name "Bodo." His original copy consists of but two run-on sentences. As he read the tale his voice indicated the punctuation used here.

and paws. She carefully closed the door of the jam closet and, wearing a smile at the edge of her whiskers, she slipped past all the mean chattering cats whose noses were all so uppity they did not even see her.

A third-grade girl

❋ ❋ ❋

Bojo, the elephant, was talking to the man who ran the steam shovel. He wanted to take over his work for his lunch hour. He started to tell the man that he used to run a steam shovel himself. Of course it wasn't true.

"Well," said the man, "If you are sure you can do it—"

"Of course I can do it." Of course he was talking through his hat.

Then Bojo climbed into the steam shovel and began to pick the dirt. Suddenly the clutch flew back. He lost control of the steering wheel. The steam shovel turned over and Bojo was underneath.

Then the man came running. "Now look what you've done."

Bojo slowly got out of the pieces that used to be the steam shovel. The manager called the police. The police [came] with sirens ringing. The police grabbed Bojo. There was a barbed wire fence close by the policeman and Bojo gave him a big push into the fence.

The policeman shouted, "OW! My seat!"

Bojo ran away and Bojo never, never said that he could run a steam shovel again.

A third-grade girl

❋ WINDOW TROUBLE

Mo and Nig, the play detectives, were washing the windows of their house when they broke a window.

Nig said, "I think we had better get out of here."

"So do I," said Mo.

So Nig hid behind the water barrel and Mo climbed up the drain pipe only to find Mother Bear climbing up the other side.

"Here comes Mom," said Mo and he slid down the roof, BUT he forgot Nig! Down the drain pipe he went and right into Nig's lap.

"Nice landing," said Nig as Mo got up.

Just then Uncle Upper Bumper heard the noise. Around the corner came a big fat stomach, then a very little head and a big twenty-five gallon hat.

"Well," said Uncle Upper Bumper, "a fine mess! Two little bears nice and wet! I thought you were washing the windows."

"You think too much," said Nig very softly.

That was too much for Uncle Upper Bumper. He called Mrs. W. Y. L. P. Q. Bear to spank them.

Nig said, "Get us out of this, Detective Mo."

"Shut up! You know I can't," said Mo.

"Here comes Mom," said Nig softly.

"We were—er—washing the windows and we had a little trouble," said Mo. "Nig dropped the pail of water on my head and I fell and Nig slipped on the water that spilled."

"A very good story. Is it true?"

"Oh, yes," said the two bears.

"O.K., here's fifty cents to go to the movies."

In five minutes they were in sight of the movies. "I'm glad we got out of that one," said Nig.

Meanwhile at home—"This ought to fix them," said Mother Bear. "This is a new lie-detector machine."

Just then Uncle Upper Bumper came into the house. "What a nice chair," he said. (The chair was the lie-detector machine.) "And a very comfortable one at that."

Just then the two bears came in very tired and they went right upstairs and went to sleep.

A third-grade boy

* MUD AND TUD

Mud and Tud were two ducks that lived in Mrs. Hakelman's house in the ice box. They liked the cold spots. Mr. Hakelman is mayor of the town and is going to give a ball. Mrs. Hakelman has had to bake some cakes. She has laid them in the ice box on the second shelf down.

It happened to be that Mud and Tud were on the top shelf. Mud was holding Tud's hand. All of a sudden Mud slipped and they both went down. They landed right beside a huge cake which towered above them. It had three layers. Mud and Tud started to eat their way in. Luck was with them. The icing dripped down to cover the hole.

Mrs. Hakelman came home about four o'clock. "A-a-a-a-h, my cakes seem to be ready. Now to take them to the ball. Oh cook, oh cook! Oh, there you are. Take these cakes to the car."

Part Two: At the Ball

The thirteenth piece of cake was passed to Mrs. Bradley, the fattest lady in town. All of a sudden out jumped Mud and Tud. Mrs. Bradley SCREAMED.

A third-grade boy

* TAFFY TUGBOAT

Taffy Tugboat was in the dock when an ocean liner came in to dock in some fog and bumped Taffy Tugboat 'way under the dock. Taffy Tugboat was stuck. Taffy Tugboat tooted his whistle but nobody came to help him.

Now Taffy Tugboat was in a mess. He tugged and pulled but he could not get out. What would his master say? He would be very angry if he was not there to take him out to the big boats to pull them in.

He had to get out from under that dock. All of a sudden he heard two men coming over the dock. He tooted his whistle. The two men heard him. They were scared. They ran to the police. They said a big monster was under the dock in a very big rage and if he wasn't caught he would try to control the whole city.

The whole police department went to the dock very quietly and started to shoot at the dock. Taffy Tugboat was in a mess.

All of a sudden the shooting stopped. A man said he thought

that what they were shooting at was not a monster. It was his tug-boat and it *was his boat.* It was Taffy Tugboat.

A third-grade boy

* F U Z Z Y   G E T S   I N   T R O U B L E

Bang! Bang! Bang! There was an awful racket coming from the cellar. "Ow-w, my thumb!" Fuzzy and Billy Rabbit were making a wagon.

"Whew, thank goodness, that's done! Now let's play in it."

"Yes, let's coast down the hill by Mr. Snobbottom's house."

"O.K., but we won't be able to make any noise," said Fuzzy.

"Why not?"

"Because he'll bawl us out."

"Yeah, I guess so."

"Well, come on," said Fuzzy, pulling the wagon out of the yard. "Whee-e, boy is this fun? Hey, Billy, I can't steer."

"Help, we're going right into Mr. Snobbottom's yard," yelled Billy.

"Yes, and the drive's just been cemented."

"Get out of my new driveway," bawled Mr. Snobbottom.

"We can't," wailed Fuzzy.

"Why not?" yelled Mr. Snobbottom.

"Because we're stuck in the cement."

"Well, get out anyway. Walk off. You can get the wagon later," he yelled, "but get off my new driveway!"

"O.K.," said Billy, climbing out of the wagon. Fuzzy climbed out too.

"HELP!" yelled Fuzzy.

"Help!" echoed Billy.

"Oh, I can't walk. I'm cemented in," wailed Fuzzy.

"So'm I," cried Billy.

Then the front door opened and Mr. Snobbottom waddled out of the house, for he was very fat. "Well, why don't you take off your shoes?"

"O.K. Now we're stuck again."

"Well, take off your socks."

"I can't because they're wet," said Billy.

"Oh, I'll get them off for you," said Mr. Snobbottom, walking onto the cement. He had gone a few steps when he let out a yell. "HELP! I'm stuck too!" Then he forgot all about being scared and started bawling Fuzzy and Billy out. "I'll get the police on you if I have to use hounds."

"First you'll have to get a tow truck," said Fuzzy under his breath.

Now really Fuzzy and Billy were on a dry part of the driveway, but Mr. Snobbottom wasn't. So Fuzzy and Billy just walked away laughing.

BUT (a small word with a big meaning) the next day Mother Rabbit opened the door on a much battered-up cross man. "Mrs. Rabbit, I demand to take your son to the police."

"Why—what do you mean?" asked Mother Rabbit, a bit astonished.

"Just what I said," and he told the story.

BANG! The front door slammed in his face. He was so astonished he lay down and died; so that was the end of Mr. Snobbottom.

The End

A fourth-grade boy

* CLEAN HANDS AND A PURE HEART

Tommy Rabbit tried to sit down at the table without being noticed by his mother. But she saw him all right.

"Let me see them," she said.

Tommy showed her his right hand which was pretty clean.

"Now the other," she said.

He had to show her his left hand which had a big ink spot on it.

"Now, Tommy Rabbit," said his Mother, "you know better than to come to the table with hands like that, especially today when all the mothers are going to school for a program. You go right upstairs and wash them again."

Tommy went upstairs grumbling to himself about how silly grownups were about clean hands. While he was upstairs he got an idea. That bad little rabbit tip-toed into his mother's room and there was her hat and her gloves laid out for the program at school. Very quietly Tommy put a lot of black powder from his chemistry set into each glove. Then he washed his hands and went downstairs.

After lunch Mrs. Rabbit put on her hat and pulled on her gloves and started off with Tommy. While they were walking along, Tommy picked up some stones and a piece of dirty string and in no time his hands were dirty again. Of course, Mrs. Rabbit had to notice that.

"Tommy," she said, "you will be the death of me. Look at your hands."

"Oh, well, Mother," said Tommy, "boys always have dirty hands."

"No," said Mrs. Rabbit, "your father never had dirty hands and anyway I always say, 'Clean hands and a pure heart.' I am very careful to see that MY hands are always clean." When she said this Tommy began to cough and look up at the sky.

When they got to the school, Miss Fluffy, the teacher, came out to meet all the mothers. Mrs. Rabbit pulled off her glove as she shook hands with Miss Fluffy. Of course her hand was black with powder and in a minute so was Miss Fluffy's. Neither of them noticed it because they were so busy shaking hands with the other mothers.

Suddenly Mrs. Rabbit looked down at her black paws.

"Oh, my heavens," she said and fainted.

When she came to, Tommy said, "You had better go right upstairs and wash your hands, Mother. How about clean hands and a pure heart?"

And from that day Mrs. Rabbit was never quite so fussy about Tommy's dirty hands.

A fourth-grade boy

* SPANKED TOO MANY TIMES

"Goodbye, Mother," said the five bears. They were going away to Grandma's farm.

The five bears got on the train and waved until the train was out of sight. Then Mother Bear went into the station to send a telegram to Grandma. Mr. Brown the telegraph man was a very good friend of Mother Bear.

"Hello, Mr. Brown," said Mother Bear. "Nice morning, isn't it."

"Yep," said Mr. Brown.

"Can I send a telegram now?" said Mother Bear.

"Yep," said Mr. Brown.

This is what Mother Bear said in the telegram:

DEAR MOTHER,

I AM SENDING MY FIVE LITTLE CHILDREN. I HOPE THEY'RE GOING TO HAVE A NICE TIME.

YOUR LOVING DAUGHTER

ANNABELLE

R.S.V.P.

Mother Bear said to Mr. Brown, "Can I wait for the answer?"

"Yep," said Mr. Brown.

The answer came and this what it said: "OH NO!—MOTHER."

Mr. Brown giggled. "I have a feeling they're going to be home pretty soon."

But up on Grandma's farm we find our five heroes having to have a pail of water thrown on their seats. "I'll get even with Grandma for this," said Nig.

Later we find them toasting marshmallows twenty years old that Grandma's husband gave her as an only wedding present. Grandma was shopping, but not for long because she had met Reverend Jones running down the street toward the fire station.

"What's wrong?" said Grandma.

"My prize rosebush is on fire."

With that Grandma knew something was very wrong. She hurried home to find nobody there. But when she got out in the backyard she could hardly keep herself from screaming. Her best sheet was on fire. The Bears didn't know she was there. But they did when she took them by the ears and reddened their seats.

A few hours later they were home and taking turns sliding down the rain pipe into the water barrel.

"You and your Big Ideas," said Mo to Nig.

Splash—Blub—Blub.

A fourth-grade girl

* CALIFORNIA OR BUST

One summer morning Eenie, Meenie, Meinie, Mo, and Nig started out. Each had a bundle under their arm. Nig was the last. On his back hung a sign, "California or Bust." As they went along a tribe of Indians came down the hill. Nig was last and an Indian caught him and took him home to the tribe. They put him in a big pot. They were just ready to cook him when there was a big noise. The Bears had put a jazz record on the victrola and were playing it full blast. The Indians went over to see what the noise was. Meanwhile the bears untied Nig.

Meanwhile at home Mother Bear said, "Such peace and quiet without those pesty bears."

The next morning Mother Bear went into Eenie, Meenie, Meinie, Mo, and Nig's room. She almost fainted. There in bed were Eenie, Meenie, Meinie, Mo and Nig. On the bed hung a sign:

"WE BUSTED!"

A fourth-grade girl

* MOTHER'S DAY

It was Mother's Day in Bearville and the Five Bears were looking in the dictionary to see if they could find something to give Mother Bear for a Mother's Day present.

Just then Mo interrupted, "Why don't we earn some money and get her that perfume she wanted."

"Oh, you mean that stuff that smells like gas poisoning?" said Nig.

"Well, I guess that's what you call it."

"O.K. We'll go to the grocery store and see if we can deliver groceries."

"Let's go!"

At The Grocery Store

"Hey, Mister," said Eenie, "we want a job."

"O.K. Here, take these to Mrs. Bottom-Puss at 44 Killiver Lane.

At Mrs. R.F.D.'s House

"Come in, you darling boys. It was so nice of you to bring my groceries. Here you can each have a candy bar."

Just then the clock struck six.

"Oh! We better go home. We were meant to be home a long time ago!"

At home a robber was stealing Mother Bear's best china. Just then the Five Bears walked in. Nig grabbed his B-B gun and shot the robber.

"My heroes!" said Mother Bear. And Nig got rewarded.

A fourth-grade girl

❋ ❋ ❋

Wham! went the door of the Bear home. "Ma," cried Nig and Mo together. "Ma, can we have the living room for our club?"

"Well—" said Mother Bear.

"*Please*, Mom."

"Well—all right."

"Yippy," cried Mo and Nig. "Let's tell the gang."

Next day the five bears were decorating the living room. Nig and Mo were giving orders. In two more days the living room was a sight. The wallpaper had been peeled off and in its place were crayon Indians drawn by Mo. The drapes had been pulled together and the room was very dark. The carpets had been rolled up and sheets had been put in their place. All the tables and chairs in the house were put in rows and Eenie was getting the gang together.

All this time Father Bear was away (Thank goodness!). But the *day* the first meeting was to be held was the day Father was to come home. Father opened the door of his home to find the living room in the sight it was. Father grabbed all five bears BUT Mother Bear saved the bears from a sore seat that night by telling Father. *And* Father saved the bears from another sore seat. Because if Mother had heard what kind of a club the Bears were running, she would have spanked them.

P.S. The bears were talking about cookies and cake and ice cream. (at the club meeting) They were going to take them from Mother Bear. She was making them for the County Bazaar.

A fourth-grade pupil

° STARRY LIGHT-UP

Now Starry Light-Up was a little star that lived in the town, Invisaville. One night, he and his brother, Mego, were shining down on a meadow when Starry spoke up and said, "I wonder if Mom and Pop are awake, yet."

"No, I doubt it. They never are awake this early. Then why don't we go to the moon?"

"Excellent idea," exclaimed Mego, "but what about Mom and Pop?"

"Oh, they'll never guess we went there."

So, off they flew, gaining more speed as they flew. And in a whoosh they were on the moon.

"Wow, it's windy," Starry said.

He was only one foot three inches high and weighed only seven pounds, which was underweight for a star of seven years. So he was blown into a gravity pit which held three times as much gravity as there is in the earth. (The moon really doesn't have that much gravity.) What will Starry do? Mego has fallen into one, too. Fortunately, Starry knew how to use wind. He blew as hard as he could upward. He started falling up. It was working. Soon he was out and told Mego to do the same. Both boys had starchutes. They were like parachutes. But it was so windy that the starchutes blew away and they forgot all about them.

For an hour or two they were hunting for rocks to take home when suddenly, from out of the rocks, came something. Starry shouted to Mego, the expert on Nature, but it was only a rock lizard which were very common. Then Starry noticed that they had no starchutes and told that to Mego. They decided to shoot. This was very difficult, and they hit Earth. Mom and Pop were still asleep. It must have been strange to see stars in the daytime. They had to shoot again. This time they hit Rockway, a village far from Invisaville. Again they shot and landed right on their house on the chimney and slid right down with a big thump. All this awoke Mom and Pop. If you ever see marks of a shooting star in the daytime, you'll know it's Starry and Mego.

A fourth-grade girl

* NIG'S NOT THE ONLY TOUGHIE

The five bears were playing checkers on their father's red and black fishing jacket. All of a sudden there was such a big roar you would think it was all the earthquakes in the world put together. Suddenly Paddy, their father, came barging into the room with his fishing pole in his hands. In a few minutes there was a broken fishing pole and five sore seats.

The next day Miss Grump, their teacher, told the children to put their tables in test position for a reading study hall. After ten minutes the teacher got discouraged at the five bears and said, "SIT DOWN, for heaven's sakes."

The five bears said all together, "We can't."

"Why not?" asked the teacher.

"Because we don't have anything to cover our seats with so they won't sting when we do," they said.

After school the five bears went down to the penny bubble gum store where they were to meet rich Aunt Ethel and her very naughty boy named Brownie.

"I ain't gonna go," said Nig.

"Why not?" said Mo.

"Dat kid is gonna break my record," said Nig.

"How?" asked Eenie.

"He's tougher'n me!" said Nig.

At the penny bubble gum store we find four bears screaming with laughter while we find one bear screaming with pains from the seventy hundred millionth hair on his head to the last fraction of an inch on his toe nails.

Later we find out why Nig didn't want to meet his cousin. Nig was crying because a tornado had just hit his room. Brownie, his tough cousin, had beaten him up. Now Nig knew just what Mo hated.

The End

A fourth-grade girl

* STARRING HORNY HORNET
IN
RELATIVE TROUBLE

One day Horny Hornet was flying along and all of a sudden to his surprise it was his cousin, Wilbur Warbler, who probably ran away from home because his mother never let him out of the house.

Horny was surprised. "Hey—what are you doing here?"

"Yipes!" Wilbur turned around and flew as fast as he could. Something white fell from his tail feathers.

Wilbur was wanted by the police because he ran away from home. Horny buzzed as fast as he could and "Ouch!" Wilbur zoomed—crash!—right through his bedroom window.

Horny got a beautiful wool stinger-cover for a reward.

A fourth-grade boy

* DANNY WOODCHUCK

Once upon a time there lived a little woodchuck named Danny. It was winter, and all little woodchucks were very fast asleep and the winds were cold and sent a whisk of winter cold through Danny's door and made him shiver in his winter blankets.

Funny enough, he started to yawn and woke up and stared all around him because a witch in his dream was about to eat him up. But remembering his house he laughed, but the cold wind broke his laugh and he remembered it was winter and crawled to the door. Sure enough, there was snow on the earth everywhere.

He said, "I have never seen snow. It looks like white frosting"—and so he ate some birch bark, jumped in some clothes, and went out the door.

Before you knew it, he bumped into Mr. Squirrel and WHOO-OOOOOOOO SMACK! A landslide of snow came down on him.

Finally he got out and walked home and from that day on he had to take sleeping pills!

A fourth-grade boy

* MAC-THE-WORM STORIES

One day Mac got tired of mowing the lawn, and so, after ten hours of sweating he said, "I will build a robot."

And as you came by his apple-born house, you would hear a rat-a-tat-tat and a bang-bang.

That afternoon Mac came out with a robot who could cut the grass for him. At three o'clock he took it for a trial run. B-r-r-r-r-rm! Crash, boom! The race is on. Z-z-z-z-z-z. It went right through the hedge. Pow—right through Mr. Talk-a-lot's apple. Z-z-z-z-z-z. It crashed right into a police car.

Just then a policeman came out and said, "Get this contraption out of here."

Poor Mac had to go to prison for the rest of his life, but that's not the end of his stories 'cause there's another old worm in prison named Charlie Hill and every day Mac dictates to him.

The End

* * *

One fine morning, Mac said to himself, "I need a vacation."

So Mac-the-Worm called the airport. Yes, there was a plane leaving for Florida in just six hours. Mac packed in a hurry. When he got to the airport, some men took his baggage. Then he plopped down on a seat to rest.

After four hours there was a great commotion. It startled Mac. Mac got up and went to the window of the plane. Then someone shouted "Plane buzzards! Plane buzzards!"

Now if you don't know what plane buzzards are, you rightly

now should know. They're giant ropelike birds. Then Mac heard, "Get the guns! Get the guns!"

Pow, pow, pow, pow! BANG!

"Bye, bye, Bud—er—I mean Buzzards," said Mac.

But one of the bullets had hit the only good propeller. Mac cleared his throat, and said, "Er—bye-bye to me, with tears!"

Mac jumped off the falling plane, but he forgot he had a parachute on. Mac was relieved. But he also saw an island below. Then Mac saw a cannibal. When he landed, lots of cannibals were around. Poor Mac!

Mac got taken to a big pot. "Not me," he grunted. "Worm stew!"

But the cannibals let him go. Mac saw a boat with a motor. He ran, jumped in the boat, and put-putted away. Soon he saw a tugboat coming.

The captain said, "I'll take you ashore, young feller."

So Mac got home and said, "I lost my clothes, but I had an exciting trip." And he fell fast asleep.

The End

A fourth-grade boy

❋ ❋ ❋

One day (his room looked very gloomy) Joey Bear said to Moey Bear, "Let's go swimming."

"But Mommy said—"

"Aw 'fraid cat! I don't care what she said. I'm going to swim."

"Oh, you are, are you?" said Mother Bear as she walked in the door.

Two minutes later Joey Bear was wishing he hadn't talked to Moey. Then he had a bright idea (he thought). He went into his closet, rummaged around in the junk until he found the rope to his cowboy suit. Then he tied it to the radiator just inside the window. He let down the rope very carefully. Then he made sure the knot was tight enough. He looked down. Suddenly it looked very far to the ground but he just had to do it. He was halfway down the rope when there was a distinguished squeak from the front door. Joey saw to his horror that it was Aunt Brown Bear. He moved very fast. As he went past the hall window he saw something which made him panic-stricken because he saw Mother Bear *going into his room!* And a few strands of the old rope were broken and he was slipping.

Just then the last of the rope gave way and he fell right on his aunt's new porcupine quill hat. "Yow-ow-ow! My seat! Ow-ow! Jeepers, it hurts. I give up," Joey cried.

Mother Bear came out. "I am going to give you something you deserve," she said.

"No—no—not the hair brush?"

"No, you've learned your lesson. I'm going to give you a new cowboy rope."

The End

A fourth-grade boy

* WASH DAY

"Children," said Mother Bear, "today is Monday and a holiday from school—and now," she said in a low tone with a little gleam in her eye, "you can do some washing. Wash day, you know—YOUR WASH DAY."

The five bears slowly, inch by inch, got up from the dinner table, but in the wink of an eye Mother Bear caught them by their big floppy ears and dropped them one by one ker-splash into the tub.

A fifth-grade boy

*   *   *

"Children, I have a treat for you," said Miss Flower, the bears' teacher, "a special treat."

"What is it?" asked the class in chorus. "Is it ice cream and cake?"

"Oh no, much better than that," said the teacher. "Miss Brown—she is one of the teachers in a western university—she has come to see how boys and girls act."

Miss Brown smiled and began to speak. "I love to come and

visit schools and see the boys and girls. You remind me of my childhood. I teach older boys and girls, but they are almost grown-up while you are just beginning life. How I envy Miss Flower, your beloved teacher, for she has you with her every day."

Miss Flower was very jealous of Miss Brown, but she hid her own feeling and offered Miss Brown her chair. She didn't know that Nig had put a tack in the chair. Miss Brown sat down. Miss Brown got up rather fast and started for the door.

"I never did like children," she said as she started through the door.

"You shouldn't have done that, children," said Miss Flower, but she gave them each ten cents to buy a Good Humor with.

A fifth-grade girl

* THE PORKVILLE ARMY

"Left, left, halt." There was a moment of confusion and the Porkville Army came to a halt.

"Now we'll have roll call," said Tit, who was the general. "Ezra Squirrel?"

"Here."

"Tat?"

"Here."

"Toe?" There was no answer. "Well, what are you waiting for?" shouted Tit. "Go and find him."

In a minute the whole of Porkville was in a hubbub, but Toe couldn't be found. After the army got reassembled Tit screamed, "Well, where is he?" Then he sent them off a second time and retired to his tent.

Very soon a little pink head appeared from behind a crate of turnips and quickly disappeared again as a mud ball hit the wall above him. When the army got to the crate there was nothing but a hole in the turnip crate and a lot of footprints. Meanwhile the body that owned the little pink head was running hastily to the Porkville Army headquarters, where Tit sat lazily chewing a stick of molasses candy. The little pink head and body, in other words Toe, began quietly to cut a hole in the back of the tent. A minute later when Tit reached down to the molasses box he couldn't find anything. Two minutes later he was struggling to get out of a fallen-down tent.

"Let me out of here. Help. Splutter," he mumbled.

A peal of laughter came from outside the tent, but shortly it turned into angry squeals for the Porkville Army had come back.

"Livingston, I presume," said Nig as he entered Tit's tent.

"Yeah," said Tit, kicking Nig into the empty molasses box.

"Whee," said Nig as he went whizzing through the air, "now for a three-point landing."

Crash! Nig had got stuck in the molasses box. "Blubbity blub," was the only thing Tit could hear. Then Nig shouted, "Let me out of here! Why, I'll sue you for this."

"All right. I challenge you warmly. You can go home now," said Tit to Nig, whose head was still stuck in the molasses box.

Next morning Tit and his army were getting ready for the fight with wooden swords and mud balls. Then Tit gave his last orders and saw that Toe was well-guarded. Just then over the hill crest came Nig and his twenty Rough Riders, and with this army came marching a flag. From the flag came a voice saying, "But, Nig—"

"Shut up!" came the reply. But Mo, who was the flag bearer could not finish his sentence because a mud ball found its mark.

"Men," said Nig, "there is the enemy. Are you scared of a little mud? Why look at me. I'm facing—"

Spleosh, oo, blub, splutter.

After wiping the mud off his face, Nig, under a small cloud of swearing began his speech again. With a big, confident smile he said, "Everybody who's with me say 'yah.'"

A hushed silence came over the army of bears huddled closely together. Nig's smile became almost invisible. Then he shouted, "Charge!"

Alone he rushed forward. Before he could do anything the army of pigs was upon him. There was a splash, a splosh, and a hollow-sounding bong as a wooden sword hit a bear's head.

The bears did not wait to see what happened to their general, Nig, but retreated with the flag straggling after. There was a gust of wind as Nig passed them, doing what he called "covering the retreat."

A fifth-grade boy

✿   ✿   ✿

The five little bears were in school one afternoon. "Now," said the teacher, "I will tell you something. On your way home will you hunt for signs of spring?"

Nig shot a bean out of his beanshooter.

"Ouch! Oh-h-h!" said the teacher.

"That's a sign of spring," said Nig.

"You're dismissed," the teacher said.

"Good!" said all the bears except Mo.

The next day the bears went to school bright and early. But Nig decided to play hooky. He sneaked away from the other bears.

"I hope," said Mo, "that we won't be late.

"Come on. Let's run or we will be," said the other bears.

When they got to school the teacher asked if they had seen any signs of spring. Meenie raised his hand and said, "I was digging and I found a worm and it was growing pink."

"No, Meenie-a-I-er-a don't think that's a very good sign of spring," said the teacher.

"You don't say so," said Meenie. "Why, where is Nig?"

The teacher said surprised, "Huh?"

The bears said, "I guess he must have played hooky, don't you?"

"Yes I do," said the teacher. "Eenie, Meenie, Meinie, and Mo, go out and find Nig."

"All right," they said. They went outdoors and saw a truck.

"I'll tell you what let's do," Eenie said. "Let's get up in the truck and ride all over town and maybe we will find Nig."

"I see," the other bears said.

They got up in the truck and lay down as flat as they could. Mo whimpered a little after they were on the way. "Oh, stop your crying and look," said Eenie.

They finally saw a little ash can walking around on two brown fat, chubby bear legs.

"I think that I see Nig," said Eenie.

"Where?" the other bears said.

"Over there," he pointed to the ash can. The bears tumbled out of the truck. "Oh dear—oh dear—oh dear!" they said. They ran over to Nig. "Hey, you've got to go home."

They pulled off the ash can. Nig did not want to go home. The four little bears pulled and pulled. They got Nig home. About an hour later Nig was rubbing his seat. The other little bears were eating a nice piece of cherry pie. "Um-m-m—" they were saying when they got to bed.

A fifth-grade boy

* MO'S NEW COAT

"Nig," called Mother Bear, "come here and bring Mo."

In came Nig, dragging Mo by the ear, but he let go when he saw Mother Bear, and held him gently by the hand.

"Why are you crying so, Mo dear?" asked Mother Bear.

"Oh," said Mo, sniffling and holding his ear, "—er—" Just then he saw Nig with his fist in fighting form. "—er—nothing, Mother."

"Well, I want you, Nig," said Mother Bear, raising her voice for she saw Nig sticking his finger in the sugar bowl.

Nig turned around and started twiddling his sticky thumbs angelically. "Yes, Mother," he said.

"I want you," repeated Mother Bear, "to go with Mo and get him a new coat. Be sure to see that it fits well. I'm too busy to go. Please be back quickly," she added, jerking Nig's finger out of the sugar bowl again. "And charge it," she said, pushing them out. "Goodbye. Oh, if there ever was the likes of them. Whew!"

Meanwhile at the store Nig was trying coats on Mo. He took the biggest one. "This will fit you nicely, Mo darling," he said, and he wrapped it on Mo. He told the man their address and left.

"But, Niggy dear," said Mo, "it's too big. Mother said I should have a size thirteen and you've got size forty."

"Aren't you satisfied?" said Nig, showing his fist.

"Why—er—yes, Niggy, I am," said Mo trembling. "Y-y-yes, sh-sh-sure I a-am."

"Come on then," said Nig roughly. "We'll never get home if you don't hurry."

Ding, ding.

"Why, hello, Nig," said Mother, "where's Mo?"

"There," said Nig, pointing to a large coat with two legs sticking out. "There he is."

"Oh," said Mother sternly, "is that Mo's new coat?"

"Yes," said Nig backing away, "that's Mo's new coat."

"Well, young bear," said Mother, taking Nig over her knee, "you can march right back to the store and get the coat changed and no allowance for you this week."

Five minutes later a bedraggled bear started off in the direction of the coat store, holding a coat and his seat.

A fifth-grade girl

° NIG SHOWS OFF DAISY MAY

The bears were coming home from school. Nig was running so fast that the other bears had a hard time keeping up with him. Now this was very unusual for Nig, for he always dallied on the way, stopping at the baseball field to bat a few balls. But today he hurried; no one knew why. But Eenie suspected that he had a date with Susie Bear.

When they got home Nig ran up to Mother Bear's room. The other bears followed him because they wanted to know where he was going. When they got up to the room Nig was talking breathlessly.

"There's a new girl in school called Elizabeth Ann, and I am going over to see her this afternoon, and bring Daisy May for she wants me to."

"Well, all right," said Mother Bear. "Wrap her up warmly in a blanket and you will have to dress her."

"So he is going over to see Elizabeth Ann," thought Mo, "and show her Daisy May, and I wanted to. Well, I'll fix him." Then Mo said in a very sweet voice, "Let me dress her for you."

"Oh, all right. Put on her best dress and her best coat and hat and put her in her new carriage and put on her new blanket."

With these instructions Nig straightened his tie and combed his hair while Mo went to fix Daisy May. Ten minutes later Mo wheeled Daisy May's carriage into the living room where Nig was.

"Don't pull the hood up," said Mo, "for she is asleep."

"All right," said Nig. Taking the handle of the carriage in one hand and his father's cane in the other he started over to Elizabeth's. When he got there Elizabeth ran down to meet him.

"Oh, let me see Daisy May!"

"Why, Nig, you deceitful thing. Don't you think I can tell the difference between a person and a doll? You are teasing, you mean thing!" With that she went into the house and Nig was left with the doll.

That night at supper, Mo had a black eye and Nig had a warm seat.

A fifth-grade boy

* THE FIVE BEARS START AN ORCHESTRA

One day the five bears decided to start an orchestra. Mo was to the play the drum. He couldn't quite reach the top, but he had talent. They discovered it one time when Nig was fighting Mo, and Mo started pounding on his back. Meinie played the tuba. He did it 'cause it hid him, and if he struck a sour note, nobody would know who did it. Meenie played the flute 'cause he knew Joy Bear was coming, and she could see him easily with the flute. Eenie played the violin. When he was small he had swallowed a toy whistle; so he said he wouldn't mind the squeaks. Nig had the bass violin 'cause he liked to take up a lot of room to be noticed.

One day their school decided to put on an amateur hour, and the bears decided to enter their orchestra. Finally the great day arrived and they were very much excited. They just got there in time.

"Ladies and gentlemen, and contestants, we present to you tonight Major Blows, who is to judge our contest. The first contestants are Eenie, Meenie, Meinie, Mo, and Nig Bear, who have an orchestra."

They all took their places and began. Mo and Nig started a piece called "Thunder," while the rest played a piece called

"Twinkling Stars." The discord was enough to blow everybody out of the auditorium. They finally finished quickly and took their seats. At the end everyone was supposed to clap for the best, but when the orchestra went on the stage, nobody made a sound.

"Aw gee," said Nig, "nobody appreciates good music."

A fifth-grade girl

* TALL, MIDDLE-SIZE, AND SMALL

Once upon a time in a little house lived three otters. They lived with their mother and father (of course). The tallest otter's name was Tall; the middle-sized otter's name was Middle-Size; the little wee otter's name was—What do you think it was?— Small!

One day Tall, Middle-Size, and Small said to their mother, "Mother," said Tall.

"Mother," said Middle-Size.

"Mama," said Small in his small wee voice.

"Mother," they said all together, "Mother, we are going to do something, but we can't think what it is. What are we going to do?" they asked.

"Why, don't you know? You are going to the fair with your father and me."

"Oh, yes, yes, yes! Now we know," they cried.

"Now we know! Now we know! Now we know!" repeated Small.

"Oh, shut up," said Tall, "or it will be the worse for you." Small began to whimper but brightened up at the promise of an ice cream from his mother.

"You spoil him," said Tall who was just like his father.

"What's that about spoiling somebody?" came a cheery voice.

"Oh, nothing," said Tall grumpily. "She's just spoiling Small just 'cause he's the littlest."

"Well, Oscar, after all he IS the littlest and—" said Mrs. Otter.

"I know, Ophelia," said Mr. Otter "but you shouldn't baby him."

"Well, why shouldn't I? After all, he's our smallest child—"

"Well, why don't you do something about it? Why don't you give birth to another baby otter? That's an idea!"

"That's an idea! I'll do it. I'll have another baby."

"She'll have another baby," echoed Small.

"Oh, hush up," said Tall.

* CHAPTER TWO: THE BABY'S ARRIVAL

When it came, it was a girl and on the day of its arrival the mother called the children into her room. When all were assembled (even the father), the mother said, "Now children, what shall we call the baby?" Silence . . . "Well?"

"We're thinking." More silence.

Then from Tall, "We could call it Ophelia after you, Mother."

"And call her Ophy for short," put in Middle-Size and then he giggled. "Can you tell why?"

Then Small said, "We could call her Small Junior after *me*."

"Who would want to name anything after *you*? You're the smallest." Tall is speaking.

"I'm the smallest," echoed Small regretfully.

But then Mother said, "Not any more, sugar plum. That little girl in the cradle is the smallest *now*. But come, can't anybody think of a better name than Ophelia or Small Junior? Papa, can you think of anything?"

"Why not call her Tiny? That's a good name."

"Yes, yes," said everybody, "let's call her Tiny."

"Let's call her Tiny," echoed Small but nobody said, "Hush up," this time.

* CHAPTER THREE: GOING TO THE FAIR

Coming to the fair had to be delayed a few weeks 'til the baby should be able to sit up in the baby carriage. But animals grow very fast and Tiny was no exception. So in a few weeks Tiny could walk, a little wobbly perhaps, but still she could walk.

So one sunny morning they started out for the fair. As soon as Tiny was tired, Mr. Otter picked her up and carried her. It was plain that Tiny was Mr. Otter's favorite for nobody likes to have all boys however nice they may be. After all, one likes to have at least one of a different sex.

Finally they reached the fairgrounds. Small shrieked with delight when he saw the Ferris wheel. Tall and Middle-Size acted more grown-up than Small but they were pleased nevertheless. Tiny could not go on the ferris wheel as she was still a baby but she did not seem to know what she was missing and gurgled and cooed all the time.

When Tall, Middle-Size and Small came down from the Ferris wheel, they all went to the merry-go-round. Small and Tiny wanted to try it immediately but Tall and Middle-Size said, "Ach, such babies to ride on a merry-go-round."

But Small and Tiny didn't mind. Indeed, Tiny *could* not understand a word they said as she was only a few weeks old.

All afternoon they gorged themselves on hot dogs and soda pop and ice creams—that is, all except Tiny. *Her* diet was limited to one ice cream and a glass of orange juice.

What a happy afternoon they had! And when it was all over and they were riding home in the wagon, Small said, "Gee, we had fun!"

The End

A fifth-grade girl

* SMALL GETS A HAIRCUT

"Why does everything have to happen to me?" Small sighed. "Huh! I don't need a haircut anyway. Women are so silly, always thinking little boys need haircuts. Well, here I am. Should I go in or should I stay out? Oh, I might as well go in—but—Oh, I'll go in."

He walked slowly into George Goat's barbershop. "I want a crow-cut," he announced.

"Don't you mean a crew cut?" asked the attendant.

"No," said Small, "I mean a crow cut. Just like the crows wear."

The attendant finally got Small settled in the barber's chair. "Now you say you want a crew cut," he began.

"A crow cut," said Small firmly.

"But—but there isn't any such thing as a crow cut," said the bewildered attendant.

"I don't care," said Small; "I want one anyway."

The attendant said he'd try and was just about to put the sheet about Small's neck when Small suddenly said, "I don't need a bib. Watcha putting a bib on me for?"

The attendant's pride was hurt. "Young man," he said sternly, "this is not a bib. It is merely a sheet to keep the hair off your clean suit—"

"Tain't clean," said Small sullenly.

"So you won't get it dirty," continued the attendant.

"Don't care if I do get it dirty," pouted Small.

"Now *will* you sit still?" asked the attendant impatiently, after a vain attempt to cut Small's hair straight.

"Why?" asked Small impishly.

"Because," said the attendant, "if you don't I won't be able to cut your hair straight and then you won't look nice."

"Don't wanna look nice," said Small. "Wanna go home."

"Go home then," said the angry attendant.

"All right, I will," and Small stomped out of the barber shop, the soap suds all over his head.

A fifth-grade boy

* THE FIVE BEARS GO DAISY PICKING

"Oh gee," said Mo, "I wish there was something to do."

"You can come and look at the postman with me," said Nig, who was perched in the window and staring at the postman. "He's coming up our front walk now."

Ding, ding. The doorbell rang.

"I hope he has something for us," said Eenie as he ran over to the door.

"Yere's a letter for ye boys," said the postman as he busily chewed his tobacco.

"Looks like it's from Sue Bear's house. Hey, look, it's an invitation to a-a-a-aoh-h—" Eenie collapsed.

"Read it, Nig," said Mo excitedly. "What's it say?"

"We're invited to a—oh, my gosh—to a daisy-picking party."

"Oh-h," they all moaned, "I've got a stomach ache," and they all dashed upstairs, that is all but Mo. He stopped to look at the invitation.

"Golly, of all the stupid things to ask he-men like us to go to. I—Gee, what's this? Refreshments will be served. Golly, I'm going."

* CHAPTER TWO

"Now children," warned Mrs. Bear, "don't go near the railroad tracks."

"We won't," and then they all started picking. After about half an hour Mo spied a wonderful, big daisy a few inches away from the tracks. He quickly ran over and looked down the tracks. Then he stooped over. A train from the other direction came speeding down, and the cow-catcher caught Mo right in the seat of his pants.

"E-e-e-e-K," squeaked Sue. "Mo's cowed on the caughtcatcher —I mean catched on the cowcaught—I mean— E-e-ek! Look!"

As Mrs. Bear turned she just saw a quick glance of Mo speeding around the corner.

* CHAPTER THREE

It was a peaceful day for the three bulls in Farmer Brown's field as they stood there munching grass. Soon the four-o'clock train came roaring down the tracks. They all stopped and looked. Suddenly a brown and red thing flew off and landed a few feet from them. (Mo's best suit was bright red.)

"RED!" they roared and went flying towards poor Mo.

"Ah-h" he thought, "there's a place I can get through."

He started running, but there before him loomed the biggest person he had ever seen. It was Farmer Brown's daughter, who was known all over the country for her bigness and also her affection.

"Oh, oo toot wittle fing," she cried, "is oo wunning from da big, naughty bulls?" And she stood there with her arms waiting to clasp Mo.

"Oh, golly," said Mo, "I'm stuck."

An unfinished story
by a sixth-grade boy

* MORNING EXERCISES

It was five o'clock in the Bear house. Nig was tuning in his radio.

"This is Station XQZV calling all of Professor Getemup Gush's members to the Exercise Club."

"Now, members," the professor said, "jump out of bed and stretch."

Nig jumped out of bed and stretched.

"Now bend down and touch your toes," he went on. "Now stand on your bed and touch the ceiling."

Nig climbed up to the bunk above his. There he stood up and touched the ceiling. As he was coming down, he put his foot on what he thought was the ladder. Instead he stepped on some fuzzy, furry stuff. He looked down and saw a man.

"It's a robber," he thought, and fell back on the bed in a daze. On the wall hung his cork gun. He reached for it. Just when he was about to hit the bad man with it, the professor on the radio said, "Put up your hands."

The man put up his hands, and Nig reached down and shut off the radio. Then he hit the man over the head with his cork gun and yelled, "Get out of here, you bad man!"

The gun broke, and the man looked up. Nig looked down.

"Ow!" he exclaimed, for the man was Nig's father. Nig didn't know what else to say and so he didn't say anything. Then Nig remembered. It was like this. Father Bear was getting too fat, and so he had told Nig the day before that he would do exercises with him. Meanwhile Nig had forgotten.

"Nig!" said Father Bear.

Nig hardly breathed. It was sure to be either castor oil or a spanking; maybe both.

"Nig," his father repeated, "you'd make a mighty good watchman. Here's twenty cents for a new cork gun."

A sixth-grade girl

* EAU DE COLOGNE

"One more tack," said Nig to Mo. "When we get this sign up our luck begins."

Nig was pasting a sign on the door. It read:

Classical Beauty Parlor

Mud Packs		Hand Permanents
	Manicures	
Haircuts		Back Massage
	Children Only 3¢ to 13¢	

The five bears had decided that they would have a beauty parlor and get rich. They had fixed up the attic. In it was a bucket of mud, a bucket full of water, four chairs, Eenie's toy cash-register bank, which was on top of the bookcase which had three or four Mickey Mouse magazines on it, a copy of Red Riding Hood, Grimm's Fairy Tales with three pages out, a funny page from the Saturday paper, a Big-Little book, and a cupboard, which contained miscellaneous things such as water paints and bobby pins. The last had come from Mother's room, and there was a table with a vase which had some withered daisies which Mo had contributed. The beauty specialists were in the attic when the bell rang. Nig opened it with a bow. There stood Ann Bear.

"Are you the manager of the beauty parlor?" she said.

"Yes," said Nig, guessing that he was.

"Well," said Ann Bear, "I want a mud pack, please. Where shall I go?"

"Er—uh, right upstairs. Follow me," said Nig. "Here we are," he said as they came to the attic. "Sit right down, please. Hey, Meenie, how do you give a mud pack, anyhow?"

"I don't know," answered Meenie.

"'Well, I guess you just put mud on a person's face. Yeah—well here I go. Now, Madam," said Nig, "please sit back."

He picked up a rag, dipped it in the mud, and washed Ann's face with it.

"There," said Nig. "Four cents please."

"But you're not finished," said Ann Bear, "you have to wash it off."

"Why," said Nig, "our sign didn't say so. It says MUD PACKS. It didn't say a thing about washing it off, but since you're so unhappy about it I will take it off for one cent."

"Oh, all right," said Ann, who had been wondering what she was going to do. Nig got another rag, dipped it in the water, and washed it off. Nig thought it was a perfect job, but he did not see how Ann's yellow fur was still striped with brown.

"Well," said Ann, "here's your five cents. Goodbye."

As soon as Ann had gone Eenie said, "Nig, it's my turn now."

"O.K.," said Nig, "you can take care of the next customer, but" he warned, "do it good."

Eenie had just mumbled something under his breath about he wasn't so hot when the doorbell rang. Eenie slid down the bannisters and opened the door. "Why," he said, "it's Louise Bear."

"Yes," said Louise Bear, "I have come to have a hand permanent."

"O.K.," said Eenie; "follow me."

"All right," said Louise Bear.

"Er," said Eenie as they got up to the attic, "would you pay me in advance, please?"

"I suppose so," said Louise Bear, "how much?"

"Three cents," said Eenie, "for the rubber bands, two cents for the trouble, one cent for doing it. That adds up to um—er—let me see—three cents and two cents makes five cents plus two cents more makes seven cents exactly."

"Very well," said Louise Bear, "where shall I sit?"

"Over there," said Eenie, thinking that the water pail was a chair.

Louise Bear sat down, "Oh," she cried, "my new dress! Give me back my money!"

"Now, now," said Eenie, "you know it was just a mistake."

"Wasn't," yelled Louise Bear. "I'm going to tell my mummy." And she ran home.

"You're not so good," said Mo timidly. "Let me try."

"Oh, all right. See what you can do," said Eenie.

"Oh goody," said Mo. "Just watch me."

Just then Mother Bear, who did not know what the bears were doing, led the real-estate man upstairs to the attic. He had come to see about repairs and Mother was saying to him, "And the attic needs repainting."

She opened the door of the attic.

"So," said the real-estate man, "this is the way you take care of your house. The company shall hear of this." And the man started to go out the door.

"Wait, Sir," said Mo. "Would you like a haircut?"

"How much?" said the man.

"Three cents, Sir," said Mo.

"O.K. Clip away," said the real-estate man softening.

Mother Bear was so grateful to Mo for saving the day that she called up the drugstore and ordered five chocolate ice cream cones for the bears. Meanwhile Mo started cutting. Cut-cut, cut, cut.

"Are you finished?" said the man after a while when Mo stopped.

"Yes," said Mo, innocently, "there isn't a hair left on you."

"What?" yelled the man.

"I said," said Mo, "that there's not a hair left on you by this time."

Mo Bear, Eenie, Meenie, Meinie, and Nig were laughing so hard they were crying.

"Well," said the man cooling off, "since you are so sorry I shall not report this."

That night Mother Bear was so mad about the attic not being painted that she took the five bears to the drugstore and got them five sodas each.

A sixth-grade boy

* THE LOVE STORY

The clock struck twelve. A silent figure slipped down the Five Bears' lane. It was carrying something that looked like a guitar. The figure was humming a love song. "Oh love, oh love," the figure was whispering.

Next morning came, Sunday morning. Mo found a note pinned to Nig's empty bed. It read:

"I have gone to sing a love song to Patricia Bear. If she refuses me, I don't think I shall ever come home. If she loves me I shall come home with her as my bride."

Mo giggled his silly little giggle. He knew that the letter had come out of the book of etiquette for the man in love.

"Father," Mo exclaimed, "Nig is in love."

Father Bear grunted sleepily. It wasn't news to him, but he got up and sloshed his feet into his heelless slippers and scuffed down the hall to Nig's room.

At eight when the four bears and Daisy were eating breakfast there came a feeble knock at the door. In stepped Nig with two black eyes, and a very red ear, and he was limping. The once beautiful guitar was hanging around his neck.

"She has refused me," he broke out tragically.

"So I see," barked Father Bear unsympathetically.

"You'd better go to bed," said Mother Bear coldly. It was the only way she could think of to get rid of him.

"You, my dear Mo," Nig said, "may have the pleasure of taking Daisy May to Sunday School." Nig was still feeling romantic. Mo groaned. He knew what it was to take Daisy to Sunday School.

Finally the Four and Daisy were off. They had left Nig in bed, smelling terribly of liniment and reading *How To Win Your Love*. When they got to church Mo warned Daisy about how quiet she must be.

"Aw wight, Mo," she said.

When they got in Daisy went prancing up the aisle, saying hello to anyone she knew. Mo was so mad at her that he forgot himself and yelled at the top of his lungs, "You—you thing! Come here this instant."

Daisy turned slowly around. "Oh, Mosy," she squeaked, "you are in church. You mustn't yell." Then she put her fingers to her mouth. "Shush," she said, and turning she scrambled up the aisle to the front row and sat down.

Mo was so mad that he didn't know what to do. He started to let out one of his famous screams, but then a thought came to him. He stopped with his mouth open. He was in church. Mo blushed and blushed. Everyone was looking at him. Slowly he walked up the aisle, looking very silly with his hair going every which way and a face that looked like a tomato with hair. He grabbed Daisy May by one ear and scrambled to a seat. Then Sunday School started. He found himself beside Patricia Bear. Patricia Bear was feeling very sympathetic and good that morning after having beaten up Nig the night before.

"She—she isn't very good, is she?" she whispered, nodding at Daisy.

"Oh," said Mo, a little upset, "why, yes. No," he added giving innocent Daisy a kick.

Everything was all right till the plate was passed. Mo was so nervous that he still shook, and in reaching for the plate he gave a jerk and dropped it. Crash, bang. Money bounced everywhere. Everybody started scrambling for it. Mo thought he had come to the end and would die presently. He made one last effort.

"Patricia," he said above the noise, "make up with Nig for my sake. Please, please. He can take care of Daisy, he can."

"Oh," said Patricia, grabbing a quarter on the roll. "I have. I called him up this morning."

Mo, who was Mother's pet and not used to any strain, quietly fainted. From then on Daisy May had more respect for Mo.

"My bruvver can faint," she would say proudly.

Mo was proud of her, too. "My sister can make more trouble than a thousand bandits."

Nig never had any quarrel after that about taking Daisy May out.

A sixth-grade girl

* FIVE BRAVE KNIGHTS

Once upon a time Nig said, "I am going to read my new book."
"I will read it with you," said Mo.
"So will I," said each of the other three bears.
They all ran into Nig's room. Nig said, "I am in Chapter Fifteen." So he began to read: "The knight vowed to kill the giant, and so he went to the giant and cut him with his sword."

"He did not," said Mo. "He killed him with his sword."

"Well, that's what the book says," responded Nig.

"I have an idea," said Eenie suddenly. "I saw five suits of armor down in the living room. We can each wear one and then we will go out and slay a giant." And they all ran down into the living room.

"Help me into this suit of armor," said Eenie. The other bears helped him squeeze into it. Then they got into suits too, all except Mo. Mo went over to examine Eenie's suit.

"You look nice," said Mo, lifting up the armored arm. Suddenly he lost his grip. The heavily armored arm crashed down on Mo's head. A huge crash echoed through the house. The other bears were so scared that they jumped right out of their armor and sailed six feet into the air. They came crashing down to the ground, and their suits of armor fell on top of them, breaking all to pieces. Meinie stuck his head out of the pile of broken armor.

"What happened?" he asked.

"Mo got squashed," said Nig carelessly.

"Well, then we'd better unsquash him," said Meinie.

"I don't know how to do that," said Nig, and so they put Mo in his room and started on their adventures. Before long they heard a great crashing noise.

"It's a giant," whispered Eenie fearfully.

"I'll get him," said Nig, and he ran up and stuck the sword into the giant's leg.

"Ow!" yelled the giant, so loud that it seemed to make the whole village shake.

"I will kill him now," said Nig, and he started to climb up the giant's leg.

"So will we," said all the other bears, and they followed Nig up the giant's leg.

"Get off!" screamed the giant, and he kicked his leg so hard that Nig lost his grip and found himself flying through the air. Luckily he landed in the giant's hair and yelled, "Come on, you fellows," to the others.

Meanwhile Mo, back in the house, was very much disappointed because he could not go along with the rest.

"Oh dear me," he said, "if I weren't squashed I could go along with the rest of them." Then suddenly he had an idea. "If you hammer down a person," he said to himself, "he would be squashed, and so it is very reasonable to suppose that if you hammer up on a person he would be unsquashed." So at once he ran down to get the hammer, and he unsquashed himself as far as he could. Then he ran out to where the other bears were fighting with the giant.

"Now I will show them," said Mo, and he began to climb up the giant's leg. Now Mo was a very bad climber, and every time he climbed up the leg he slipped down again. This tickled the giant so much that he began to laugh. He laughed till he sneezed and he sneezed till he fell over backwards. Then the five bears all ran up and down his stomach and made the giant laugh himself to death. Mo was so happy that he sang this song all the way home:

> Who slew the giant?
> Five brave knights;
> But it was really I
> I killed the giant.

A sixth-grade boy

VERSE SUPPLEMENT

Just as hearing children's stories often starts a wave of story writing so, too, does listening to verse composed by other children serve as a touchstone for poetry making. We find it productive to have a collection of children's poems to read aloud. We use them to provide contagion for poetic expression—sometimes to set a mood, to show how differently people feel about the same thing, often to build confidence, but never as models to be imitated or copied.

For these reasons we present here a supplement of verse by children seven- to ten-years-old. It is not children's "best"; rather it represents a broad spectrum of their writing and dictation. We purposely have included many poems that illustrate unevenness of quality. For the brief flash of individuality along with the matrix of pedestrian language in which it is imbedded, serves to fortify another beginner's belief in himself. We offer also some examples which show merit in the elements that are the essence of poetry.

＊ ＊ ＊

There are four blue eggs in the brown nest;
The mother robin gentles her red feathers
Down over them
And never makes a sound.
Then suddenly there are four baby birds
Squawking with surprise
To see the great brown world of the nest.
And the mother bird
Stands on the edge of the nest
And sings to everyone,
"Look, Look,
The world is full of baby birds."

❋   ❋   ❋

Who scratched the sky?
Last night some clumsy giant cat
Roared over the edge of night,
And blackly reached his giant paw
To scratch with gold the sky.

❋   HIGHWAYS

Leaves are like a highway
With thousands of roads:
Big ones for big insects,
Small ones for the small.
They are painted green;
Every winter they are covered
With rust
And break down;
But every spring
They are rebuilt
And given another coat of green.

❋   ❋   ❋

Oh, Little Rose Bush,
How you fight
When a weed is strangling you!
Your thorns are pricking him
But he still fights on;
Finally your friend, the human, comes
And pulls him away.
You show your thanks
By becoming the most beautiful rose
In the garden.

❋   ❋   ❋

❋ T H E   S K Y

When I was young
I used to look up at the sky
And think that the sun
Was the father,
The moon the mother,
And the stars the babies.
People say the sky
Is the wonder of the earth,
And the trees have the advantage
Of being in the sky's beauty.

❋ F R O G G Y

Froggy,
Why do you have
Such a big Adam's apple?
How is it to be bothered
By all the fish?
Don't you ever get tired
Jumping around?
How is it to be in shallow water
All the time
Under the beautiful shade
Of the trees?
And, by the way,
Are you going to be home
Tomorrow?

❋   ❋   ❋

A holy thing is a little sort of free thing
That you really believe in
And don't force on anyone else.

Oh, Moon above me,
Where do you go
When you are gone?
Do you go visiting?
Make the next person
On your visiting list
Be me!

* CLOUDS

Clouds are like a white, lovely pillow
Where you can lay your head down
For a hundred years.
Every minute a baby cloud is born.
Sometimes the clouds aren't so lovely:
Sometimes they fight
And all the rain falls,
But it quenches the flowers' thirst.

* HOW TO MAKE A POEM

Don't say "pretty" or "nice",
That's not very good,
It doesn't have a color in it.
Don't say "pretty" or "nice"—
It's no good at all,
Just like a flower when it's dead.

It isn't like a paint picture
Because *it* runs down the paper;
It's like a story
That's a short one;
The words are a good kind of words—
Ones that you know about.
It isn't anyone else's poem;
It's yours!

❋   ❋   ❋

❋   T H E   S E A S O N S

When spring comes I'm ever so glad,-
It's not because it's spring or I can pick flowers;
But it is that summer's coming soon
And my birthday's in summer, too.
That makes it very nice:
I can go swimming, and have picnics,
And romp in the woods.

I like winter, too,
Because it's almost Christmas
And Halloween comes around.
I play in the snow and have such a jolly time.

It's just like a ball of string
That keeps unwinding all the time
And winding back again.

❋   ❋   ❋

❋   T H E   H A L L O W E E N   N I G H T

The two pumpkins sit on the back fence,
And their fire is shooting up.
And the cats are sneaking behind them;
And the witches
Are riding
In mid-air,
As the light
Of the pumpkin's candle
Touches the tree above it.

The tree throws back its branches with anger,
And the wind comes along
And scolds the pumpkins
And blows them out.
The witch is very annoyed,
And rides furiously away with the wind carrying her.
She casts a magic spell on the wind and it dies away.

✿   ✿   ✿

Over by the sweet lily pond
Where the frogs
Do their little dance
And sing their merry little tune,—
Over by the sweet lily pond
All of a sudden
A big blow
Comes to their little home
And they jump up
And skip into the water.
Then sunshine comes
Through the shadows of their rooms,
And they pop up
And sing
Their merry little tunes,
Down by the sweet lily pond.

✿   ✿   ✿

The lily of the valley
Looks like an old fashioned lamp.
I wonder if it ever
Would light up in the dark.
If it would,
I would pick one
So it would guide me home.

✿ THE STAR'S MOTHER

In morning when the sun rises
All the little star children
Twinkle themselves to sleep.

The mother moon watches over them
So they will not wake up.
They sleep so soundly in the blue sky
That they sink into their cloudy pillows
And you can't see them.

      ✿   ✿   ✿

Was it the wind?
NO!
Creeping, creeping,
Though you could hear nothing
Save the low steady growl
Of the giant's cat.
Like a wild bear
He was purring contentedly
As though he had his fill of milk.
Putting his head against the furnace
He meowed once,
Yawned, showing his teeth
Like the fangs of a hungry wolf.
He put his head on his paw,
Stopped his purring,
Curled his tail around his legs,
And went to sleep.

      ✿   ✿   ✿

One day I was walking along
In the city;
The streets were black,
The people weren't gay
As they are in the country.

In the country
You see men

Driving cows home,
But in the city
There are no cows
To be driven home,
Or no cows to be milked.

I like the country
Better than the city
Where the hills
Stretch far and clear.
Nothing can stop them
Since nothing's strong enough
Except an earthquake.

＊ ANOTHER WORLD

Once I saw an army of ants marching,—
They marched and disappeared
Through the blades of grass,
And then appeared again.
Then I saw them disappear
Down a hole.
I saw another army
March into that same hole.
Ants seem to have
A world of their own;
I wonder if
I'll ever see them again.

＊ MAKE BELIEVE

The clock is chatting all the time.
He never can close his mouth;
His tongue is going back and forth
Because he's out of breath
From talking so much.

❋ ❋ ❋

Leaves look like an army
Going to war;
Leaves look like fighter planes
Flying in formation.

❋ ❋ ❋

What is gloom?
Gloom is a sticky, messy day,
Gloom is a disappointment,
Gloom is a misunderstanding.

❋ ❋ ❋

The water comes tumbling down
The stone wall.
When it meets with the river
They turn together;
The river runs to the ocean.
The Baby Waterfall, Mother River,
    and Father Ocean
Join together.

❋ ❋ ❋

The trees look like an upside-down broom
Sweeping the sky;
They sway back and forth
Just like a real broom,
And clean all the dust
Off the clouds.

❋ ❋ ❋

The tall flag pole
With its ball of gold at the top
Looks bare without a flag
Swinging on it.

Most poles
Have a design at the bottom,
With names engraved
Of the soldiers that died.

The flag pole
Represents our country
And peace.

*　*　*

Leaves have beautiful talents—
When they fall
They make me
Think of a bird
Diving down to earth.
Then they blow in the wind;
They look like clowns
Doing somersaults.
Birds make patterns;
Rivers have a twisty-turn flow;
The world seems like a circus.

*　*　*

When the moon is happy
It is very, very small;
But, when it's sad
It's very big,
And the shadows
You see on it
Are the tears.

*　*　*

A lot of things can happen
On a bright spring day:

Birds will be flying
Above you,
Maybe you'll even see
A little field mouse,
Or a chipmunk
Running around,
Enjoying the springtime
As we do.
The grass will be light green,
Ducks will be swimming happily
In the pond they like so much.
A lot of things can happen
On a bright spring day—
More than I have told you.

* * *

A best friend
Is someone you can love
All your life—
A friend to play with
And to do what is fun;
It may be dolls,
Or riding a bike;
It may even be baseball
If that is what you like.
But best of all, I think,
Is to sit on a leafy branch
Where no one can see you,
And talk and plan the things
You are going to do
In the summer to come.

* THE TREES

Whenever I'm in trouble and talk to myself out loud,
The trees nod their heads to and fro,

They know what is troubling me;
They hold out their arms
As if to make a bed for me.

* SPRING IS IN THE AIR

You can tell when spring is in the air
For you can smell the trees.
The grass and the brown earth
Smell the nicest.
The butterflies come out of their cocoons
And fly around so smoothly,
The bees come buzzing around you
When spring is in the air.

* * *

Come with me, my little child,
And walk through the dark night.
I'll hold your hand,
So don't be scared, my little child.

Hush, Hush! She is asleep.

* THE CLOUDS

I look up, up to the clouds and think
What a beautiful bed with lovely white sheets
Has God!

* SOME THOUGHTS ABOUT SPRING

When Spring comes
The sun takes its place
As a comforter to the world.
It sends its hot rays,
And makes a blanket
Around the cold earth.

The ground feels soft again,
There are fairy rings on the grass,
Crocuses are popping out of their beds—
Little fairies dressed in yellow.

Spring has a happy thought
Of seeing flowers and leaves sprout;
Mother Nature is painting the grass and trees
Green again;
And when we walk in the rain
We can smell the spring coming.

Spring makes us think
That summer is on its way,
With the busy times
When all the animals
Are feeding their young,
And the birds
Are on their nests.

We trust spring—
That it will bring us
Warmth and happiness;
We feel free
When spring is here.

Dictated by a fourth-grade class

❋ ❋ ❋ ❋ ❋ ❋ ❋ ❋

BIBLIOGRAPHY

APPLEGATE, MAUREE, *Helping Children Write*. New York: Harper and Row, Publishers, 1954.

ARNSTEIN, FLORA J., *Adventure into Poetry*. Stanford, Calif.: Stanford University Press, 1951.

——, *Poetry in the Elementary Classroom*. New York: Appleton-Century-Crofts, 1962.

BARUCH, DOROTHY WALTER, *Parents and Children Go To School*. Chicago: Scott, Foresman and Company, 1939.

BETZNER, JEAN, *Content and Form of Original Compositions Dictated by Children Five to Eight Years Old*. New York: Teachers College, Columbia University, 1930.

BURROWS, ALVINA TREUT, "Children's Writing and Children's Growth," *Elementary English*, XXVIII (April, 1951), pp. 205–210.

——, (editor) "Children's Writing," *Research in Composition and Related Skills*. Champaign, Ill.: National Conference on Research in English, 1960.

——, *Teaching Children in the Middle Grades*. Boston: D. C. Heath and Company, 1952.

——, *What Research Says to the Teacher*. Washington, D.C.: American Educational Research Association, 1958.

——, "Writing as Therapy," *Elementary English*, XXIX (March, 1952), pp. 135–138, 149.

COLE, NATALIE ROBINSON, *Arts in the Classroom*. New York: The John Day Company, Inc., 1940.

——, "Creative Writing as Therapy," *Elementary English Review*, XX (January, 1943), pp. 1–6.

DAWSON, MILDRED, "Guiding Writing Activities," *Elementary English Review*, XXIII (February, 1946), pp. 80–83, 97.

DE LA MARE, WALTER, *Early One Morning in Spring*. New York: The Macmillan Company, 1935.

279

DEWEY, JOHN, *How We Think*. Boston: D. C. Heath and Company, 1933.

DIMNET, ERNEST, *Art of Thinking*. New York: Simon and Schuster, Inc., 1929.

DOWNEY, JUNE, *Creative Imagination*. New York: Harcourt, Brace & World, Inc., 1929.

FEREBEE, JUNE D., "Form through Creative Expression," *Elementary English*, XXVII (February, 1950), pp. 73–78.

————, "Gaining Power Through Writing," *Elementary English Review*, XIX (December, 1942), pp. 282–285.

————, "Increasing the Writing Productivity in Children," Philadelphia: University of Pennsylvania Bulletin, *36th Annual Schoolmen's Week Proceedings* (March 30–April 2, 1949), pp. 47–53.

————, "What is Important in the Language Arts?" Philadelphia: University of Pennsylvania Bulletin, *36th Annual Schoolmen's Week Proceedings*, (March 30–April 2, 1949), pp. 26–30.

————, and DORIS C. JACKSON, "Working with Children in Creative Writing," *Journal of the Childhood Education Association*, XVII, No. 6 (February, 1941), pp. 258–262.

GETZELS, JACOB W. and PHILIP W. JACKSON, *Creativity and Intelligence*. New York: John Wiley & Sons, Inc. 1962.

HENRI, ROBERT, *The Art Spirit*. Philadelphia: J. B. Lippincott Company, 1939.

HERRICK, VERGIL E. and LELAND B. JACOBS, *Children and the Language Arts*. Englewood Cliffs, N. J.: Prentice-Hall, Inc. 1955.

JACKSON, DORIS C., "Poetry Making With Children," *Elementary English Review*, XX (April 1943), pp. 129–134.

LA BRANT, LOU, *Study of Certain Language Developments in Grades IV–XII*, Worcester, Mass.: Clark University Press, 1933.

————, *We Teach English*. New York: Harcourt, Brace & World, Inc., 1951.

MARKSBERRY, MARY LEE, *Foundation of Creativity*. New York: Harper and Row, Publishers, 1963.

MEARNS, HUGHES, *Creative Power: The Education of Youth in the Creative Arts*. New York: Dover Publications, 1958.

————, *Creative Youth*. New York: Doubleday & Company, Inc., 1929.

National Council of Teachers of English, *Language Arts for Today's Children*. New York: Appleton-Century-Crofts, 1954.

SCHMIDT, BERNARDINE, G., "Creative Ways of Retarded Children," *Elementary English*, XX (January, 1943), pp. 16–19.

SHANE, HAROLD G., MARY E. REDDIN, and MARGARET C. GILLESPIE, *Be-*

ginning Language Arts Instruction with Children. Columbus, Ohio: Charles E. Merrill Books, Inc., 1961.

SHANE, HAROLD G., JUNE G. MULRY, MARY E. REDDIN, and MARGARET C. GILLESPIE, *Language Arts Instruction in the Elementary School*, Columbus, Ohio: Charles E. Merrill Books, Inc., 1963.

SMITH, DORA V., "Growth in Language Power as Related to Child Development," *Teaching Language in the Elementary School*, 43rd Yearbook of National Society for the Study of Education, Part II. Chicago: University of Chicago Press, 1944.

SMITH, ETHEL E., *Procedures for Encouraging Creative Writing in the Elementary School* (Ph.D. Thesis, Typewritten). Evanston, Ill.: Northwestern University School of Education, 1943.

STRICKLAND, RUTH, *The Language Arts in the Elementary School*. Boston: D. C. Heath and Company, 1951.

TORRANCE, E. PAUL, *Guiding Creative Talent*. Englewood Cliffs, N.J.: Prentice-Hall, Inc., 1962.

WALTER, NINA WILLIS, *Let Them Write Poetry*. New York: Holt, Rinehart and Winston, Inc., 1962.

WATTS, A.F., *The Language and Mental Development of Children*. Boston: D. C. Heath and Company, 1948.

WILT, MIRIAM E., *Creativity in the Elementary School*. New York: Appleton-Century-Crofts, 1959.

WITTY, PAUL, "Creative Writing Climates," *Journal of the Childhood Education Association*, XVII, No. 6 (February, 1941), pp. 253–257.

———, "Encouraging Growth and Development through Language Arts," *Arts in Childhood*, Bulletin No. 3, Series VI (1951), pp. 14–18.

———, "Opportunity To Write Freely," *Elementary English Review*, XIX (May, 1942), pp. 171–174.

———, and WILLIAM I. MARTIN, "An Analysis of Children's Compositions Written in Response to a Film." *Elementary English*, XXXIV (March, 1957), pp. 158–163.

ZIRBES, LAURA, *Spurs to Creative Teaching*. New York: G. P. Putnam's Sons, 1959.